B+ T
35

CRANFORD PUBLIC LIBRARY NJ

3 9520 00207 0227

JUN 0 1 2007

Food Fight!

W9-DDX-069

Food Fight!

The Battle Over the American Lunch in Schools and the Workplace

JULIE L. LAUTENSCHLAGER

McFarland & Company, Inc., Publishers
Jefferson, North Carolina, and London

LIBRARY OF CONGRESS CATALOGUING-IN-PUBLICATION DATA

Lautenschlager, Julie L., 1973–
    Food fight!: the battle over the American lunch in schools and
the workplace / Julie L. Lautenschlager.
        p.   cm.
    Includes bibliographical references and index.

    ISBN-13: 978-0-7864-2670-6
    ISBN-10: 0-7864-2670-5
    (softcover : 50# alkaline paper) ∞

    1. Food habits — United States.   2. Luncheons.   3. Lunchbox
cookery.   4. School children — Food — United States.
5. School lunchrooms, cafeterias, etc. — United States.
6. Work environment — United States.   7. United States — Social
life and customs.   I. Title.
GT2853.U5L38   2006
394.1'2 — dc22   2006025398

British Library cataloguing data are available

©2006 Julie L. Lautenschlager. All rights reserved

*No part of this book may be reproduced or transmitted in any form
or by any means, electronic or mechanical, including photocopying
or recording, or by any information storage and retrieval system,
without permission in writing from the publisher.*

Cover images ©2006 PhotoSpin; cowboy lunch box
provided by David Alff

Manufactured in the United States of America

McFarland & Company, Inc., Publishers
    Box 611, Jefferson, North Carolina 28640
        www.mcfarlandpub.com

To my parents,
The Reverend Luther W. and
Mrs. Linda M. Lautenschlager

You were the ones who tied those baby high-tops and encouraged my first steps, and now, more than thirty years later, you are still my cheerleaders and safety net as I continue to take new and uncertain steps in life. From saddle shoes, to clogs, to ballet shoes, to Reeboks, you have always kept me in my "walking shoes"—both literally and figuratively.

The path from Mr. Jefferson's alma mater to his Monticello has been an exciting and rewarding one, but like all journeys, it has also presented challenges and struggles. Your support, and often consolation, has kept me true to the course in spite of the hurdles. Chessie Cottage is my house, but my "home" will always be with you.

When I thought that this project would consume every word that remained in my brain, I saved five of the most important ones for you — Thank you. I love you.

Acknowledgments

If no man is an island, certainly no book is either. This book is the result of the kind support and encouragement that I received from many people.

First, I'd like to extend my gratitude to the American Studies Program at the College of William and Mary, Williamsburg, Virginia. The assistantships I held at the *William and Mary Quarterly*, Yorktown Victory Center, Jamestown Settlement, and the Swem Library Archives and Special Collections helped me develop valuable knowledge and skills beyond the classroom. A very special thank you to my advisor, Dr. Scott Nelson, who gave his time, attention, and commitment to this project from the moment he came on board. Also thanks to committee members Dr. John Haskell, Professor Barbara Carson, and outside reader Dr. Shirley T. Wajda, Kent State University.

Thanks to the History Department at Kent State University, Kent, Ohio, whose master's program helped me build a foundation for my future educational pursuits. Thanks to my advisor, Dr. Clarence Wunderlin, who helped develop and guide my thesis and who introduced me to documentary editing on *The Papers of Robert A. Taft*. A round of special accolades to Dr. Wajda, who not only shepherded me through my years at Kent, but also helped make my William and Mary dream a reality.

Thanks to all of my colleagues at *The Papers of Thomas Jefferson: Retirement Series*, particularly project editor Dr. J. Jefferson Looney. Thanks to Dr. Kristofer M. Ray, for his willingness to read my draft and his insightful comments. Special thanks to Dr. Robert F. Haggard, who advised and edited with care, listened to my questions and concerns, and encouraged me throughout the process.

Thanks to Janet Metzger of the William McKinley Presidential Library, Canton, Ohio, for her help in securing images. Thanks also to Dr. John Kaminski, of the *Documentary History of the Ratification of the Constitution* at the University of Wisconsin, Madison, for much appreciated guidance and encouragement.

Thanks to friends and to my family — Grandmother, Aunts, Uncles, Cousins — and all those who came before me.

And thank you to Chessie — the delight of my life.

Table of Contents

Acknowledgments   vii

Preface   1

Introduction: American Eating Ideology and the Noon Meal   5

1. From Full Dinner Pails to Empty Market Baskets:
   The Debut and Demise of a Political Symbol   19

2. Creating Efficient Workers and Students:
   Reformers Take Up the Lunch Cause   44

3. Kitchen Commandos: Government, the Media, and
   the "Marketing" of Food Rationing during World War II   75

4. Sharing in the Sisterhood of Sacrifice:
   The Recipe for a "Homogenized" Homefront Housewife   102

5. A Nutrition Victory: World War II and the Noon Meal   122

6. Staking a Claim on Lunch:
   Eating on the Job after World War II   145

7. Carrying Lunch to School: Players in the
   Institutionalization of Students' Noon Meals   162

8. Lunch Ladies: Magazines, Advertising, and the
     Construction of Women as Lunch Box Packers   181

Conclusion: Blame Not the Oreo   201

Chapter Notes   217

Selected Bibliography   231

Index   241

Preface

What did Thomas Jefferson eat for lunch? It is an interesting question with a yet more fascinating answer. The fact is, Mr. Jefferson did not eat lunch. That's right. According to the reminiscences of his granddaughter Septimia Anne Randolph Meikleham, after breakfast, Mr. Jefferson "retired to his library" and was not present for another meal until he greeted his family and guests in the drawing room where they assembled for dinner, which was served at half past three. Although Mr. Jefferson probably never partook of it, there was a noontime repast at Monticello, but it was "quite informal & handed around to the guests."[1] Clearly, the culture of food and eating which Mr. Jefferson and his contemporaries understood was quite different from that which has developed with the industrialization and growth of modern American society.

This project began as a material culture study of lunch boxes. In my efforts to answer questions about the origins and use of lunch boxes, I discovered that these objects were part of a much larger story about the transformation of American society and the American diet. Lunch became a part of many Americans' days around the turn of the nineteenth century when changes in the national economy and educational system caused alterations in long-held eating patterns and moved more people away from the homes and farms that had earlier been the nucleus of productive activity. Although some of these lunching pioneers were indeed purchasing food at various public establishments, many needed or preferred to carry their food along with them. Hence, the need for

1

a product arose, and through a combination of American ingenuity, industrial development, and marketing, the lunch box was born.

Early lunch containers did not simply carry food to the sites of labor and learning; they were also conduits of information, ideas, and culture between these locations and the homes and families of their carriers. With the transition to more public meals, the floodgates were open for an assortment of industrial managers, social workers, medical and experimental scientists, manufacturers and processors of food, advertisers, and representatives from all levels of the public and private sector to center their attention on the contents of Americans' lunch boxes. This is the story of how these interests, through united efforts and individual crusades, have worked to modify and change Americans' eating habits for a variety of reasons ranging from socialization and improved health to increased productivity and greater expenditure on consumer goods. These various interests carved out overlapping territories in the contest to gain access to, influence over, and control of American's eating habits; in essence, they "colonized" lunch.

During the late nineteenth- and early twentieth-century, the progressives started the ball rolling when they drew public attention to the relationship between good nutrition and "good" workers. Then, World War II changed the rules when food became a national concern on the battlefield and the homefront. The arrival of federally mandated food rationing meant that the army of colonizers who had been focusing their efforts on the most public meal of the day could justify their attempts to intervene everywhere from the family dining room to the factory canteen and school cafeteria. Following the war, the legacy of the colonizers' work echoed in the form of friction between management and unions, but the school lunch gained the most attention. Although over time the national defense character of the school lunch receded into the background, educators, legislators, dieticians, and others saw in the school lunch promise for the promotion of burgeoning equal opportunity programs. Lastly, while the postwar era ushered in redefined gender roles in families and workplaces, packed lunches continued to function as the focal point for members of the public and the media to debate the ideals of American motherhood.

The modern American obsession with food and diet bears witness to the effects of the colonization process. We are now at a crossroads

Opposite: **Illustration from L. Frank Baum's *Ozma of Oz*.**

THE LITTLE GIRL PICKED ONE OF THE LUNCH-BOXES

in that process. The colonizers may prove to be the victims of their own successes. With recent lawsuits alleging that fast-food restaurants or food processors are responsible for the overweight and ill health of some people, it seems that the "colonized" are attempting to impose their will on the "colonizers." What will be the ultimate outcome of this interaction remains to be seen, but this colonization process is not a conspiracy, and the best corrective to counterbalance its negative influences and effects is education. Whether their lunch comes from a lunch box, cafeteria, or the microwave at home, individuals retain the responsibility and accountability for the personal food choices they make.

Introduction:
American Eating Ideology
and the Noon Meal

It is time for breakfast in the Land of Ev, and Dorothy, the little American heroine of L. Frank Baum's *Ozma of Oz*, the 1907 sequel to *The Wonderful Wizard of Oz*, is hungry. Even as a young girl, Dorothy understands that certain foods are to be consumed at certain times. Meals have a name, a schedule, and an acceptable bill of fare.

> The little girl stood on tip-toe and picked one of the nicest and biggest lunch-boxes, and then she sat down on the ground and eagerly opened it. Inside she found, nicely wrapped in white papers, a ham sandwich, a piece of sponge-cake, a pickle, a slice of new cheese and an apple. Each thing had a separate stem, and so had to be picked off the side of the box; but Dorothy found them all to be delicious, and she ate every bit of luncheon in the box before she had finished.
> "A lunch isn't zactly breakfast," she said to Billina, who sat beside her curiously watching. "But when one is hungry one can eat supper in the morning, and not complain."[1]

By the late nineteenth and early twentieth centuries in the United States, a specific midday meal known as lunch had evolved in response to the changing needs of a growing industrial society. The story of lunch in American workplaces and schools is a part of the history of

5

the industrialization and commercialization of American society. These twin engines have animated American culture even as they have worked to transform it. As the work and education routines of many Americans moved them away from home for the better part of the day, the act of eating became more public and it also entered a new realm of scrutiny. The character of the noon meal consumed in public work or educational spaces is the product of an interactive colonization process[2] that brings a variety of interests into the act of fashioning, sustaining, and revising the meanings communicated through food and the environment in which it is consumed.

Understanding the significance of lunch for modern Americans involves sorting out intricate relationships among food, ideology, and power.[3] The history of organized feeding programs in workplaces and schools reveals a complex tale of coordinated efforts toward the primary goal of altering an individual's eating habits. A secondary benefit of this process accrues when that individual spreads the new ideas to others. From the progressive reform movement aimed at improving labor conditions and the general welfare of workers, to the penny lunch movement in American schools, to World War II food rationing and the effort to improve the meals of wartime industrial workers, many different characters have played a part in structuring lunch for workers and students. Some were affiliated with reform movements, such as progressive era experts in the fields of science and nutrition. Business and government leaders, the media, and advertisers have also contributed. Working both in concert and isolation, these various interests, both individuals and organizations, have attempted to alter the eating habits of their subjects toward the goals of increased Americanization, socialization, or productivity. Together, they have shaped the role of lunch in modern American food ideology.

Late nineteenth- and early twentieth-century progressives drove the opening wedge, introducing the debate about the relationship between nutrition and industrial or educational efficiency. Then, during World War II, business and government experts transformed lunch from a matter of primarily private concern into one of military necessity. After the war, issues over employee lunches remained a contested terrain in many union–management conflicts. Also during the postwar era, the national defense character of the school lunch faded while educators, legislators, dieticians, and others who had become enamored with statistics, used the school lunch as a tool to "even up the starting line" through equal opportunity programs. Such experiments on young Americans have had both positive and negative outcomes ranging from the institutionalization of the federal free and reduced-price lunch program to the sometimes troublesome effects of distribution of excess agricultural commodities among school cafeterias. Finally, although the twentieth century was one of significant changes in women's roles both inside and outside the home, ideals of motherhood proved to be less elastic and amenable to shifting work and family patterns. The packed lunch, as a public demonstration of maternal commitment, also became the material site of conflict and contestation as to the very nature of motherhood.

Throughout this work, I employ the colonization metaphor to represent the highly diverse corps of individuals and groups who have been involved in efforts to control, change, and generally influence the ways in which workers and students have consumed lunch during the twentieth and twenty-first centuries. In a general sense, the term *colonization* describes a process by which powerful interests, including intellectuals, the government, and the media, adopt persuasive tools to rationalize and bring a routine to the world around them. This process reflects what the German philosopher Jurgen Habermas called the colonization of the lifeworld. Habermas called communication the central feature of modern society. The open exchange of ideas among individuals and groups provides the basis for democratic forms of government. Along with the positive progress associated with modernity, however, Habermas described an equally negative disintegration of this communicative core. The emergence of the mass media, the blurring of the lines between public and private, and the growth of bureaucracy and interest groups have led to a crisis in legitimacy for both individuals and institutions. Quite simply, systems controlled by money and power have come to dominate and undermine open discourse and debate — they have "colonized" the communicatives sphere. The size, diversity, and complexity of modern society tend to perpetuate this process. Ultimately, systems and forms of economic and administrative rationality prevail as colonization ushers in new levels of standardization and homogenization.

Between the late nineteenth and early twenty-first centuries, the various interests involved in the process of colonizing American lunch habits have been propelled by a wide array of motivations and goals. Generally, however, some combination of concern for human well-being, national welfare, industrial efficiency, or financial reward, has constituted their efforts. The mixture of philanthropic and capitalistic impulses has meant that often the colonizers have ignored or simply misunderstood the significance of certain eating habits to individuals and ethnic or minority groups. People have endowed their food with special meanings and significant social roles in processes ranging from religious rituals to the performance of ethnic, familial, and personal identities. In their efforts to rationalize and homogenize lunch choices, colonizers have drawn increased attention to social classifications evidenced by eating habits. The way a person consumes the noon meal, whether carried from home in some type of container or obtained at some public location, has been manipulated by the colonizers. As anthropologist Mary Douglas writes, food is a code that contains a message about "different degrees of hierarchy, inclusion and exclusion, boundaries and transactions across those boundaries."[4] The efforts of the colonizers in the environments of workplaces and schools demonstrate how much power and control they have exercised over the food codes or food ideology sent to and shared by American workers and students.

What Is Lunch About?

By dictionary definition, *lunch* is a light meal, often comprised of sandwiches, that is consumed generally at some hour near noon, although the term may apply to a light meal eaten at any other time. While many different people certainly eat some form of midday meal, students and workers are significant because they must generally consume their lunch away from home. Lunch poses special concerns for anyone who spends the day away from home. For those who live far from their workplace or school, or have only a short break for lunch, the midshift meal presents a problem of logistics. The problem can be solved either through specialized containers to transport food from place to place (e.g., lunch boxes to carry food from home to factory,

Opposite: **Although this 1865 advertisement does not include a lunch box, it demonstrates an early use of the term in conjunction with other school supplies (Library of Congress, Printed Ephemera Collection; Portfolio 711, Folder 59).**

BOYS' REINS,
WITH BELLS ATTACHED.

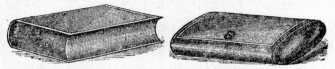

LUNCH BOXES,
ALL SIZES AND STYLES.

BOOK STRAPS,
OF ALL KINDS, AT

NEAT, KEARNEY & CO.'S
TRUNK STORES,

336   Washington Street,   336

((OPPOSITE THE ADAMS HOUSE,)

And 52 Elm and 24 Friend Streets, Boston.

J. H. & F. F. Farwell Printing Office, 112 Washington Street, Boston.

office, or school) or through the provision of food services on or off the site of labor or educational activities.

Questions about the best method of providing lunch for workers arose early in the history of America's shift from an agrarian to an industrial nation. In many respects, the noon meal is an appendage of the industrial system. Early disputes between labor and management often involved the time allowed for breaks and meals.[5] Although a three-meal-a-day pattern is neither divinely ordained nor necessarily healthful, it has nonetheless been the standard pattern throughout American history. It has been the titles and timing of the meals that have varied according to the social and economic growth of the nation.

The agrarian economy demanded a schedule of meals whereby a hearty breakfast was followed by the main noon meal, called dinner. A farm family's day closed with a light evening repast known as supper. With the onset of industrialization, a new pattern emerged. People working in factories and other businesses found that a considerably lighter breakfast better suited their schedules. Then, a simple midday meal, called lunch, was consumed at the workplace and followed by the most substantial meal of the day, known as dinner. For much of the twentieth century, a quick test of a person's rural or urban affiliation was asking him if he ate breakfast, dinner, and supper or breakfast, lunch, and dinner.[6]

This story of lunch begins in the late nineteenth century, when for the first time in American history, for much of the population, the consumption of the noon meal took place outside of the home environment, most often at the workplace or in a school. This is not to say that before this time people always ate at home, nor that they did not possess the means of carrying food from one location to another prior to this shift. It is merely to point out that beginning at this time, the act of eating lunch became more public for more classes of people. Moreover, the mere fact that one spends the day outside of the home environment does not necessarily always translate into "public" meal consumption. One could eat in a closed office, outside beneath a shade tree, or in any number of places away from peer review or supervision. However, for the reformers interested in reshaping people's eating habits, the focus has been on the experience of eating in shared spaces.

The history of dining provides us with information on the extravagant foodways and entertainment practices of the elite from colonial

Photographed in July 1937, these Brookeville, Maryland, farmers (names unknown) eat their noon meal family-style (Library of Congress, Prints and Photographs Division, FSA-OWI Collection, LC-USF33-004321-M4).

times to the present. We can also find mention of the slave diet in ante-bellum America and general commentaries on the eating habits of the poor through the centuries.[7] There is, however, a gap in historical coverage when it comes to the lunchtime habits of working-class people and schoolchildren. For these groups in particular, the changes wrought by increased industrialization and the rise of public education meant coping with the necessity to eat away from home, in an environment that might or might not have lent itself to accessing food from a local source. The character of a person's lunch experience is directly related to two significant variables — his or her environment and cultural realities.

A fact of life in America's industrialized society is that much of the work of the day is completed between the hours of nine in the morning and five in the afternoon. Most Americans complete their business transactions and attend school between these hours. Thus, for most people, the meal between breakfast and dinner must be consumed in a public place. Those with freedom of movement, who are not expected to punch the clock or remain within the confines of a schoolyard, have the advantage of going out to lunch. Executives, at-home parents, and retirees can take their noon meals in a restaurant or café. In contrast, hourly workers and schoolchildren can seldom leave the premises because of time constraints and safety concerns. In addition, the modern factory system, with its staggered shifts covering twenty-four-hour periods, means that some workers may be eating their lunch at midnight rather than noon. Hence, many workers and students must choose between purchasing the selections offered at an institutional cafeteria, or they must transport their meals from home. In either case, their lunch experience is shaped by environmental constraints.

Eating lunch involves more than just the rote consumption of food. The public forum of the cafeteria or restaurant transforms a simple meal into a sort of social barometer. In an increasingly impersonal world of machines and mass education, when little else is known about a person, his or her lunchtime routine, be it consuming fare in an institutional cafeteria or from a lunch box, provides spectators with one means of assessing the social origins of their fellow diners. The lunch box or lack thereof is a highly visible, though potentially inaccurate indication of a person's place in the social hierarchy.

This project focuses specifically on the modern American experience of lunch as a lens through which to view and understand more general efforts to achieve a rational society in an industrialized and commercialized world. It shows how the meaning of food for a noonday meal, carried in some type of container or alternatively obtained at a central location, has been manipulated by individuals, corporations, the government, the media, educational institutions, and assorted experts. In the hands of these individuals and groups, lunch and the material culture associated with it have functioned as an indication of social status, a badge of personal or group identity, and also as an instrument of power, control, and reform. The story of lunch is a chronicle of the politicization of what was once private and personal.

Lunch is partly about the encounter among home, workplace, school, and the marketplace. Throughout the twentieth century, women were key elements in the equation that linked colonizers representing food producers, distributors, and nutritional science. Regardless of their other duties within or outside the home, women have historically been the ones responsible for the procurement, preparation, and serving of family meals. Though women's work is generally invisible in terms of paid labor, it has been and remains a public standard by which women are judged in their capacity as caretakers and mothers.[8]

In some cases, the role of women in packing lunches has been the subject of jeremiads from individuals and groups associated with the goals of rationalizing eating habits by focusing increased attention on nutritional quality and the efficiency of preparation and consumption. Sometimes, these interests cast women as their most powerful allies in the effort to provide healthful, satisfying meals to America's families. At other times, however, a goal of this discourse has been to deny women their role in lunch packing in favor of a more rational and efficient system of meal production or for the promotion of commercial products. A result of the interplay among these diverse interests has been the creation of a body of prescriptive literature aimed at assisting women as they pack "proper" lunch boxes and hence maintain their "proper" social roles. A tension has arisen from the fact that working women must often be both the packers and the consumers of lunch. This fact is problematic for its basic inconsistency with still powerful cultural ideals of women as wives and mothers.

As historian Leila Rupp notes, regardless of whether women fulfill their socially prescribed roles, they are cognizant of their conformity or lack thereof. Further, Rupp notes that although "popular ideologies" are often "at odds" with reality, these prescriptions play an important role in women's perceptions of themselves.[9] An historical examination of American household advice manuals, cookbooks, and ladies' magazines certainly supports this argument. Over the centuries, many of the authors and editors of these works have perpetuated the identification of women with domesticity. Sisters Catherine E. Beecher and Harriet Beecher Stowe dedicated their 1869 household manual *The American Woman's Home* to the women of America, "in whose hands rest the real destinies of the Republic, as moulded by the early training and preserved amid the maturer influences of home."[10] In the tradition of republican motherhood, stretching back to the American Revolution, the appropriate venue for female political participation was in the creation of a home that would serve as a civic incubator for the nurturing of patriotic, virtuous citizens.[11] Although during the late nineteenth and early twentieth century crusaders like Fannie Farmer emphasized the scientific aspects of domestic life, pushing the bounds of female domestic activity through the incorporation of scientific principles, they did not extend women's reach outside of the traditional domestic sphere.[12] Soon thereafter, popular media and advertising, including magazines, cookbooks, newspapers, radio, and television, took hold of the traditional association between women and food and used it to sell products and encourage consumer activity. All this combined with the influence of home economists, nutritionists, the public schools, and the increased numbers of women working outside the home, has resulted in a gradual reinterpretation of how women can fulfill their responsibility for family nutrition.

Finally, lunch is about the tension between people and the homogenizing influences of technology. An important thread that runs through this study concerns the mechanization and progressive rationalization that characterizes life in a modern, industrial democracy.[13] Corporate power, in the shape of directives from the state, educational institutions, the media, and industry, has worked to direct the creation of an idealized American consumer. Feeding human bodies, unlike machines, is not a simple matter of providing electricity, gasoline, oil, coal, or steam. Although people can perform several activities at the same time, they require a time and a place to eat. As industrialization mandated that people adapt to a clock-based society, it also required that they relinquish some measure of control over their eating patterns. The ultimate outcome of this accommodation has been the creation of a more homogenous approach to eating lunch.

Progressive efforts at Americanization and socialization of immigrants encouraged uniformity in the eating habits of ethnic groups, minorities, and the poor. Food historian Harvey Levenstein offers the hypothesis that the "square meals" served to military personnel during World War II "played a major role in speeding the process of nationalizing and homogenizing American food tastes."[14] Similarly, the experience of eating lunch in a public setting such as a workplace or school, influenced by the work of the colonizers, served to inculcate a common understanding of how to be an American consumer and, more broadly, how to be an American.

The effort to encourage individual participation in the culture of production and consumption has resulted in a sort of masked individuality that some social critics say creates an illusion of individual choice. On one level, the ability to choose among an Oscar Mayer Lunchable, a home-packed brown bag lunch, or a hot lunch in a cafeteria or local eatery seems to provide plenty of options for personal decisions, but these alternatives are products of the corporate structure of American life. The range of choices available to the American worker/student is evidence of what sociologist George Ritzer calls the McDonaldization of America. He describes the progressive dehumanization that is at the core of progressive rationalization. As people are guided by "institutionalized rules, regulations, and structures," there is "less room for individual variation in choice of means to ends."[15] Even so, viable choices do remain, albeit often shrouded beneath the layers of colonizers' spin. The colonizers' efforts have indeed reshaped and to a certain extent directed Americans' eating ideology, but individual choice is persistent, and it keeps homogenization from becoming complete.

World War II and the Homogenization of the Homefront

In terms of organized intervention into American's food habits, no other period in our history rivals World War II. The stark reality of homefront mobilization, the drive to lend assistance to our allies, and national commitments to soldiers at home and abroad placed an enormous burden on the American government and industrial core that was passed along to the American people in the form of rationing. Rationing of durable goods and foodstuffs introduced a new level of outside involvement in the simple process of providing for a family. Food rationing in particular allowed a bevy of colonizers to gain access to the inner sanctum of the family table, and the impetus of war lent an increased aura of legitimacy to their efforts. The exigencies of balancing the provisioning of the battlefront and the homefront meant that colonizers no longer needed to rely on the publicity of lunch to tap into broader family eating habits. War made food in general fair game. By equating patriotism and a consumer's willing compliance with rationing guidelines, colonizers transformed food into a weapon of war. At the same time, a rising tension between traditional feminine household roles and the demands created by the exodus of so many men from the pool of available labor resulted in mixed messages about the propriety of women in the workforce but consistent information about women's retained responsibility for family meals both inside and outside the home. With victory in the war, food rationing was retired into the government's arsenal of mothballed weapons, but the effects of food mobilization on the American psyche and diet were not so quick to vanish.

The Battle over Lunch

By opening up Americans' lunch pails, buckets, boxes, and bags, and peering into the cafeterias, lunch rooms, and kitchens where lunch is prepared, served, and consumed, this project will demonstrate how an historical understanding of that meal provides clues about who Americans have been, who they are, and who they are becoming. As French gastronome Jean Anthelme Brillat-Savarin commented: "Tell me what you eat, and I'll tell you who you are."[16]

The story of lunch in American workplaces and schools is complex. Importantly, the players involved in shaping the way lunch is consumed in these environments have often carried both complexity and confusion into policy. "Battles" over lunch have resulted from the contest among those with differing ideas about how best to shape the way lunch is consumed and the wills of those doing the consuming. During the twentieth and early twenty-first centuries, the intentions of progressive reformers, assorted experts in education and industrial

Several varieties of lunch containers await their owners in a rural Wisconsin school. Note the presence of dome-style boxes and covered tins (Library of Congress, Prints and Photographs Division, FSA-OWI Collection, LC-USF33-T01-001536-M4).

efficiency, the government, and commercial enterprises became mixed and often indiscernible from one another. These various interests carved out overlapping territories in the contest to gain access, influence, and control over Americans' lunch habits — they "colonized" lunch. Sometimes their efforts have resulted in significant improvements in the health, well-being, and productivity of workers, students, and Americans in general. At other times, however, when the colonizers' interest turned from the provision of good nutrition to more overt efforts at intervention in foodways, the result has been the elimination of cultural traditions and introduction of homogeneity. In such cases, recognition of different ways of thinking about health and nutrition have taken a backseat to such goals as increased Americanization or the creation of revenue through the sale of commercial products.

As Ann Hulbert, the author of "'I Say the Hell with It!' School Lunches Are Making Kids Fat — But Collard Greens Aren't the Solution," observed: "Dietary issues have always tended to inspire zealotry in this country."[17] This history of the enthusiastic and sometimes fervent efforts to gain control in the battle over lunch cannot hope to provide answers to all of the questions about why Americans think about and consume lunch as they do. It can, the author hopes, help us understand how we have arrived at this point and how best to move forward from here.

1

From Full Dinner Pails to Empty Market Baskets: The Debut and Demise of a Political Symbol

A Novel Hot Lunch Box

The complex gastronomic problems with which mankind has been struggling ever since the dawn of civilization set in at last promise to be solved by a simple little device, which not only enables urbanites to defy anti-free lunch legislators and smile in serene contentment at the rebellious domestic cook, but threatens to put cheap luncheon counters into innocuous desuetude. It enables the tourist to penetrate the desert of the Sahara without a thought of where he is going to strike a restaurant. It will make travelling or exploring of any kind unalloyed delight, for whenever sustenance or inner comforts are needed all that is necessary is to unstrap the Bon-Vee-Von, and bring forth from its recesses the viands and liquid refreshments with which its different compartments have been provisioned.

The miraculous Bon-Vee-Von, so lauded in the July 5, 1903, *New York Daily Tribune*, was produced by a firm in New York City known as the Union Lunch Box Company. Although the above summation of the Bon-Vee-Von appears in a newspaper article, its language suggests more of an effort to encourage the distribution of lunch boxes than an unbiased, factual report. According to the article, the "ingenious little affair" offered features and benefits that would suit the needs and desires of everyone from the "traveling man," to the miner, to the factory girl.

Among the qualities that might interest such pers4ons in this box were its sturdy construction, its many separate compartments for "solid food, a pint flask for liquid refreshment, tea, coffee, soup, etc., an alcohol lamp and storeroom for knives, forks, napkins and toothpicks." Measuring a compact size of "eight inches wide, five inches deep and seven inches high," the box was touted as "not a burdensome piece of luggage." It would indeed appear that the Bon-Vee-Von could be all things to everyone saddled with the necessity of carrying a lunch. For "miners, watchmen, farmers, laborers, and all other workers whose work exposes them to all conditions of weather, and who have no facilities for procuring hot food when needed," as well as for "working women who do not wish to go to a crowded lunchroom, or who are in factories away from such places, the luncheon box will prove a great boon." In addition to its "low price of $2," which "places it within the reach of everybody," perhaps its greatest attribute was its "neat, attractive appearance," which "especially recommends it to that class of people who desire to carry their luncheon in a receptacle that will not arouse comment."[1]

The preceding description of the Bon-Vee-Von may seem a trifle bombastic, rather like a piece of grandiloquent advertising copy. It nevertheless reveals a great deal about the genesis of American lunch culture. The beginning of the twentieth century is in fact a very significant moment in the development of the circumstances, ideas, and objects that helped shape modern lunch. A key factor in the evolution of lunch may be found in the process of industrialization and urbanization that firmly gripped the nation by the turn of the twentieth century.

Following the Civil War, the United States began the long endeavor of recovery. Politically, economically, and socially, the country had suffered under the strains of war. The rifts and dislocations wrought by the experience of sectional affiliation were difficult to repair. To many Americans, the evil twins born of immigration and emigration were unemployment and poverty. While railroads, telephones, and telegraphs promised to improve communications, and emerging national markets eased the distribution of goods, economic instability remained a constant irritant to industrial workers, farmers, and the numerous newcomers to America's cities. The result of this cauldron of change, risk, and failure, was a series of financial crises and depressions that rocked the nation in the late decades of the nineteenth century.[2]

Data from the cities revealed that many immigrants and poor urban dwellers were locked in a struggle to provide even the basics of food and shelter for themselves and their families, and many rural folk were no better off. Jacob Riis's contemporary graphic portrayal of the "other half" during the late nineteenth century emphasized the fact that the problem of poverty should be of concern to everyone, if not out of humanitarian concern then out of fear for the ultimate demise of American society: "Philanthropy we call it sometimes with patronizing airs. Better call it self-defence."[3] Riis articulated a middle-class view of the social dislocations wrought by industrialization and immigration. In his 1892 work, *The Children of the Poor*, Riis proposed an environmental interpretation of the causes of poverty. He saw cities, particularly New York City, as the breeding ground for crime and assorted other vices. People driven to the cities by "the era of steampower and industrial development" found themselves crowded into inadequate tenements and faced with the reality of hunger and its attendant physical maladies.[4] Riis exhorted his middle-class readership to action by appealing to its sense of foreboding that arose from the threat it perceived from living side by side with the underprivileged and idle masses. He capitalized on anxiety about the growth of social classes that might lead toward violence. Riis's solution to the problem was to avert danger by improving the educational and material condition of the urban poor. It was in this super-charged atmosphere that the dinner pail and lunch box first emerged as political and status symbols.

1896: A Promise of Prosperity in the Dinner Pail

The year 1896 found the nation in the midst of a series of rapid and decisive alterations. Since the economic depression of 1873, the economy had cycled through periods of depression and recovery. Still, industrial development continued. The growth of railroads greatly simplified the distribution process and, in combination with land and water routes, made the majority of urban and rural consumers accessible to manufacturers and merchants. In the wake of economic change came social change. As America's population boomed, so did her cities. The population of the United States in 1880 was 50 million with 28.2 percent living in rural regions. By 1900, those figures had increased to a population of nearly 76 million with 39.6 percent rural.[5] Then in 1920, the census revealed that for the first time in American history the majority of the population of the United States resided in urban rather than in rural settings. These cities were replete with opportunity, but also harbored discrimination, poverty, and vice. Progress was not without its tolls.

As America's rural contingency shrank, it began to feel the pinch both politically and economically. Although productivity was on the increase as more land came under cultivation, surplus crops did not necessarily translate into excess cash for the farm belt. In fact, during the long agricultural depression between 1873 and 1900, prices for commodities fell sharply. The greater national economic perils combined with the uncertainties and traumas of poor environmental conditions caused many farmers to lose their farms during this period.[6]

Some farmers responded to the tough times by uniting into political and social organizations to demonstrate their solidarity. An outgrowth of these various agrarian associations was the Populist Party. People who subscribed to this political affiliation met for their first national convention in Omaha, Nebraska, in July 1892. The Populist platform found favor with many rural and urban Americans who identified with the deplorable conditions the party leadership sought to eliminate. By 1896, the major parties could not ignore the influence of Populist agitation. The Democrats were particularly amenable to Populist ideals. Even so, when the Democrats met in 1896 for the purpose of nominating their presidential candidate, they faced extreme rancor and division within the party ranks. At the convention, delegates had difficulty coming to agreement with regard to both the monetary question and the selection of a candidate. Some Democrats considered the possibility of forming a coalition with the Populists to broaden their popular appeal and in an effort to siphon Populist supporters to their side.

William Jennings Bryan, the national standard bearer for the Populist movement, took the 1896 Democratic convention in Chicago by storm. A lawyer and congressman, Bryan's greatest asset was his amazing oratorical skill. He captured the convention's attention with his famous "Cross of Gold" Speech. In this fiery response to the debate over the currency, Bryan challenged those favoring the gold standard at the convention and outlined a prosilver platform wherein he identified the Democrats as the party of the downtrodden and under-represented. Many farmers, miners, and debtors believed that the unlimited coinage of silver would expand currency in such a way as to increase the price of their crops and render debts more easily payable. The gold standard, in contrast, was far less flexible and limited the power of the government or banks to influence inflation. Bryan asserted, furthermore, that Democrats backed legislation to bring prosperity to the masses, benefits that would work their "way up through every class which rests upon them."[7] He concluded with a stirring religious metaphor:

Photograph of William Jennings Bryan taken during a speech circa 1896 (Library of Congress, Prints and Photographs Division, LC-USZC2-6259).

Having behind us the producing masses of this nation and the world, supported by the commercial interests, the laboring interests and the toilers everywhere, we will answer their demand for a gold standard by saying to them: You shall not press down upon the brow of labor this crown of thorns, you shall not crucify mankind upon a cross of gold.[8]

Both Bryan's rhetoric and the language of the Populist platform referred to a social divide between two distinct classes. The Populists tended to see a simple separation between wealth and poverty, while Bryan honed in on an urban/rural or eastern/western divide. Either way, the goal remained the same: to carve a unified coalition out of divergent interests. The significance of their arguments was not in the

SECOND COPY.

OCT 1899

VOL. 37 NO. 939   OCTOBER 14 1899   PRICE 10 CENTS

Judge

55515
Aug. 30. 99.

PROSPERITY.
MEN WANTED
MILLS AND FACTORIES
RUNNING NIGHT and DAY
INCREASED WAGES
EVERYBODY SATISFIED
WORK FOR ALL
GOOD PRICES
EVERYTHING BOOMING
MEN WANTED
McKINLEY PROSPERITY

FULL
DINNER PAIL

16 to 1

GRANT HAMILTON

ENUFSED.

The 14 October 1899 cover of *Judge*, depicting William Jennings Bryan trapped beneath a larger-than-life "full dinner pail." The sign by his side reads: "PROSPERITY/MEN WANTED/MILLS AND FACTORIES RUNNING NIGHT AND DAY/INCREASED WAGES/EVERYBODY SATISFIED/WORK FOR ALL/GOOD PRICES/ EVERYTHING BOOMING MEN WANTED/MCKINLEY PROSPERITY" (Library of Congress, Prints and Photographs Division, LC-USZ62-56909).

geographic affiliation of their audience, but in the symbolism of the honest laborer and diligent farmer. These were the images that encapsulated the constituency targeted through the broader progressive movement of which Populism was a part.

Progressivism was a somewhat generic label applied to a wide range of reform movements beginning at the end of the nineteenth century and continuing into the early decades of the twentieth. According to historian Lewis Gould, the progressive impulse grew out of the "social change and political ferment" that followed in the wake of rapid "industrialization, urban growth, and ethnic tension."[9] Under the umbrella of progressivism came such movements as the social gospel movement and those favoring municipal reform, woman's suffrage, and child welfare legislation. Among the leadership and rank-and-file of these social reformers, motivations and goals often differed. For example, some business leaders might become involved in a movement for better working conditions if such improvements might also lead to higher worker productivity and lower costs. Clearly, workers crusading toward the same goal did not evaluate their efforts from the same point of view. Many progressive reformers expressed confidence in the overall goodness and moral perfectibility of humans. It was a commonly held tenet of their philosophy that by improving the environmental conditions of a person's daily life, they could bring about a strengthening of character and thereby create a more virtuous American citizenry. Sometimes, however, their efforts to achieve social amelioration resulted in the suppression of immigrant cultures or the institutionalization of bureaucratic procedures.[10]

Although progressives tended to downplay the existence of discrete classes in an effort to foster feelings of unity, many refused to acknowledge that any nonspecialists should be allowed to make decisions or affect public policy. A progressive belief in a proactive government called for the intervention of experts to remedy the social and economic problems that plagued the nation. This lack of confidence in the farmers and urban workers who comprised the main voting bloc for progressive candidates, combined with an overall weakness in the party leadership's ability to unite these distinct interests, frequently spelled failure for the progressive agenda. Limited successes at the local and national level were not enough to propel a completely progressive politician to the presidency.[11]

The Republicans, like the Democrats, faced a momentous challenge when the time came to choose their candidate for the 1896 presidential race. In the shadows of the 1873 depression, in spite of the fact that Republican Ulysses S. Grant had been president at the onset of economic turmoil, Republicans had fared well over Democrats in the national elections. The Democrats began to lose increasing numbers of urban and rural votes to their Republican competitors. The result was a political realignment whereby immigrants and working-class people who had traditionally cast ballots in the Democratic column shifted their loyalty to the Republicans.[12]

As it was for the Democrats, the currency issue was a major source of internal discord for the Republicans. Western Republicans tended to support the silver standard. Having their roots in states where sil-ver mining and agriculture predominated, many of these Republicans deserted the party and joined the more progressive Populists. After rejecting a proposed international bimetallic standard, the party finally closed ranks around the gold standard. A reliance on silver, they argued, would have a negative impact on foreign and domestic credit and, by retarding American business growth, would be injurious to the welfare of farmers, merchants, and laborers.[13]

American farmers and working men became the focus of the political campaign. The Republicans, like the Democrats, knew that to win the election, they had to appeal to these groups. The Republicans chose as their candidate a man who they hoped would be able to attract the broadest level of support.

Photograph of William McKinley, taken circa 1896, during his first term as president (Library of Congress, Prints and Photographs Division, LC-USZ62-97097).

A political cartoon from the 1900 McKinley presidential campaign (image from Richard L. McElroy, *William McKinley and Our America: A Pictorial History.* Canton, Ohio: Stark County Historical Society, 1996).

William McKinley, a lawyer by trade, two-term governor of Ohio, and congressman, based his platform on strong protectionist policies and the gold standard. He ran a successful "front porch" campaign during which he spoke from the front porch of his home in Canton, Ohio, to groups of people who arrived by train from all over the nation. When election

The 15 September 1900 cover of *Judge*, with a disgruntled William Jennings Bryan lost amid a sea of "full dinner pails" (Library of Congress, Prints and Photographs Division, LC-USZ6-793).

day finally arrived on 3 November 1896, the nation's voters turned out in large numbers to cast their ballots. Ultimately, candidate McKinley reigned supreme, and he sailed into office on the promise of a "full dinner pail."

Dorothy's Dinner Pail

This tale of the dinner pail begins once upon a time, in the far-away land called Ev. One day, a little girl named Dorothy, who is from Kansas, and the veteran of many other adventures in the land of Oz, finds herself lost in this magical place. She has been traveling with "her Uncle Henry to Australia, to visit some relatives they had never before seen. Uncle Henry, you must know, was not very well, because he had been working so hard on his Kansas farm that his health had given way and left him weak and nervous." During a sea voyage to Australia, the ship carrying Dorothy and Uncle Henry encounters a terrible storm. While searching on deck for her uncle, Dorothy clings to a chicken coop to steady herself against the howling winds. The powerful gusts are too great, however, and Dorothy and the coop are swept into the turbulent sea. The rightful inhabitants of the coop are sent "fluttering away in every direction, being blown by the wind until they looked like feather dusters without handles." Eventually, the winds subside, and the tired and wet little girl falls fast asleep. She awakens to the incessant clucking of a yellow hen who is also a stowaway on the coop-turned-raft. Soon, Billina, the hen, who speaks English quite fluently (this is Ev after all) informs Dorothy that land is in sight.[14]

The land of Ev is a magical place, described by Dorothy as "a new, wild country, without even trolley-cars or tel'phones. The people here havn't been discovered yet, I'm sure; that is if there *are* any people." While the question of human inhabitants in Ev remains outstanding, Dorothy makes another interesting discovery — trees bearing fruit in the form of lunch boxes:

> One was quite full of square paper boxes, which grew in clusters on all the limbs, and upon the biggest and ripest boxes the word "Lunch" could be read, in neat raised letters. This tree seemed to bear all the year around, for there were lunch-box blossoms on some of the branches, and on others tiny little lunch-boxes that were as yet quite green, and evidently not fit to eat until they had grown bigger.
>
> The leaves of this tree were all paper napkins, and it presented a very pleasing appearance to the hungry little girl.

Illustration from L. Frank Baum's *Ozma of Oz*.

But the tree next to the lunch-box tree was even more wonderful, for it bore quantities of tin dinner-pails, which were so full and heavy that the stout branches bent underneath their weight. Some were small and dark-brown in color; those larger were of a dull tin color; but the really ripe ones were the pails of bright tin that shone and glistened beautifully in the rays of sunshine that touched them.[15]

Later, when she samples the contents of the pail she finds them pleasing as well:

> In the cover she found a small tank that was full of very nice lemonade. It was covered by a cup, which might also, when removed, be used to drink the lemonade from. Within the pail were three slices of turkey, two slices of cold tongue, some lobster salad, four slices of bread and butter, a small custard pie, an orange and nine large strawberries, and some nuts and raisins. Singularly enough, the nuts in this dinner-pail grew already cracked, so that Dorothy had no trouble in picking out their meats to eat.[16]

Dorothy is well sustained by the pleasant meals she harvests from the trees of Ev, but she soon discovers that her actions have not gone undetected by some of the pseudo-human inhabitants of Ev. A Wheeler, one of a great army of beings who "had the form of a man, except that it walked, or rather rolled, upon all fours," interrogates the newcomer to his domain: "Did you not pick our lunch-boxes and dinner-pails? Have you not a stolen dinner-pail still in your hand?" As Dorothy equivocates, the Wheeler declares: "It is the law here that whoever picks a dinner-pail without our permission must die immediately."[17]

"Ozamerica?"

Although we must, for now, leave the fairy land of Ev and return to the United States, the two are not separated by as wide a gulf as one might think. To understand the significance of the comparison, it is necessary to look to the one man who inhabited both of these countries — the royal historian of Oz himself, L. Frank Baum.

Both Baum's personal beliefs and the volatility of the American political landscape are reflected in his work. His most famous children's book, *The Wonderful Wizard of Oz,* was an immediate success in 1900. The American public raved over this story of an American child that was not based on some distant European myth. The book resulted in the creation of numerous sequels, promotional products ranging from dolls to wrist watches, and several stage and film versions. The year 1939 brought a new interpretation of Baum's work in the form of Metro-Goldwyn-Mayer's timeless movie. The youthful energy and charisma of talented actress Judy Garland, along with her costars, Ray Bolger, Jack Haley, and Bert Lahr, transformed the popular American fairy tale into a motion picture spectacular.

Today, the *Wizard of Oz* is nothing short of a cultural icon for many Americans. Knowledge of the story and its characters enables one to participate in a cultural dialogue where the phrase "There's no place like home" has special meaning. *The Wonderful Wizard of Oz* is indeed an American fairy tale. There is more, however, to this story than might appear from a casual, superficial reading. Beyond the obvious adventure tale lie the roots of a political satire.

Lyman Frank Baum was born into the successful oil drilling family of Mr. and Mrs. Benjamin Baum on 15 May 1856 in Chittenango, New York. As a boy, he loved to read and, like his father, had a bit of the entrepreneurial spirit within him. He experimented in such areas as chicken breeding, newspaper printing, and, after an unsuccessful stint as an actor, he attempted play writing. Baum's plans changed after he made the acquaintance of Maud Gage, the daughter of the prominent women's suffrage crusader, Matilda Gage. The couple was married on 9 November 1882. By 1883, they began their family, and Baum discovered his newest forte, that of being a father.

The year 1888 found the Baum family in a difficult financial situation. Like many Americans, Baum suffered from the effects of a volatile national economy. News of great prosperity in the Western United States convinced him that it would be in the best interest of his family to relocate. So the family moved to Aberdeen, South Dakota, in search of a new life. In Aberdeen, Frank opened his own store called "Baum's Bazaar." This venture did not prove very fruitful and lasted only about two years. He then purchased a small local newspaper and returned to his natural talent of writing. As owner and editor of the *Aberdeen Saturday Pioneer*, Baum authored a weekly column titled "Our Landlady." He wrote his stories in the form of a dialogue among residents of a boarding house, and according to his biographers, he used it to comment on "affairs close to the hearts and purses of Aberdeen readers. It was a device he used for humor, social satire, character portrayal, personal comment, and fantasy."[18]

During his time in South Dakota, Baum experienced firsthand the suffering of the Western farmers. One of his "Our Landlady" columns featured a farmer and a federal land agent. When the land agent inquired of the farmer whether he had enough food for his horses, the farmer responded: "No, I put green goggles on my horses and feed 'em shavings an' they think it's grass, but they ain't gettin' fat on it."[19] Poor growing seasons meant that farmers had little ready cash for purchases such as newspapers. As a result, in spite of Baum's editorial skill, the circulation of the newspaper dropped to such a low level that he could no longer sustain his commitment. In 1891, the Baum family moved to Chicago. While living in the Windy City, he was able to break into the printing business and begin publishing his own works. Baum also found himself immersed in the politics of a presidential

Photograph of Lyman Frank Baum, circa 1908 (Library of Congress, Prints and Photographs Division, LC-USZ62-103204).

election. Although he had not been active in politics before and would end his involvement after Democrat William Jennings Bryan's second failed presidential campaign in 1900, being in the heart of Populist country raised Baum's level of awareness and concern about the direction of the country.

Baum's setting for *The Wonderful Wizard of Oz* and his characters have uncanny similarities to the important places and influential people of American life circa 1900.[20] Indeed, historians and literary critics alike have speculated over the possibilities for "Ozmic-American" parallels. Although Baum himself never stated publicly that he intended his story to contain allegorical elements, his documented Populist leanings,

involvement in the 1896 Bryan campaign, and predominantly Democratic voting record, attest to the possibility that such allusions may
have been planned. By using the lens of political satire, a timeless fairy
tale is transformed into a temporally and culturally specific narrative
where the yellow brick road is akin to the gold standard; Dorothy represents the "everyman" Western farmer; the Wizard equals William
McKinley; the Cowardly Lion mirrors William Jennings Bryan; and
the Tin Man stands for the dispirited industrial laborers.[21]

Cross of Gold and Pail of Tin

In view of the theories regarding Baum's use of symbolism, it is
profitable to examine one of his later works, one of the sequels to the
adventures in Oz, from a similarly critical perspective. Again, there is
no tangible evidence that Baum constructed his stories with an eye to
political, social, or economic satire. However, as a product of a distinct cultural moment, his tales are useful in the effort to unlock the
mysteries of symbolism and dialogue shared by people from the past
but lost to the modern audience.

Ozma of Oz, the third book in the Oz series, was published in 1907.
Baum had never planned to write additional works chronicling the lives
of the characters from the original Oz work, but the outcry from the
petite readers in his audience was such that he eventually responded
with fourteen books on the fairy land of Oz. Some of the key imagery
in the early part of this work revolves around the lunch-box and dinner-
pail trees from which Dorothy harvests her meals. In the magical world
of Oz, anything can grow on a tree, but the fact that Baum chose to
make these trees bear food containers as fruit begs questions regarding
the symbolism of this choice.

Baum's use of lunch boxes and dinner pails suggests that these
were objects with which his readers had some familiarity. Indeed, during McKinley's second presidential campaign 1900, the dinner pail took
on special significance. It became a rallying point to gather the forces
of the farmers and factory workers whom McKinley needed to ensure
his victory. In 1900, as in 1896, McKinley found himself running
against Bryan. Although his first term witnessed significant international challenges in the form of the Spanish-American War, on the
domestic front, prosperity seemed to be the general national condition.

In a speech at Kewanee, Illinois, on 7 October 1899, the president claimed: "The hum of industry has drowned the voice of calamity, and the voice of despair is no longer heard in the United States, and the orators without occupation here are now looking to the Philippines for comfort."[22] McKinley capitalized on this sense of economic prosperity by using the "full dinner pail" as a symbol of the absence of hunger for Americans, both urban and rural. The dinner pail was an object that each of these contingencies could relate to and understand as a promise of the good times and plenty to come.

Let's Do Lunch: The Social Performance of a Meal

Dorothy's pattern of dining in Ev exhibits a preoccupation with the propriety of food consumption. She clearly understands the day as divided into breakfast time, lunch time, and dinner time. Each of these meals occurs within a specific time frame and is defined by certain signatory foods. When Dorothy cannot find anything appropriate for her breakfast, she breaks the standard pattern and eats lunch: "'A lunch isn't zactly breakfast,' she says to Billina, who sits beside her watching curiously. 'But when one is hungry one can even eat supper in the morning, and not complain.'"[23] Still, Dorothy eats the food from the lunch box first and saves that from the dinner pail for later.

In Dorothy's Oz drama, it is clear that meals have certain significant names. Outside of Oz, the lexicon of food consumption is even more complicated and meaning-filled. Breakfast, lunch, luncheon, brunch, dinner, supper, and tea are among the many labels given to the various meals of the day. Usage of these terms varies across cultures and even within them. The sharing of meals is both a physical act and a cultural and social interaction that may include a variety of transactions for both business and pleasure. Decisions such as what to eat, when, where, and with whom to dine carry consequences for social status. The word *lunch* can be defined several different ways, including "A light meal, less substantial than dinner"; or "The regular midday meal, so called by those who eat dinner in the evening"; or "Food, frequently sandwiches, a piece of pie, etc., put in a pail or package, and eaten by school children, workmen, etc., esp. at noon"; and finally "A light meal eaten at any irregular time."[24] This denotation of lunch demonstrates two important features of the noon meal. First, that it is "so called" by people who consume a "dinner" later in the evening. Second, that the term *lunch* is often used specifically to describe the types of food carried in a container and eaten by workers and students. These two criteria suggest that a hierarchy exists in Americans' interpretation of what lunch means for different people in a variety of circumstances.

Historically, making food portable has been a common concern for a wide range of people, including agricultural and factory workers, soldiers, explorers, settlers, students, and travelers. Although each of these workers and adventurers had different reasons for being unable to return home for a meal, they all faced the similar conundrum of how to select foods that would not be damaged by changes in temperature and could be transported easily.[25]

Evidence of the need for portable food appears in many early American cookbooks in the form of recipes for dishes such as "johnny-cake" or "journey cake." Generally, these recipes called for a combination of cornmeal and water or milk that was baked on a flat board so that it could be cut into squares and packed neatly. Mary Randolph, a native Southerner, introduced a regional variation when she published in her 1860 edition of *The Virginia Housewife* a similar recipe based on rice or a cornmeal and rice mixture. Another comestible of this type was hardtack. A mixture of flour and water, hardtack was baked until it hardened, rather like a modern cracker. Hardtack's durability and hence transportability made it a staple of the Civil War soldier's diet. Many enlisted men derided these wafers for their primary, indeed perhaps only notable quality — tastelessness.

What these portable foods may lack in gourmet appeal they make up for in their ability to provide nutrition on the run. The need to carry lunch from one location to another has led people to the creative adaptation of foods and containers to suit their needs; a process that continues even as mass producers and marketers endeavor to provide products for this purpose. Accounts of lunch carrying in historical and literary sources list lard and molasses buckets, shoe boxes, tea and tobacco tins, and simple paper bags among the objects people have employed for this purpose.

Material culture theory is grounded in the assumption that objects, as tangible and visual evidence of daily life, exude powerful messages in their roles as decorative arts, tools, and commodities. Although scholars approach this field from many different disciplinary traditions, many material culture theorists agree that things do social work. The production and consumption of material goods by members of a culture is a part of a process that serves to create and sustain relationships among human beings. In this context, objects are not valuable simply because of their materiality but also for their role in structuring the chaos of the social environment and contributing to the evolution and perpetuation of cultural systems.[26]

The advent of the modern consumer-oriented society and questions as to when and how people came to possess and value objects constitutes a common area of investigation and debate in recent material culture studies. Scholars of material culture, history, and anthropology often disagree over the exact period during which the transition from a producer- to a consumer-based economy occurred. Some researchers locate its beginnings as early as the sixteenth century, many others suggest the eighteenth century as the true locus of change, and still others argue that full development cannot be claimed until the late nineteenth and early twentieth centuries.[27]

For the purposes of this study, the precise timing of the shift from a producer-based to a consumer society is not as significant as the fact that it was unquestionably evident in the United States by the end of the nineteenth century. By this point in American history, industrialization and commercialization had proceeded far enough to make lunch boxes commonly understood objects. Because they were culturally familiar artifacts, manufacturers, advertisers, the government, interest groups, and individuals could easily manipulate how they were perceived. This process resulted in the creation and attachment of a battery of social and symbolic meanings to a simple, utilitarian object — the dinner pail or lunch box.[28]

In Dorothy's experience in Ev, lunch boxes and dinner pails grow on separate trees and contain different types of food. The contents of the lunch box are simple but hearty: a sandwich, fruit, cake, a pickle, cheese, and an apple. Through John R. Neill's captivating illustrations, readers see Dorothy reaching up to pick one of the ripe boxes from a low branch of the tree. The lunch boxes grow in orderly rows attached to the limbs by what appears to be a string stem. While the lunch boxes are made out of paper, the dinner pails are made of tin. Neill's illustrations show an oval-shaped tin container with a removable lid sporting a built in "tank" and cup for beverages. In addition to their contrasting physical appearances, the boxes and pails differ most significantly in the nature of their contents. The fare within the dinner pail is much more elegant than that in the lunch box. The pail contains such delicacies as lobster salad, cold tongue, fresh strawberries, nuts, and lemonade. These differences are not insignificant. As was demonstrated in the definition of lunch, the labels applied to meals can have certain specific class-related connotations.

The dictionary definition of *dinner* is: "The principal meal of the day; an elaborate meal served on a particular occasion."[29] Both imply a sense of solemnity that is lacking in the definition of lunch. The "luncheon," more formal than lunch, and "less substantial than dinner," carries a similar air of importance. In an 1899 issue of *Scribner's Magazine*, Robert Grant, author of "The Search-Light Letters: To a Young Man or Woman in Search of the Ideal," queries: "Speaking of democracy and culture, my dear sir, I should like to inquire if you have any authority for your use of the word 'lunch'? As employed by the appropriating and the arrogant it has long meant a meal or a bite between breakfast and dinner; but as used by democracy, it seems to apply to afternoon tea or late supper equally well." He asks this question when a visitor refers to a midnight repast as a lunch. Later, Grant comments: "Confound the man! Why should he call my supper a lunch?"[30]

It is interesting then, that during the late nineteenth century, when the prefixes lunch- and dinner- were applied to the suffixes -box and -pail, the issue of class affiliations as evidenced through the monikers applied to one's meals seemed to evaporate. Under the dictionary entry *lunch pail*, "dinner pail" appears as a synonym. It did not matter whether one carried one's lunch in a dinner pail, or dinner in a lunch box, the significance was not in the name of the object, but in the need to carry it. The terms were interchangeable because the objects they described both branded users equally with the status of worker. In both the *Oxford English Dictionary* and *The Dictionary of American English on Historical Principles*, the terms *dinner pail* and *lunch box* are described as originating in America in the latter half of the nineteenth century. The dinner pail is described exclusively as an object utilized by working men, laborers, or students. Lunch boxes, in contrast, may be found in the hands of the aforementioned as well as the occasional traveler. No matter what it was called or what its recesses contained, a dinner pail or lunch box was a clear emblem of one's affiliation with the laboring classes. These objects were politicized by their popular social significance.

In this consumer-centered society, the advertising industry helped people internalize new meanings for their consumption activities. Advertisers worked to establish connections between people and objects that would encourage buying and create product loyalty. What was particularly remarkable about this process, as historian Alan Trachtenberg points out, was the separation of consumer and laborer that occurred when advertisers addressed their audience. Advertisements spoke to people as if each and every one of them was "already 'middle class' in its tastes, outlook, and expectations."[31] In the sense that they targeted all Americans as if they were members of this vaunted middle class, advertisers made two important assumptions. First, they promoted a society wherein middle class equaled normalcy, virtue, and patriotism. In crafting their appeals, they equated the language and images of their advertisements with an idealized notion of American life. Second, by aiming their advertisements at a monolithic group, they denied the existence of class divisions and thus sidestepped the envies, dislocations, and conflicts inherent to the competition between the classes. Viewers of these advertisements imbibed a vision of American society that emphasized harmony, order, and unity achievable through the vehicle of consumer goods.[32]

The Mechanization of Society: Technological Dislocations in Imaginary and Real Worlds

The type of labor most commonly associated with those who carried their meals to work involved very little in the way of abstract thinking. While the work might have required specialized skill in a particular process, it could be performed through rote, mechanical action. As industrialization placed greater emphasis on the distinction between workers and managers, many people experienced new levels of discomfort with the system. Trachtenberg writes: "The momentous event of mechanization, of science and technology coming to perform the labor most significant to the productivity of the system, reproduced itself in ambivalent cultural images of machines and inventors, and in displacements running like waves of shock through the social order."[33] Factory work demanded a certain time and work discipline that was not new to American workers but was different in that it was imposed rather than self-directed.

Although Ev is a fairy land, life is not all sunshine and happiness for everyone. Similar to late-nineteenth-century America, some inhabitants of Ev are experiencing the sometimes negative effects of mechanization. Tiktok is a mechanical man. Though he has the capacity for thought, he is unable to engage it unless someone else winds him up first. He is a diligent and devoted worker — and that is all. Tiktok does "Everything but Live." Baum's Tiktok is an example of the dehumanization that was a direct result of the industrial process. Tiktok cannot run without the intervention of an outside party that can wind his clockwork mechanism. When wound, he can think, act, and speak, but he remains always completely dedicated to the service of his master. When Dorothy offers him a taste of the victuals from the dinner pail, he politely refuses because, as a mechanical man, he does not need food. For him, the tin dinner pail becomes most useful as a weapon with which to defend himself, Dorothy, and Billina from the advances of the Wheelers. Tiktok's individuality and humanity is a casualty of mechanization.

Curiously, Tiktok's creators, Smith and Tinker, have both vanished

Illustration from L. Frank Baum's *Ozma of Oz.*

from the land of Ev. Tiktok tells Dorothy and Billina that Mr. Smith, both an artist and an inventor, one day painted a picture of a river that was so realistic, "as he was reach-ing a-cross it to paint some flow-ers on the o-po-site bank, he fell in-to the wa-ter and was drowned." Mr. Tinker, loyal servant of the king of Ev, endeavored to construct a lad-der to the moon so that he could harvest stars for the king's crown. When he reached the moon, he found it to be such a wonderful place that he pulled up the ladder and never returned. In the tragicomic tale of Smith and Tinker, Baum satirizes the tension inherent in the tran-sition from a rural, agrarian society, to one dominated by technology and industry. The shift was not an easy one in Ev or anywhere.[34]

Trachtenberg has described the phenomenon that transformed American life in the late eighteenth and early nineteenth centuries as "incorporation." He argues that the corporate business model also came to define American culture and society, and that corporate organiza-tions affected people's perceptions of time, space, leisure, and knowl-edge. In Trachtenberg's estimation, by the 1870s, incorporation had become commonplace, to the great dismay of many social critics. The transformation process was swift and frequently brutal. It involved the breakdown of traditional paradigms of work and compensation. The demands of rapid economic growth and different interpretations of the nature of labor and entrepreneurship resulted in the creation of a new American working class. Between 1870 and 1900, the percentage of the population engaged in industrial labor nearly doubled. By the close of the nineteenth century, more than one-third of Americans counted themselves among these ranks. Trachtenberg comments: "Wage labor emerged, unequivocally, as the definitive working-class experience, a proletarianization no longer the imagined nightmare of independent artisans and failed entrepreneurs but the typical lot of American work-ers."[35] Baum's Smith and Tinker were not alone in their distress with a changing world.

Another important consequence of the incorporation process was a growing specialization in the type of knowledge required to function at the highest levels of industrial society. In this new economic system, technical knowledge was the handmaiden of power. Trachtenberg chronicles the path whereby traditional artisanship and empirical skill was eclipsed by an educational hierarchy based on scientific calcula-tions and efficiency. To achieve the important designation of "profes-sional," Americans who possessed the means to do so increased their level of education and embraced the use of consumer goods as indicators of status and wealth.

The Eclipse of a Political Symbol

For those who struggled to maintain their identity against the encroachments of industrial life, the dinner pail or lunch box could be both a symbol of unity with other workers and an expression of increasing modernization. McKinley's campaign strategists knew that to succeed, their candidate had to maximize his appeal to the new industrial working class and to the diminishing yet still politically significant American farmers. He capitalized on the unifying aspect of the dinner pail and its positive associations with prosperity and plenty. The dinner pail conjured up imagery familiar to each of these important groups. Those who were still members of the farming community understood dinner as the biggest, most formal, and substantial meal of their day. Although they probably returned to their homes at noon, they would have understood McKinley's full dinner pail as a symbol of positive economic conditions that contrasted with the despair and hardships of the past. Similarly, industrial workers, many of whom originally hailed from rural areas, still associated the term *dinner* rather than *lunch* with their noon meal. They recognized McKinley's promise of a full dinner pail as an insurance policy against the economic uncertainties of the modern industrial economy. The full dinner pail was a comforting, calming image for those living in the midst of tremendous economic and social changes. The soothing message of the full dinner pail slogan helped weld the farmers and working class into a solid McKinley vote.

Although McKinley was able to use this symbol effectively, within a short period after his reelection in 1900, the dinner pail followed Populism onto the dustbin of history. As the rural population continued to dwindle, political concerns shifted further away from them and toward the booming cities and suburbs. Moreover, the ideal American life, as depicted in popular literature, focused increasingly on the middle-class urban household.

In fact, during the 1912 presidential contest, which included Democrat Woodrow Wilson, Republican William Howard Taft, and Progressive Party candidate Theodore Roosevelt, the Democrats used the contrasting image of the housewife's "empty market basket" in an ultimately successful effort to capitalize on the Republicans' failure to deliver the full dinner pail as they had promised. The power of the market basket symbol is strong evidence of a growing political focus on consumers in American society.

The path leading to the extinction of the dinner pail as a political symbol had begun long before the McKinley era. In its incipient stages, it was expressed as an undercurrent of mistrust and fear of the changes that industrialization brought about in the social and economic structure. Whereas manual labor had once been associated with virtue and skill, the new industrial labor force, comprised as it was of immigrants and the urban poor, came to represent the antithesis of the American dream. Membership in this new working class was neither an emblem of virtue nor an indication of skill. Most disturbing of all, the lines of demarcation that defined this class did not allow for the fluid movement upward that was such a vital part of the American promise. In the language of objects, the dinner pail screamed "working class" at a time when the popular imagery of the good life was becoming distinctly middle class. As Americans grew more comfortable with the new industrial economy, they cohered into "a mass of new consumers anxious to exchange their incomes for the assurance promised by goods of immunity from poverty, insecurity, the increasingly degraded status of the manual worker."[36] Hence, people became more conscious of the outward signs that classified them in the public eye. In a culture where people read appearances as evidence of status, items as simple as a dinner pail or lunch box could broadcast undesirable messages. In such a culture, continued reliance on the dinner pail as a political tool would have been unwise, at best.

The character of the American lunch box today owes much to an evolutionary process that began with the humble tin dinner pail. While its construction and the foods commonly found in it have changed over the years, one role that has remained constant is its role as material communicator. With the politicization of the dinner pail in the late nineteenth and early twentieth centuries, the lunch box, its contents, its "toter" and "packer" became acceptable subjects of public praise, scrutiny, and, sometimes, social ostracism.

2

Creating Efficient Workers and Students: Reformers Take Up the Lunch Cause

Unfair Luncheon Fare

Let us consider for a moment the sheer variety of luncheon fare one might encounter in late-nineteenth- and early twentieth-century American factories. A high volume of immigrants to the United States coincided with the boom in industrial capacity; hence, many newcomers found themselves employed in often low-paying production jobs. In his 1905 book *The Jungle*, Upton Sinclair exposed the working conditions and questionable processing techniques of meat packing plants of early twentieth-century Chicago. He also illuminated the struggle to feed workers an ample supply of calories on the limited incomes they brought home. The immigrant family in Sinclair's story clings to many of its traditional foods and items of minimal cost. Teta Elzbieta, the matriarch of the family, rouses the men for work and prepares the daily rations: "She would have ready a great pot full of steaming black coffee, and oatmeal and bread and smoked sausages; and then she would fix them their dinner pails with more thick slices of bread and lard between them — they could not afford butter — and some onions and a piece of cheese, and so they would tramp away to work."[1] These workers carried

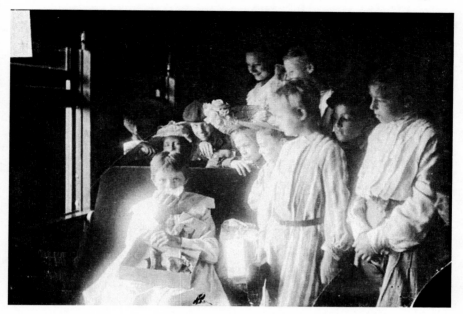

This unidentified young train passenger is eating her lunch from a paper box, circa 1905 (DN-0002902, Chicago Daily News negatives collection, Chicago Historical Society).

two social brands out the door each morning: the obvious one of status as a worker, based on the nature of the lunch container, and the equally potent label of immigrant communicated by the nature of the food within their pails.

Another literary character from the turn of the century, Theodore Dreiser's Caroline Meeber, boards a train outside of Chicago with only a trunk, a satchel, a lunch in a paper box, and a purse with her train ticket, as she sets out to find a new life with her sister in the city. Later, as an employee of a shoe factory, Carrie experiences the feeling of being transformed from a human being into a machine. She is a captive of the equipment in front of her, making unnatural, mechanical movements with little or no control over the speed of her work. When, on her first day, the bell for the lunch break finally rings, Carrie welcomes the opportunity to leave her station, stretch, get a drink of water, and perhaps eat a little bit of the lunch she had carried with her. What she discovered was, however, not a pleasant room for workers to relax and refuel, but a dingy, smelly place with poor sanitation facilities, and

Young workers (names unknown) leave a Cincinnati paper box factory to purchase items for their lunches in August 1908 (Library of Congress, Prints and Photographs Division, LC-DIG-nclc-01310).

almost no provisions for comfort. After leaving to take a drink from the water bucket in the corner of the room, Carrie finds all of the seats in the break area occupied by other workers.

As the novel unfolds, Carrie meets some very wealthy individuals who can afford to dine in the more refined Chicago establishments. When she joins them, Carrie is mesmerized by the service, comfort, and food she receives: "She felt a little out of place, but the great room soothed her and the view of the well-dressed throng outside seemed a splendid thing. Ah, what it was not to have money!"[2] The contrast was, after all, remarkable. By the end of the book, some of the characters experience a reversal of fortunes. The once prosperous Hurstwood finds himself dependent on the local charities of New York City for his lodgings and meals. Without exception, the services he receives are the result of concern on the part of private individuals or religious groups. From the Sisters of Mercy he procures a free noon meal in a situation that highlights the dehumanization caused by poverty:

> Space and a lack of culinary room in the mission-house, compelled an arrangement which permitted of only twenty-five or thirty eating at one time, so that a line had to be formed outside and an orderly entrance effected. This caused a daily spectacle, which, however, had become so common by repetition during a number of years that now nothing was thought of it. The men waited patiently, like cattle, in the coldest weather — waited for several hours before they could be admitted. No questions were asked and no service rendered. They ate and went away again, some of them returning regularly day after day the winter through.[3]

A later work, Thomas Wolfe's 1929 *Look Homeward, Angel,* confirms Carrie's observations regarding the relationship between the material culture of lunch and one's social status. Wolfe describes the paper bag of food carried by a school boy, the lard bucket lunches of black workers, and the shoe box lunches toted by travelers. Paper bags, which were first patented in 1859, were remarkably versatile and easy to use. They could be used as a packaging tool or to carry goods home from stores. Fairly inexpensive, the paper bag could be plain or decorated, often with the name of a commercial establishment.[4] In the early twentieth century, people who traveled from the western shore of the Chesapeake Bay to the eastern shore were often called shoebees because they toted their lunches in shoe boxes that had been lined with wax paper. Shoe boxes were not used as everyday lunch containers, because

people bought shoes relatively infrequently, so the boxes were somewhat rare and saved for special occasions such as a journey by train or
steamboat. The shoebees held their lunches safely inside the boxes by
wrapping a rubber band around the outside. In their estimation, a person who had the wherewithal to purchase a picnic basket was "well-
off."[5] Other manufacturers in the late nineteenth and early twentieth
centuries were not blind to the potential for reusing their product packaging. When tobacco processors found that people were reusing their
tins as lunch boxes, they redesigned the packaging to make it more
appealing for that purpose.[6]

For turn-of-the-century factory workers like Carrie and her
cohort, the combination of poor pay and short breaks meant that carrying lunch from home in some type of container was logical. Yet for
some, particularly male workers, the saloons and bars that were often
situated close to factories provided their noontime food and drink.
Whereas drink in eighteenth- and early nineteenth-century workplaces
had been common, indeed almost expected, by the mid-nineteenth
century, the change from a craft-oriented workshop labor force to a
more industrially regulated one meant a new demand for regularity
and system that translated to a need for temperance — at least during
the working day. Factory owners often suppressed the sociability associated with workplace drinking. Ethnically segregated saloons became
the place where working-class men ate lunch and did their drinking at
the end of the working day. Temperance and prohibition movements
dominated by middle- and upper-class, often nativist men and women
targeted these saloons. Drinking and/or dining in a saloon, like carrying a dinner or lunch pail, served as an automatic symbol of membership in the working class.[7]

Nor were students protected from the classifying eyes of their
peers, as Harper Lee, the author of *To Kill a Mockingbird*, demonstrated with this scenario. It is noon in a small southern classroom during the Great Depression. When the teacher instructs her class:
"Everybody who goes home to lunch hold up your hands," the "town
children" send arms into the air. That leaves students who bring their
lunches, or the "country folks." At the appropriate moment: "Molasses
buckets appeared from nowhere, and the ceiling danced with metallic
light. Miss Caroline walked up and down the rows peering and pok-
ing into lunch containers, nodding of the contents pleased her, frown-
ing a little at others. She stopped at Walter Cunningham's desk.

'Where's yours?' she asked." As the narrator, Jean Louise Finch, tells readers: "He didn't forget his lunch, he didn't have any. He had none today nor would he have any tomorrow or the next day."[8] In this world of home lunchers and packers, there are clear distinctions along social lines. Walter, unlike his other country counterparts, has not even the economic wherewithal to bring a humble snack in a recycled molasses container. For such children, the possession or lack of a lunch box serves as an easy barometer of economic status.

The consumption of the noon meal in each of these situations — in the schoolhouse, on the factory floor, at the elegant restaurant, in the mission house, or in the saloon — was conspicuously public, and yet for the poor student, worker, and impoverished unemployed, it was scarcely visible to the broader society. Sinclair, Dreiser, and other writers and social critics began to tug at the veil of poverty, exposing the other side of capitalist expansion. Still, lunch, although often taking place in a public location, remained at this time essentially a private concern, best handled at the individual level. Not until the growth of progressive and other reform movements with an emphasis on alleviating poverty and Americanizing immigrants, along with advances in nutrition science and rising concerns about industrial and educational efficiency, did the personal matter of lunch become the focus of outside parties.

Are You Going to Eat That? Changing the Eating Habits of Immigrants, the Poor, and the Uneducated

For the worker, a cafeteria was a convenience and perhaps a health benefit. For the factory owner or manager, understandably focused on the financial stability of his enterprise as well as the stamina and effectiveness of his employees, food service was less about catering to individual dietary tastes and needs than about providing fare that would be filling for the workers and would contribute most to their energy levels and ability to produce.

The carried lunch became a prime target for the jeremiads of nutritional reformers. The food consumed out of working-class dinner pails was often linked to the worker's ethnic heritage or to poor, albeit inexpensive foods associated with poverty. Early proponents of factory cafeterias attempted to convince managers that providing food and improving both employee diets and eating spaces would raise profits. Properly fed workers would be productive and tractable. Growing working-class militancy and resentment toward owners and managers during World War I propelled a new class of industrialists, proponents of the "enlightened corporation" and welfare capitalism into leadership positions. They saw themselves, rather than labor unions or the state, as responsible for "the creation of a more benign industrial society."[9]

These industrialists' newfound feelings of responsibility involved more than the employee alone, they spread to include the broader community as well. These reformers hoped to push improved dining habits from the factory to the home. A member of the medical department at Standard Oil of New Jersey, Ernest F. Hoyer, discussed some of the practical considerations involved in providing a hot meal in a factory canteen: "There are, of course, many pros and cons to the canteen idea — yet the fact remains, that it will not only stimulate the output — steady the efficiency — but also, besides helping physically, will eventually teach how and what to eat and so carry the good work to the homes."[10]

Some reformers were aware of the difficulty involved in altering working-class eating habits. Particularly among the immigrants, the foods one ate gave expression to one's cultural heritage and identity. The anonymous author of a November 1923 *Literary Digest* article titled "Decline and Fall of the 'Full Dinner Pail,'" warned that no matter how reformers might view the contents of workers' lunch boxes, for many people, these foods provided a "certain individuality" that appealed to "certain persons who do not like the idea of 'massed feeding.'"[11] Reforming and improving people by targeting their "bad" (read "different") habits and ameliorating the unsanitary and inefficient environments in which they lived and worked motivated these progressive reformers. Food consumption came under special scrutiny, because the lunchtime food habits of workers and students threatened to perpetuate potentially dangerous distinctions of class and ethnicity that might bring about social upheavals and general discontent at the local and, some feared, even the national level.

A general progressive belief in a proactive government called for the intervention of experts to remedy the social and economic problems that plagued the nation. Many progressive reformers hoped to end poverty through the influence of expert advice and by setting a good example. On the surface, this appeared to be a faultless undertaking. Sometimes, however, the efforts to achieve a certain level of social and economic parity resulted in the suppression of immigrant cultures and the institutionalization of bureaucratic procedures.

Reformers often rightfully condemned unsanitary food gathering, preparation, and storage methods of immigrants and the poor, but based on minimal general knowledge of health and nutrition, they sometimes inaccurately painted individual food choices as contributing to low energy levels and debilitated health. No amount of casual coercion or ranting and raving on the part of reformers could change the emotional and psychological significance of certain foods, nor alleviate the cash burden of procuring high-quality, fresh, and nutritious foods.[12]

Pure Food and Drugs: The Government Takes a Stand

By the late nineteenth century, scientific knowledge of bacteria, germs, and disease had made remarkable strides. For example, in the 1860s, Louis Pasteur developed a process for killing off undesirable bacteria present in milk and other food products. As scientists came to better understandings of such processes as fermentation and putrefaction, the possibilities for improving the quality of human life also increased. The growth of the food processing industry in the United States during this same time raised awareness regarding the proper care and handling of food. In an era before standard label laws and inspection of food processing facilities, no one knew exactly what might be in the tinned foods they purchased. Some small-scale food processors had used various chemicals and other additives as cost-cutting measures. Sinclair's *The Jungle* had exposed the seedy underbelly of the meat packing industry in Chicago, and the resulting products of large-scale food processing were neither appealing to the eye nor healthful for the body.

Partly in response to such widespread popular concern over the quality of processed food, during Theodore Roosevelt's administration, Congress passed the Pure Food and Drug Act in 1906. The Act included provisions for meat inspection and federal regulation of other food processors. Ultimately, some food processing giants saw it as a potential boon for their industry because it would serve to reassure consumers that their products were safe and clean and drive less scrupulous competitors out of business. Henry John Heinz, for example, was instrumental in gathering industrial support for the regulations. Heinz knew that small companies would not be able to compete with larger conglomerates when the law demanded a higher standard of product quality.[13] Heinz pickles, at least, would be clean and green.

The Pure Food and Drug Act thus demonstrates an early cooperative effort among government and industry leaders. But it did not ensure that all food would be either safe or nutritious. For those who could afford better quality food, the Act ensured health and convenience. Many of the immigrants and poor, like the family of Jurgis Rudkus in *The Jungle*, could not afford such assurances. For such people, a hot lunch in the factory cafeteria or the school lunchroom might be their best hope for a safe and nutritious meal.

Making Lunch Efficient: Employers Take an Interest

Frederick W. Taylor's 1911 work, *The Principles of Scientific Management*, initiated a concern with efficiency in the workplace that soon became a rallying cry in management circles. Taylorism had the effect of making factory workers seem like industrial robots. In an atmosphere marked by nearly obsessive interest with productivity, the nature of employee's meals soon fell subject to management inquest. Under these circumstances, reformers' efforts to change workers' eating habits gained sanction from the quantitative investigations of efficiency experts.

Partially as a result of the need to mobilize American industry for production during World War I, an increasing number of workplaces began to provide access to some form of sustenance during the workday. In a January 1917 article titled "The Disappearance of the Dinner Pail," Mary Alden Hopkins wrote: "Eating is no longer a private matter. Food is potential energy. The business house that wants concentrated efficiency spreads a table before its employees and cries: 'Eat, workingmen! For the work's sake, eat!'"[14]

By the early 1920s, workers' eating habits were truly shifting from being a private matter to one in which employers took a great deal of interest. The dinner pail was well on its way to transformation from being a simple political symbol into what an anonymous author in a 1923 issue of *Literary Digest* called a "threefold evil — an evil to the

A view of the factory lunch room of the Cheney Brothers Silk Manufactory in south Manchester, Connecticut, circa 1914 (Library of Congress, Prints and Photographs Division, LC-USZ62-97479).

employee, to the factory, and to the executives who run it." Accordingly, continued the article, factory owners who had formerly expressed little interest in their workers' meals "found that it is not a matter of philanthropy, but good business, to give the worker a chance to get a different sort of meal." The author goes on to describe the reasons why even a small factory owner would want to encourage his employees to eat in an on-site cafeteria rather than bring their meals from home. The author's research took him to Jonas Howard's observations in *Plant-Restaurant Management*. Howard had performed an early feat of investigative journalism. Howard asserted: "Our data comes from sources which are beyond question. The writer, himself, has made investigations." He had traveled to various factories to inquire into the facilities and provisions for employee dining, and he found a decided lack of space devoted to employee dining that disturbed him greatly.

> Have you ever, Mr. Executive, seen a group of factory workers sitting in a gutter on a hot day, eating the lunch brought from home in a dinner-pail? Have you noticed the results of using the gutter itself for a "table"? Have you realized that, having no other convenient place to lay his sandwich, the workman will often lay it on the ground or on a newspaper.
> Have you seen him fanning off the disease-carrying fly as he tried to eat in what peace and comfort he can find on a cold, hard stone?
> In many small factories, every day, we see young girl workers eating the noon-hour meal while perched in the window-sill of a third or fourth story building. Or, we see them littering up the workroom with garbage, papers, string, and trash. You can't blame them. They have to eat. They do not eat on your property through choice, and perhaps they are perfectly average in their tidiness.[15]

As a point of evidence, to illustrate the poor quality of workers' food, the *Literary Digest* writer included a listing of the contents of three dinner pails carried by workers into a Chicago factory:

> PAIL A: Three swiss cheese sandwiches, with tomato catsup; lukewarm soup; slab of custard pie, with soggy crust; five dill pickles; vile coffee, lukewarm in a bottle; a stick of candy.
> PAIL B: One-half soggy, cherry pie; one piece of cake; cold coffee; one large, raw cucumber; cold, baked beans, half cooked.
> PAIL C: Half-cooked spaghetti, with garlic; cool coffee; soggy cake; strips of raw potato.

The tone of the descriptions provided both by the anonymous writer and by Howard suggest a disgust with the foods eaten by poor people, and especially immigrants. The lunch pail inventories emphasize that the spaghetti was with garlic, the vegetables were raw, and the coffee was of inferior quality and temperature. The food Howard described was no better:

> Cold sandwiches, doubtful pickles and food selected without any thought of its nutritive value form the contents of the average workers' lunch-box. If you don't believe, look into a few of them and see. There is almost no variety. A check made some months ago in an Ohio plant revealed a shocking combination of victuals in the dinner-pails of the workers. This plant now has its own restaurant.[16]

Both writers agreed that the conditions under which workers were consuming their meals were unclean, inconvenient, and inefficient, and

Workers (names unknown) on a lunch break at the Illinois Glass Company, Alton, Illinois, in May 1910 (Library of Congress, Prints and Photographs Division, LC-DIG-nclc-01288).

the foods they chose to eat were often of poor quality and nutritional value. They sought to remedy the ills of the situation, but in their reforming zeal were clear indications of their disdain for workers and their ability to make sound judgments about nutritious food.[17]

Though concerned about the conditions of on-site dining, Howard was equally censorious of the possibility that a factory worker might leave the factory to seek a noon meal. This could result in the employee paying too great a price for their food, moreover, they might also be late returning from a lunch break, thereby robbing their employer of valuable work time. Howard's solution to all of these problems was the establishment of an employee dining hall and food service system. He trumpeted its positive effects: "It makes for contentment and satisfaction and the feeling that the firm is more than passingly interested in the employees' happiness."[18]

The establishment of such on-site eating facilities was not a simple undertaking. Two 1918 articles in *Industrial Management* examined the benefits of factory lunchrooms and the best methods for designing them to function efficiently. The first article, appearing in May 1918, opened with a commentary on the reasons for the slow spread of the cafeteria idea in American workplaces, stating that it had long been "retarded because of the taint of 'welfare.' Employees looked upon it as paternalistic. The employers did not sift the practical from the sociological." The article, anonymously authored and simply titled "The Factory Lunchroom and Equipment," made the bold declaration that well-equipped and well-managed factory lunchrooms had been proven to be beneficial to both employers and employees. A major selling point of the on-site food facilities in this article was the observation made by one factory owner that "the greatest percentage of accidents occurred in the hour immediately following the noon luncheon period." On investigation of the reasons for this alarming statistic, the factory management learned that "many of the workmen went to a nearby saloon to lunch or had beer brought into the factory during the lunch hour." When managers barred beer and provided free milk "the number of accidents occurring immediately after the luncheon hour was reduced to almost zero." Who could argue with such positive results? Still, the article reinforced the basic fact that to achieve a similar outcome, factory cafeterias had to be equipped for maximum efficiency and managed by an "expert man or woman ... it should not be entrusted to the tender mercies of novices and theorists." Later, in September 1918, *Industrial Management* provided interested factory managers with suggestions for ensuring that factories that established a cafeteria, "one of these necessary adjuncts to their employees' maintenance service," could do so without resulting in economic loss for the company. The article included illustrations of suggested kitchen arrangements and dining room layouts, and advised first and foremost that the factory owner seek out "expert advice in regard to the utilities he should install," concluding that hotel and restaurant "outfitting firms have experts whose business it is to know every detail of the factory lunchroom proposition."[19]

During the 1920s and 1930s, support for the industrial cafeteria continued to grow. The reasons for such provisions were generally the same: "the desire to keep the employee in the establishment during the lunch hour, and frequently the wish to give employees better and more nourishing food than they would be likely to get outside, since there is a tendency on the part of many workers to economize on food to the detriment of their health and efficiency."[20] As more factories and workplaces began to make provisions for on-site feeding, a lunchtime revolution of sorts got under way. Workers came to their employers with a different set of expectations. According to a 1927 issue of *Monthly Labor Review*, many industrial managers had realized that the manufacturing of products or services for sale to customers was not their only job. Quite in contrast, they also needed to organize and provide services for the health and comfort of their employees: "Among the more important features of personnel work which contributes to the health and general well-being of the employees are the provision of adequate hospitals, with physicians and trained nurses in attendance, and of plant lunch rooms."[21] As D. R. Wilson, the president and general manager of the Wilson Foundry and Machine Company in Pontiac, Michigan, stated: "Opening the tin dinner pail used to be a universal response to the noon-day whistle. But industry has learned that it has a responsibility toward employees even during the lunch hour. The plant cafeteria was one acknowledgement of such a responsibility."[22]

Schools as Ideological Centers

Throughout the early part of the twentieth century, schools had been broadening the scope of their activities to include child welfare as much as education. The history of American education has paralleled that of industry in its increasing demands for uniformity and regimentation. Control over the time and motion of students has been a recurring theme. Another major theme has been the gradual erosion of family and community influence in favor of centralized school services. The processes of industrialization and urbanization altered the organization of family life by replacing family- and community-based social control with that exercised by the school.[23] From medical services to busing and school lunches, the school has gone from being a minor character to the central institution in the lives of children and their families.[24] As such, schools have achieved one of the long-term goals of the Progressive movement, which was to transform the public schools into social welfare agencies.[25]

This institutional transformation occurred largely because of an increased interest in creating a virtuous citizenry and providing for their social welfare. In an industrialized democracy, the maintenance of balance and order requires some measure of social control and organization.

The increased flow of immigrants in the nineteenth century made obvious the need for naturalizing the many people who were coming to America. The most effective method for creating this common sense of nationality was through a shared educational experience. The schools, therefore, have served a social and a political function that often results in conflicts of interest and control battles.

A writer in the *Journal of Home Economics* in 1940 expressed the hope that the school lunch might be used as a social reform tool, stating that it "is obvious that the easiest as well as the most efficacious plan for improvement of national nutrition is to better the feeding of children during the school years when food needs are most exacting and when nearly all the children of the community are gathered together five days a week under the observation and control of the schools."[26]

The school lunch provided a convenient vehicle for home economists, teachers, school administrators, government officials, and later

Children eating lunch in a New York City School, c.1920 (Library of Congress, Prints and Photographs Division, LC-USZ62-92386).

commercial and business leaders to gain access to the inner sanctum of the family table. Through American children, these various interests, each with different goals, hoped to influence the decisions about what foods were consumed in both school and home. When the school lunch was cast as a civic concern, it became an appropriate subject for public scrutiny and criticism. Although the initiatives and purposes of the assorted experts involved in the development of the school lunch program were often divergent, all expressed a common concern about the quality of parenting in American society. Many believed that if parents were educated as to proper methods of child feeding, there would be an overall improvement in the health of American children, resulting in a benefit that would carry over to the nation as a whole.

Feed the Children: Progressives and the Penny Lunch

"An ill-fed, badly nourished child is a menace to the community." With that striking declaration, Emeline E. Torrey opened her 1911 *Good Housekeeping* article, "The Penny Lunch Movement." The author was an ardent supporter of providing for child nutrition in the public schools, and she aimed to convert her audience to that stance as well. Toward that end, she appealed to both the heartstrings and the selfish fears of her readers: "Not only is a child in this condition likely to be mentally stupid and morally more or less vicious, but he is also an easy victim to disease. Any of these three conditions by itself alone may make the child, in course of time, a dependent upon the state; the three combined are almost sure to lead to this deplorable condition." If such predictions did not yet strike enough fear into the hearts of American women, Torrey pointed out that these children would eventually be added to the pauper rolls. The boys would become "truants, tramps, and thieves," and the girls would find themselves residents of "houses of correction and refuge." The ultimate threat, in Torrey's estimation, was that of disease, which, once it spread, would know no boundaries of class and status. She cautioned: "Where these half-fed are found in numbers, there will be found the plague spots of disease, which later stalks abroad and defies the men of science to overcome its terror until the cry of the hungry and starved is stilled."[27]

Torrey echoed the sentiments of a broad group of early twentieth-century American social reformers who took up as their cause the

A Works Progress Administration poster touting the benefits of school lunches (Library of Congress, Prints and Photographs Division, LC-USZC2-5427).

improvement of child nutrition. Such efforts were neither new nor unique to the United States. In fact, much of the groundwork for school lunches had already been laid in England and Europe. Beginning as early as the eighteenth century, some Europeans were organizing mass feeding programs for impoverished children and adults. Initially, the work was usually carried out by private individuals or charitable societies; only later was it incorporated into the services provided by the government.

Among the more notable European programs had been initiated by an American expatriate, Benjamin Thompson, more commonly known as Count Rumford. Perhaps most famous for inventing the double-boiler, kitchen range and baking oven, pressure cooker, and drip coffee pot, Rumford spent time in England and Germany during the late eighteenth century. While in Munich, Rumford founded the Poor People's Institute, a place where indigent adults and children worked making clothes for the army and in return received food and clothing for themselves. During their nonworking hours, clients of the Institute also received instruction in basic literacy and computation. Rumford's greatest challenge here was to procure and prepare nutritious food at a low cost. His invention of kitchen equipment often resulted from the difficulties he encountered in the effort to feed large groups of people.[28]

The United States lagged behind her European counterparts in the development of structured public feeding programs. It was not until the late nineteenth and early twentieth centuries that Americans turned their energies toward the organized alleviation of poverty. One certain cause of the burgeoning interest in the provision of cheap meals at this time was the rapid growth of many American cities. Industrial cities soon became overcrowded with poor workers, many of whom were immigrants. The potential for unrest among people who are worn with labor, hungry, and crowded into deplorable conditions with strangers who did not speak the same language seemed great to many people. Thus, most of the early feeding efforts were centered in large cities such as Philadelphia, Boston, Milwaukee, New York, Cleveland, Cincinnati, St. Louis, and Los Angeles. Even some rural school districts endeavored to supply some type of nourishment to students who were too far away from home to return there for lunch and many of whom were too poor to bring anything along with them. By the 1920s the movement for school lunches was well established and organized, only to be challenged by the national economic depression of the 1930s, which brought widespread unemployment and its attendant legacies of poverty and malnutrition. As hunger increased during this decade, it became more apparent that the individuals, school boards, school associations, and other philanthropic and private organizations could no longer manage to maintain adequate feeding programs without assistance. Slowly, the responsibility for such programs crept into the purview of municipalities and states, and eventually the federal government.[29]

Providing meals for schoolchildren was quite a Herculean task both in the cities and in the one-room schoolhouses of the countryside. In both circumstances, the organizers and outside observers expressed concern that the provisions be made available to those students who needed them and yet not be portrayed as handouts. Boston was one of the cities where the penny lunch movement took shape. Torrey noted that some critics of food provision programs believed that people should not give children the "necessary food for fear of pauperizing" them. Their fear was that "when we accustom him to receiving benefits without rendering an adequate return, we unfit him for his future work, sowing the seeds of a future dependency. This thought of having the child help himself, yet giving him an opportunity to get wholesome, well-cooked food once a day, started the penny lunches in Boston."[30]

In Boston, the school system provided some basic ingredients, but the bulk of the supplies used in the penny lunch experiment came from "friends" who were later repaid out of the program's profits. The first school to become involved in the experiment was the Winthrop School, which was "situated in a congested area of Boston where living conditions are hard." The program began in January 1910, offering a few simple dishes: cereal; milk soups; cornstarch, rice, and tapioca pudding; and applesauce. Occasionally molasses cookies and ice cream were served for "gala occasions." Food was not only supplied; it became an opportunity to teach. "Three days in the week the food was cooked by the children; on two days milk and jam sandwiches were served." An important aspect of the experiment

> was to teach the children that the food was not a gift, but an honest purchase, in which they paid a just price for value received. Another was to induce them to substitute this food for the cheap candy, and green pickles for which their pennies had gone before. This was slow

work, of course but there was a gradual increase in the receipts, until in March about forty-five hundred pennies were paid in.

In the end, the experiment was declared a success by the directors, children, and parents alike:

> The mothers seemed to be glad of the help for the children. One grandmother, a hard-working charwoman, asked to be paid for her day's labor partly in pennies, and when asked the reason, replied that she wanted them for her grandchildren's lunches — "they thought so much of them." The older girls themselves often told us how much better able they felt to do the last hour's school work. And even one of the tiny ones said to her teacher, on one of the last days of school, when lunches were not forthcoming, "My stomach doesn't feel right, teacher, without my lunch."[31]

Reformers were keen on the possibility that by providing children with balanced meals and educating them as to the nutritional values of various foods, they might also influence the parents, especially the mothers, of these children. A school principal in Chicago trumpeted the positive effects of learning the appropriate social skills and decorum for group eating as a "social asset."[32] The educational features of the school lunch were perhaps its greatest selling point when reformers tried to enlist support from outside the school community. If a school lunch helped teach poor children acceptable manners and the economics of proper food selection, then perhaps the dangers posed to society by poor food habits might be averted. One article from the early 1920s advised teachers and potential teachers in rural schools that if no other community organization accepted the challenge of providing a hot school lunch, the teacher should take it on herself to do so. The author said that the lessons taught through school lunches should not end at the close of the noon meal, but should "pass over into the homes of the pupils general information which will influence the selection of all the meals rather than apply merely to one part of one meal." Of the teacher, the author wrote: "Procuring a hot lunch at noon may appear as her initial aim, but in her mind it will be subordinated to that of reaching the parents through the children, helping them all to a better understanding of food values and good dietary habits, and making the school function as a civic and social center for the district."[33]

The school lunch presented the possibility for reforming the habits of poor urban and rural parents who some experts believed lacked both the intellectual ability to judge good meals and the social skills necessary for full participation in democratic society. When World War I broke out, the first selective service draft resulted in a dismal showing of national vigor. Fully 28 percent of the first men called were rejected as "unfit to bear arms" because they were underweight, undernourished, or suffered from other "defects which should have been corrected in childhood." Reformers believed that had the parents of these draftees been exposed to education about proper nutrition, many of the deficiencies uncovered might have been prevented.[34]

The disheartening selective service statistics instigated research into the causes of poor nutrition and its possible cures. A common solution was the school lunch. Studies found that both rural and urban children suffered from the ill effects of poor nutrition. There had been a prevailing belief that rural children, by virtue of their proximity to the productivity of the land and livestock, were healthier and better nourished than city children. Investigations made to support this thesis found it to be untenable. Rural children might carry food to school, but the "usual fare" that these children carried in their lunch boxes was insufficient in "needed food materials." City children suffered a similar fate from the ravages of "unwholesome food." Some, who because of distance traveled or because their "mothers are away all day working in a factory or shop," could not return home for lunch. If such children were fortunate enough to have been given "a few pennies with which to buy food," they often spent it at "the corner grocery for pickles, candies and other sweets or at the push-carts for unsanitary and unwholesome food." Even when children were able to return home for lunch, the meal they received was deemed "inadequate" because many mothers failed to "appreciate the full significance of food for children and serve a light lunch, preferring to prepare the more hearty meal in the evening when the father is at home."[35] The best solution, according to many social reformers, was to devise a method to provide a hot lunch at the school.

The literature on the subject of school lunches, similar to that of the factory canteen, exhibits an internal tension between the idea of a rationalized, cafeteria-style hot lunches prepared with the goal of nutrition in mind, and the often irrational, unbalanced lunches that might have been packed in haste and carried from home. In an article that praised the educational value of the school cafeteria, the boxed lunch was accused of having "contributed to disorder and problems of discipline." Without elaborating on the subject of how a lunch carried from home could create such conditions, the author proceeded to describe the school cafeteria as virtually "a necessity" and a "standardized cog in the well lubricated school machine."[36] The concern of some community members that school lunches might "weaken the sense of responsibility which parents should feel for the feeding of their children" was rigorously opposed. In her survey of the penny lunch movement in Cincinnati, Albertina Bechmann revealed: "The reverse frequently happened. Mothers often came to ask what foods to select and how to prepare and serve them so as to satisfy the complaints of their children that the food at home was not so good as that at school."[37] One author in the *Journal of Home Economics* suggested that especially in rural schools, teachers encourage parents to send their children to school with their lunches sealed in a glass jar that could be heated on a cookstove in a pan filled with water. This system was beneficial all around because it allowed parents to retain the "responsibility for his child's lunch," did not require much in the way of equipment or at-school preparation, and resulted in only a slight disturbance to the daily classroom routine.[38]

The financial obstacles to procuring supplies of food and equipment along with the logistical challenges of preparing and serving school meals presented problems in both rural and urban settings. An author in *Technical World Magazine* in 1914 noted that there was "abundant proof that stupid children were usually ill-nourished children and that they changed quickly to bright and receptive pupils when they were properly fed." In rural areas, the author commented further that "it was found that lunches served at cost prices averaged only a few cents a day per child, and parents were glad to be rid of the trouble of packing lunch boxes." The article also documented the efforts made by the Extension Service of the Massachusetts Agricultural College on behalf of rural schoolchildren. Employees of the Service developed a "substitute for the dinner pail," that was a type of "cupboard" equipped with the basics of cookery. Because cooking lessons were often a part of the school curriculum, "the girls who have this work can prepare and serve a lunch to twenty or more pupils under the supervision of a teacher." Under such a program, it was only "necessary that the pupils bring from home their individual knife, fork, and spoon, with a plate and saucer and cup to supplement the kitchenette."[39]

Other options for the rural school involved greater participation on the part of students' families. Irene Hume Taylor outlined some of the possibilities in a 1926 article in the journal *Hygeia*. She noted that the distance traveled to school by students meant that there was "no chance for them to have a substantial hot dish at noon unless the teacher manages to serve it at school." Taylor advised the teacher to visit the parents of her charges. She predicted that many mothers "would be glad to be relieved of the daily task of putting up a cold lunch, if they were certain adequate food would be served at school." Among Taylor's suggestions for the teacher were that she enlist the help of mothers, who would "take turns at preparing the luncheon, provided the distance to be traveled is not too great." If that proved impossible, the teacher might make out a schedule for each child to bring supplies to feed the class for one week at a time or she might collect funds from each family to purchase supplies and then either fix the meal herself or "assign to the older children the project, thus combining the teaching of cookery with other subjects taught." Taylor went so far as to include several recipes for the aspiring teacher-chefs. Among them were Cream of Tomato Soup with Rice for twenty, Cream Dried Beef on Toast for fifty, Lamb à la King for sixty, and Ham and Noodles for seventy.[40]

The school lunch held the promise of fulfilling a dual role. It could simultaneously feed undernourished bodies and train eager young minds in the habits of efficiency, cleanliness, nutrition, and decorum. A third possible benefit was that through the children, reformers might reach and affect the health of the broader community. One such instance occurred in a rural mining town in West Virginia. There, in the late 1920s, one schoolteacher, Miss Mabel Baisden, took it on herself to see that the "underweights" in her classroom who could not afford to bring milk to school for the "10 o'clock drink" would have milk to drink with their more fortunate classmates. Miss Baisden, in her role as "milkman," made sure that the necessary seven quarts of milk made it to school each day. When her "Ford broke down, Miss Baisden had to walk three miles carrying the milk."

Baisden's project soon caught the attention of the governor of West Virginia and was later replicated in other area schools. According to a report of Miss Baisden's activities that appeared in the May 1928 edition of *Hygeia*, from the simple idea of providing children with bottled milk grew an enormous drive for improving the health among the children of Logan County. The results included increased immunizations against typhoid and smallpox and a greater awareness of nutrition and food values. The anonymous author advanced the notion that Miss Baisden's milk bottle held a magic akin to that of Aladdin's lamp. Simply touch the magic milk bottle and you might see the fifteen-year-old Hungarian boy who had organized a "school sanitary squad." Or, look into another school, where the "negro children" sang "as only members of their race can sing, while the young gardeners put on a tableau showing how fresh vegetables grow." As further evidence of the magic milk, a fourteen-year-old boy dressed up "in a white frilled petticoat, not even masked," and carried a sign that read, "Celery quiets your nerves." Other classmates "were beans and apples and beets, while a fat boy personified a potato, with the slogan 'These Make You Fat.'" The writer observed that somehow, through this simple milk initiative, the children of Logan County had "developed a county health consciousness which made them cooperate not only in the dramatic public advertising of their health program, but in the simple everyday observances of the rules of the game."[41] In summary, the author proclaimed:

> You would never dream that just starting to drink milk in one school could change so many things in a whole county; that out of this project could come such county health spirit, felt by every school child. But if you go down to visit the ten white schools and the three negro schools of the Island Creek system in Logan County, you will see the results.[42]

Further evidence of the success was apparent at the time of the article, for even though the Logan County mines had entered a slackening period, the health record of the area children continued to progress "satisfactorily." In the Logan County schools, a "Gold Star pupil" was not one who achieved a perfect score in spelling or math, but "in the schools visited by the Island Creek Coal Company's health nurse, the Gold Star pupils are those who rate 100 on living." Miss Baisden, for her efforts, was awarded the "silver milk jug" as a prize for having the school with the best milk record. In addition, she won from the Island Creek Coal Company a one-year scholarship to the state normal school "because of her outstanding health work." The article closed with a statement of the standards to be used in awarding the next year's silver milk jug:

> This year the awarding of the silver milk jug will be on the basis of the by-products of health — going a step farther than the purely physical standards used last year. Aside from the regular records of weight normalizing, of those forming the habit of drinking milk at home as well

as at school, of those who did not like milk to begin with and who learned to like it through milk-drinking at school, there will be a check of each child's condition, revealed by his ability to concentrate, interest, self-reliance, cheerfulness, friendly attitude toward others, freedom from colds and other illnesses, good posture. They are all foundations that will build life success for Gold Star children.[43]

Miss Baisden's efforts began entirely out of her own initiative. She wanted to bring about a categorical improvement in the health of her students. Although she received recognition from the state government and the local mining company, there was not yet a formalized national program for the distribution of commodities and funds for the purposes of providing school lunches. Soon after her experiments demonstrated their success, the nation was rocked by the economic and social pressures of the Great Depression. The widespread nature of economic difficulties brought new urgency to the questions about how to provide cheap and nutritious meals for poor children and how to respond when they could not afford to pay. One article on lunch room management suggested that children who could not pay might be employed as assistants in the lunchroom. The only difficulty that this idea presented was that it might single out the poor children and make them the subjects of their peers' scorn. Another option was to give needy children "food checks without the other children knowing it; this may be considered a legitimate school expense, although it is frequently provided for through private philanthropy." The author concluded that the problem of "free feeding" was one of "tremendous sociological significance" but that "definite limitations should be set as to the extent of such aid."[44] This issue would continue to play a part as discussions of federal involvement in school lunch programs increased during the 1930s and 1940s.

A Role for the Home Economists

With regard to school lunches, the process begun with the first penny lunches came to full fruition with the promise of federal backing. The assurance of secure federal funding, which did not become permanent until immediately after World War II, made it possible for many more schools to participate. Increased government involvement placed concern for child nutrition fell squarely within the public realm. As in the past, however, the responsibility for child feeding continued to fall primarily on the women of America.

Women have traditionally been accountable for their family's well-being, and a central part of that job has involved procuring, preparing, and sometimes preserving of food. Responsibility for lunch preparation, whether to be consumed at home or away, has clearly fallen within the realm of feminine duties. The 1930 edition of *Good House-keeping's Book of Meals* advised readers on how best to plan for the various meals of the day and described as "fortunate" any "child whose school provides a cafeteria directed by a woman especially trained in nutrition and lunch room management where a healthful lunch, carefully planned, prepared and served, awaits him daily." In contrast, "unfortunate" children attended "a school where the lunch room is managed by an unscrupulous concessionaire who provides chiefly 'hot dogs', 'pop', dill pickles, chocolate bars, and 'loose' milk instead of bottled milk for the daily luncheon menu." This section, titled, "The Lunch Hour at School," closed with a call to action: "The women citizens of any town or city should realize that *the school lunch is a civic problem*, and that the solution of this problem, is to a great extent their responsibility."[45]

The expansion and nationalization of the school lunch program resulted in a greater need for the promotion, supervision, and development of both existing and new programs. Women who were trained in home economics seemed to be the logical choices for leadership positions in these areas. Since the nineteenth century, such women had been the backbone of the common school system because of the general cultural perception that they were by nature suited to nurturing roles. The fact that women could be paid less made them highly desirable to the male-dominated hierarchy. The feminized nature of the teaching profession was mirrored in the feminized nature of employment in school foodservice industry. Some women, following in the tradition of republican motherhood begun during the American Revolution and continued through the professionalization of home economics, saw the venue of foodservice as a way to link culturally accepted roles in the private sphere with broader interaction in public sphere and efforts to alter the dynamics of the political world.

The task of parental education also seemed particularly well suited to home economists. Women such as Lydia Roberts, an assistant professor of Home Economics at the University of Chicago, worked to make their field central to the project of improving child nutrition and, in turn, national welfare. Roberts's textbook, *Nutrition Work with Children*, published in 1927, argued that nutritional health was not necessarily linked to the outward appearance of the body. True, many economically disadvantaged people appeared undernourished and were financially unable to purchase the quantity and quality of food necessary for health. More disturbing, however, was the often invisible and far more widespread problem of malnutrition "unassociated with dearth of food or poverty."[46] The best method to remedy both sources of malnutrition was to reach parents through their children. Roberts noted: "The children constitute, indeed, a powerful machine which can put through most any task or reform if inspired and directed by the teachers." She further described the school as being in "possession" of the children and thus being uniquely qualified to change their food habits. Through the combination of trained teachers, physicians, nurses, dentists, and the provision of school lunches, schools were in a powerful position to influence children. Roberts suggested that teachers obtain the "cooperation" of the "home" because "harmony in purpose and method between the home and the school" was "essential to complete success in the establishment of desired habits." She advocated "group mother-meetings, individual conferences, notes and telephone conversations" as methods for "assuring parents that the school" was "helping them in the task of rearing healthy children."[47] While commenting that most parents were willing and enthusiastic with their support, she cautioned that in some situations the job of persuading "a mother that her duty lies in supervising personally the details of her child's life" was occasionally "far from an easy task."[48] Cases of extreme wealth, where children were cared for by paid staff, or severe poverty, where the mother had to work to keep the family alive, might make it difficult to secure parental assistance.

Roberts included in her work an extensive bibliography of sources related to child health, as well as a description of each of the national agencies and government bureaus that participated in the nutrition movement. Her book was successful enough that in 1954, Ethel Austin Martin, an associate of Roberts's at the University of Chicago and former director of nutrition for the National Dairy Council, and the director of nutrition and health demonstrations for the city schools of Akron, Ohio, published a revised and updated version, maintaining Roberts's legacy in her title: *Roberts' Nutrition Work with Children*. Martin believed that nutritional science had progressed enough since the first edition to warrant a republication. Her additions to the Roberts text came mainly in the form of new scientific data on nutrition and child development. Like Roberts before her, Martin continued to advocate a cooperation among parents, school personnel, and the healthcare community. Her general attitude toward parents' role also echoed that of her predecessor. In Martin's estimation, nutrition education belonged in the schools because they were "responsible for fitting the child for society and helping him be responsible for himself and his health."[49] Another parallel with the earlier work was Martin's inclusion of bibliographic information and an expanded chapter, "Agencies, Organizations, and Movements Which Contribute to Nutritional Well-Being of Children." To indicate changes in child nutrition and school lunch programs since Roberts's work, Martin added a new chapter, "Nutrition Services in State and Local Programs."

What both Roberts and Martin accomplished was the validation of a role for experts and schools in the movement for child nutrition. Each author supported the employment of professionals whose expertise and experience made them superior to most parents in improving nutrition for children. Martin made her position apparent when she discussed the value of the well-planned school meal. She asserted that because it did not vary in its nutritional elements as much as meals from other sources, it was one of the most important aspects of a child's daily food requirements. Martin equivocated: "This is not to disparage lunches eaten at home or even packed lunches. Both may be, and often are, completely satisfactory. Experience has shown, however, that this is often not the case unless a special program has been instituted to acquaint mothers with children's need for a nutritionally adequate noon meal."[50] Clearly, mothers only knew best when they followed the advice offered by experts.

An author in the December 1942 issue of the *Journal of Home Economics* echoed the theme of Roberts and Martin when she stated bluntly her belief that parents needed expert direction: "The education of parents is indispensable whether their children happen to be well- or ill-nourished but particularly if the family income is restricted. The expensive and careful building up of children during the school year has been only too often undone during the unsupervised vacation periods."[51] The author of this article moreover advocated a program of "action and education" that would include the feeding, physical examination and treatment of students, the "direct and indirect education of the pupils themselves," and the education of parents and the "whole community." The cause of child nutrition was too important to the welfare of the entire country to be left solely to the supervision of potentially inept parents:

> If we agree that one of the objectives of a democracy should be to wipe out the growth differences attributable to economic and social causes, we must recognize that this can be attained only by equalizing the quality and quantity of the food available to all children. Not only economic but also educational measures are required to bring this about because intelligence in the choice of food is even more important than increased income.[52]

The growth of large consolidated schools meant that fewer children lived close enough to their school to go home for lunch. Slowly, the school cafeteria lunch became a standard feature of the American educational day. According to one observer in the 1950s, some schools had begun to publish lunch menus in local newspapers to help mothers avoid duplicating foods on any given day. Though this seemed like a sensible plan, the problem was that children, too, had access to this information, and on days when the school menu featured dishes that they did not like, they tended to spend their lunch money "for a soft drink and candy at the store down the street." To foil such precocious youngsters, some schools responded by broadcasting descriptions of the daily fare over the radio for "the benefit of mothers only."[53] Thus, even if mothers were not packing lunches for their children, experts expected them to play a significant role in the school lunch by balancing meals served at home with those consumed at school.

In a nine-year study of school lunches conducted in Pennsylvania between 1935 and 1944, investigators arrived at the conclusion that the most successful lunch programs were those that were developed by "someone trained in nutrition and dietetics" and those where the children's "home dietaries" were ascertained "either through home visiting or by asking the children at frequent intervals to write out what they ate the night before and the same morning, as well as between meals." The study also demonstrated that when a group of untrained mothers was placed in charge of the cafeteria of a "neighborhood school attended exclusively by one foreign racial group," the children were fed at school the same types of food they are at home. Despite the fact that the mothers involved were generally interested in the school lunch program, the children remained undernourished and netted no improvement to their physical health.[54] Mothers were important, the study concluded, but they also needed to know their place in relation to the schools' dietary experts.

Who's the Boss?

At the heart of the debates over lunch in workplaces and schools from the late nineteenth through the mid-twentieth century is a question of responsibility. What we see over the course of this time is a progressive although incomplete shift from individuals maintaining the responsibility for carrying or otherwise finding a meal of their own volition, toward an environment where institutions accept the role of making food accessible during the work or school day. When institutions, influenced by goals as varied as productivity, socialization of workers, and even improving general health and well-being of the citizenry, make these factors paramount, the personal decisions of what to eat become less amenable to individual tastes and desires.

This chapter illustrates how early to mid-twentieth-century reformers cleared the way for the colonization of lunch. Their interference had a profound impact on the regulation of individual food choices and habits. The U.S. involvement in World War II brought a new urgency to the already complicated equation of lunchtime responsibility. Having learned from the earlier drive for industrial efficiency as promoted by Frederick Taylor and his followers as well as the contemporary interest in dietary reform sparked by professionalization of home economics and dietetics, the crucible of war led factory management, government wartime committees, and other national and local organizations to focus on the nutritional status of vital homefront workers and citizens. The demands of a wartime mobilization lent sanction to efforts on the part of these entities to direct the consumption habits of American workers as well as the general population. With the onset of food rationing, not only lunch but all meals became the target of public interest and outside intervention as food became an implement of war and a measure of defense. Rationing offered nutrition advocates the opportunity to reshape what they deemed to be the often inadequate, unbalanced diets of many Americans. Those untouched by the square meals served to soldiers on the battlefront were to become soldiers in their own right — soldiers in the coalition of forces working to engage the homefront in the food for victory campaign. The resulting homogenization of diet that was the culmination of their work was part benefit and part consequence for many Americans.

The next three chapters explore the mechanics of rationing, its effects on the family table, and the efforts made by this wartime brigade of experts to draft women into the ranks of "kitchen commandos" while at the same time attempting to reconcile the divergent messages aimed at Rosie the Riveter and Hannah the Homemaker into a unified refrain regarding rationing, patriotism, and women's responsibility for managing both.

3

Kitchen Commandos:
Government, the Media,
and the "Marketing" of Food
Rationing during World War II

Walt Disney's second full-length animated feature, *Bambi*, graced movie screens, the big bands provided rhythm for dancing feet, and heavyweight boxer Joe Louis won his twentieth world championship — this was a slice of American popular culture in 1942. But all was not quiet on the homefront. Wartime mobilization required both soldiers and civilians to adapt to rapidly changing conditions. Over the twelve-month period from the Japanese attack on Pearl Harbor on 7 December 1941 to the first anniversary of American involvement in World War II, the federal government spearheaded a massive homefront mobilization campaign that resulted in increased employment and greater industrial productivity.[1] As the nation shifted from depression to wartime boom, more men and women had the means to purchase consumer goods. Yet in an ironic twist of circumstances, money in the pocketbook did not necessarily translate into increased access to commodities.[2] Inflation had arrived in force, and the war effort meant that many goods, from automobiles to foodstuffs, were not available.

While the war raged in Europe and the Pacific, the military and the Lend-Lease nations demanded a larger percentage of American industrial output and foodstuffs.[3] Unfortunately, for members of the homefront, this frequently meant higher prices at home. Both goods and services cost more under a wartime economy. In regions of the nation where there were large populations of industrial workers, rents rose dramatically — not to mention the higher cost of fuel, clothing, and food. Beginning in 1942, the government rationed consumer goods such as coffee, sugar, and rubber. Because there was no precedent for such a widespread federal intrusion into the economy, the government engaged in a program intended to reassure citizens that their strict adherence to national policies would, in fact, further the war effort. For civilians, making sense of the morass of wartime rules and regulations was a complicated endeavor. Even before the onset of point rationing in 1943, consumers had to be educated in new ways of budgeting their resources and conserving their supplies, all the while maintaining optimum physical health and well-being for war production.

Cooperative efforts among industry, various social science experts, and the media developed tools for shaping and directing the activities of the civilian population. Earlier reformers had demonstrated the effectiveness of orchestrated intervention in food habits toward the ends of increased industrial output and educational achievement. Now, the rationing of both consumer durables and perishables necessitated that people make changes in their habits and traditions both to comply with government mandates and simply to navigate the shifting tides of wartime economic cycles. In this environment, it was necessary for the colonizers to cloak any efforts not directly related to the announced goal of winning the war in that mantle. During wartime, colonizers, many of whom needed the labor and cooperation of the American people to make the war a success, were less likely to condemn people for what they ate and more apt to focus on the overall objective of better nutrition.

While the immediate result of improved eating patterns often included better health, the change also led many people to see their old habits, traditions, and folk ways as inferior. At the same time, under the influence of a major national nutrition campaign carried out through a partnership between the public and private sectors, they were persuaded that the needs of the state took precedence, and of the superiority of quantitative and scientific methods. The door was thus open for the state and corporations to enter American kitchens.

In support of the effort to keep the homefront functioning efficiently, it was necessary for everyone to feel that they were performing a significant service toward furthering the Allies' success in the war. This often meant that war planners in the government, media, and industry equated cooperation with wartime restrictions, sacrifice, and patriotism. Members of the media performed an essential role in encouraging Americans' willingness to sacrifice and developing patriotism. The word *patriotism* covers a wide latitude of meanings. In the context of war, however, it involves evidence of love for one's country as demonstrated through loyalty, service, and dedication to the defense of the nation. On the American homefront, patriotism meant adjusting to unusual (and sometimes unpleasant) circumstances and willing acceptance and adherence to ration regulations. In essence, the war linked patriotism and sacrifice in an inextricable web of civilian responsibility or political obligation. For American women, patriotism meant doing their part to advance the war effort through their purchases at the grocery store and making careful use of the available food supply.

When people expressed dismay over the use of federal authority to ration foods and inspect private food supplies, the American media shifted from performing a strictly informative function to one of education and explanation. Although there were indeed limits on the acceptable extent of government intervention into the household, media sources tried to convince the public that wartime mobilization entailed some unpleasant forfeitures of individual freedom. During this tumultuous period, newspapers such as the *New York Times* provided readers with information about rationing from the Office of Price Administration (OPA) and other government agencies. Staff writers and reporters, along with stories from wire services reported the local and national conditions to the citizens of New York City. The newspaper provided a medium for exchange between government agencies and the citizenry.[4] In the months immediately preceding point rationing, journalists such as Jane Holt worked hard to convince the public of the patriotic importance of accepting point rationing, played an important part in "drafting" local women into the war effort, and championed the "All American Pledge": "I will abide by every ration of our nation for the duration."[5]

Food Will Win the War: The History of U.S. Food Rationing

A key element in the success of a war effort is a supportive and efficiently run homefront. Of particular importance to both the homefront and battlefront is control of the food supply. Neither can an army march nor a homefront produce on empty stomachs. During World War II, to ensure adequate supplies for both "fronts," it was necessary for the federal government to regulate the food supply.

The United States has needed to control the food supply on two occasions in this century. During World War I, the Food Administration, under the direction of Herbert Hoover, led the nation on a crusade to ensure an ample domestic food supply and sufficient surplus goods to assist the Allies. Fortunately, as Hoover successfully encouraged voluntary conservation and because the United States was involved in the war for only a short period of time, the food supply did not drop to levels necessitating rationing.[6]

In contrast, during World War II, rationing was the most effective means of maintaining a steady food supply. The recollection of food shortages during World War I and the Great Depression had become a part of the recent memory of many Americans, and false rumors of impending shortages abounded between 1941 and 1945.[7] To avert panic over possible food shortages, the government instituted a policy of food rationing under the OPA in 1941. The government issued all civilians books of ration stamps that assured them proportionate amounts of enumerated foods. Rationing introduced a new dynamic into American society and forced women to feed their families under new constraints.

When the United States entered World War II in late 1941, the reality of government-enforced food rationing was not far in the future.[8] Americans were well aware that European nations had been rationing food since the outbreak of the war in Europe in 1939. However, such a development seemed unlikely in the United States because the war was unfolding so far away from the North American continent and the United States was not yet formally involved. The bombing of Pearl Harbor on 7 December 1941 changed everything. Americans have historically viewed the United States as a land of plenty. Even among the earliest written accounts of life in North America were references to the bounty that existed on the land and in the waters.[9] It seemed as if there would seldom be any reason for people to experience food shortage in this land of natural abundance. In fact, during the period immediately after World War I through the Great Depression, as a result of efforts by the farm block to keep agricultural prices high, food surpluses had been a problem. One contemporary author noted that with the exception of a few years during the Civil War and one season during World War I, the United States had always faced the "threat of overburdening surpluses." He observed that the supply demands of World War II were such that farmers could produce freely, as there was no chance of their producing too much. He urged farmers to produce so that there would be enough to provide for American citizens and the Allies alike during the war and after. Then, he made a revealing comment about the nation's food supply: "And after that, if the fighting is over and the first hunger of Europe's population has been allayed, produce so that, if nothing more, forty millions in our own land will not be underfed as in the past."[10] While surpluses may have troubled special interests and economists, they had not apparently reached the American public.[11]

Clearly, World War I and the Great Depression had altered average Americans' conceptions of surplus and plenty. While the food program during World War I did not involve rationing, there were shortages of commodities such as sugar, wheat, and meat. Little more than a decade after the end of the Great War, the United States had fallen into a widespread economic depression. Surplus or not, one needed money to eat. The ability to purchase nutritious foods and the contents of the family pocketbook were inextricably linked, and the Great Depression strained that link. By the outbreak of World War II, many Americans had become aware of what Harvey Levenstein calls the "paradox of plenty": despite the notion that an abundant food supply in the United States was an invincible barrier protecting the nation from want, Americans were shocked to learn that they could indeed fall prey to food scarcity and even hunger.[12]

Although the food situation during World War I never reached the crisis point, the mechanisms developed by the Food Administration served as a model for World War II food planners. The purpose of the Food Administration had been to control exports and increase overall food production. It accomplished these goals through activities that "regulated distribution, trade and profits through the wholesaler level. Authority to fix margins of retail dealers was not included in the food law; but control was obtained by volunteer action through the local publication of Fair Price Lists and the conservation of foods."[13] A key element in World War I food control was voluntarism. Hoover championed the merits of voluntary conservation programs and encouraged the spirit of patriotic self-sacrifice that he believed resided in the American people. Voluntary programs like "meatless days," for example, discouraged the consumption of animal proteins without resorting to direct government intervention. The limited scope of American involvement in World War I meant that demands for supplies remained manageable and voluntary conservation was a viable option. Though the Food Administration certainly faced difficulties from loose governmental regulations and wartime profiteers, it performed admirably for the most part.[14]

In the incubator of the interwar years, the American population expanded and domestic needs increased. And as the nation shifted to a wartime economy and pulled out of the Depression, American consumers at last found themselves with more money to spend on food. Unfortunately, soon after workers saw this increase in their food purchasing power, the United States entered the war and the domestic food supply was subjected to the increased demands of the military and the Allies. Those increased demands in turn decreased the amount of certain foods available to civilian consumers. With military and foreign obligations looming and a large homefront to supply, the government soon realized that the scale of the war made a voluntary conservation effort impractical. Experts determined that rationing would be the most effective method for achieving a "fair" distribution of needed supplies.

The people of plenty were struck by the contrast between their financial ability to purchase goods and the rapid disappearance of those goods from the marketplace. Fear of shortages reminiscent of World War I and the Depression drove many people to engage in buying frenzies. William Ahlers Nielander, the former associate director of the food rationing division of OPA, recalled his impressions of the prerationing period:

> It became clear long before Pearl Harbor that World War II was not a repetition of World War I. This is a total war, and nearly everywhere is evidence that people are aware of this fact. The current war brought forth a striking illustration of the first law of nature, and people have shown little willingness to share scarce supplies with strangers. Food

runs on sugar, coffee, canned goods, cheese, meat and soap took place before either Pearl Harbor or the beginning of respective rationing programs ... there has been a widespread lack of appreciation that food supplies, irrespective of who produced them, are a part of the national food supply and should be shared.[15]

As in World War I, food had become an implement of war. The task at hand was to allow food to fight for freedom while at the same time eliminating the prospect of it becoming the focus of battles on the homefront. Federal officials gave food production and distribution a high priority in the war effort. They were cognizant of the fact that a well-fed homefront was necessary to maintain morale and high levels of production. Convincing the American public that rationing was necessary and would, in fact, ensure all civilians a proportionate amount of the goods rationed was no simple matter, however.

Although the United States did not become involved in the war until 1941 and did not institute rationing until 1942, it was clear that unlike many European allies who faced the specter of war in 1939, the United States was unprepared for the potential emergency. Nielander recalled that "when Poland was invaded in 1939, few Americans foresaw the impact which this seemingly remote incident would have upon our economic life." He described many people in both business and government as continuing to operate with a "business as usual" attitude that seemed to place only the issues which were "under the imperative of imminent emergency" at the top of the priority list. In contrast, Nielander called attention to Germany, where "in times of peace developed practically a full war economy," and England, "which had — with respect to food, at least, laid plans for the contingency of war." He concluded that America had "practically no plans and no organization to guide it through the mazes of protracted war."[16]

An additional obstacle to wartime mobilization was the fact that isolationist or "anti-interventionist" sentiments dominated American politics and society. Many Americans, who were still suffering from the nagging effects of economic depression, remembered the lessons learned in World War I and opposed United States involvement in another European war.[17] Nevertheless, by 1939, the machinations of Hitler and other fascist leaders proved to many government officials that preliminary planning for economic mobilization was necessary. If civilians were unaware of the dangers ahead, at least the government would be girded for battle.

The first step toward government-sponsored wartime planning came in 1939 when Franklin D. Roosevelt established the War Resources Board (WRB). A rather powerless body, the WRB was supposed to work in conjunction with the Army and Navy Munitions Board to establish an economic mobilization program. Abandoned shortly after its inception, the WRB was the first in a confusing array of war-related administrative agencies to appear and disappear in mysterious fashion.

During the tenure of the WRB and the ensuing period between the German invasion of Poland (1 September 1939) and the invasion of the Low Countries (May 1940), the federal government took few additional measures to proceed with planning. Sometimes dubbed the period of the "Sitzkrieg" or "Phony War," it was so called because the relative inactivity on the western front that caused many people to slip into a state of disinterest. When Hitler stirred his army and swept across the Low Countries and then into France in spring 1940, however, the era of denial came to an abrupt conclusion. Soon, the government began to set aside increased defense appropriations, organized the Office of Emergency Management, and reestablished two agencies from World War I: the Council for National Defense and the Advisory Commission. With these agencies at the helm, the United States moved toward increased involvement in the War.[18]

Roosevelt's bureaucratic touch was conspicuous in many of the war agencies. Some historians credit his leadership style with creating the "imperial presidency." Whether or not he merits such a label, he did exercise a vast amount of control over the planning, organization, and execution of homefront economic mobilization. He exuded an aura of confidence and wisdom that smoothed the ruffled feathers of an uncertain populace: "Better than any other personality of his time, Roosevelt combined the two major techniques of democratic political leadership: the achievement of a sense of direct identification with the people and the construction of formidable organizational support."[19] To maintain this level of control throughout the war, he engineered the war-related organizations so that he remained the primary executive. Economic historian Harold G. Vatter has characterized the president as having the "desire to spark, direct, and coordinate the defense effort himself."[20] Thus, the war agencies amounted to a "one-man show" with Roosevelt as the star. The resulting menagerie of advisory councils and boards with superficial authority hampered the efficiency and progress of the planning effort, however. As the war progressed and the United States became more directly involved, the lack of centralized authority to direct the mobilization effort meant that various groups worked at cross-purposes and that no one knew who was ultimately responsible for the war-related programs. With regard to food rationing specifically, an unwieldy conglomeration of agencies with their own agendas presented the public with a perplexing command structure.[21]

In 1941, the government implemented the Lend-Lease program, committing the United States to provide Allied governments with supplies, including food products. On 3 April 1941, the Roosevelt administration launched the Food-for-Defense program to encourage increased production so that the federal government could fulfill the promises of the Lend-Lease agreement. A few days later, on 11 April 1941, with authority delegated by the president, the Office of Price Administration and Civilian Supply (OPACS) undertook the responsibility of allocating goods for civilian needs and developing price control measures. After a brief period, the agency split into the OPA and the Division of Civilian Supply. Prior to American entry into the war, the outline for economic mobilization was in place, and the national government was ready to shift from defensive preparations to a full war economy.[22]

By 1942, the combined effects of military demands, Lend-Lease commitments, the conversion of domestic manufacturing and transportation capabilities to wartime production, and shipping difficulties on the high seas led to the need for rationing. With the passage of the Emergency Price Control Act of 1942, OPA received the formal authority necessary to control prices, and later it garnered the power to institute policies for civilian rationing. Although OPA was responsible for determining rationing methods, it did not exercise absolute control and had little autonomy in the process of food rationing. The Food Distribution Committee decided which items would be rationed and the quantity that would be made available to consumers.[23]

In determining the quantity of an item to be rationed, government planners established a set of priorities: the needs of the military were considered first, then the civilian population, and finally, the Lend-Lease nations. The first food commodity to grace the ration lists was sugar. Sugar rationing was announced on 23 January 1942 and went into effect on 5 May 1942. By the end of 1942, coffee, processed foods, meats, and fats were also being rationed.[24]

Rationing meant "the control and direction of consumption, distribution and production."[25] In the United States, it took four different forms, including certificate, differential coupon, uniform coupon, and point. OPA introduced certificate rationing first. This system involved issuing a certificate redeemable for a single item, such as a tire, automobile, stove, or a pair of rubber boots. The differential coupon method applied to products such as gasoline and fuel oil. Because people's needs for these commodities varied, this program allowed for flexible allocations. The differential method was problematic, however, because "every case had to be reviewed individually and appeals and applications for additional allotments were frequent."[26] Unlike the differential plan, uniform coupon rationing ensured that everyone received the same share of essential supplies such as shoes, sugar, and coffee. The administration of this plan required the use of individual stamps with specific validation periods, so that each person could obtain his quota. Thus, OPA introduced War Ration Book 1 to fill this need. Initially, when Book 1 appeared in May 1942, it applied to sugar only, but it was later extended to cover shoes and coffee.[27]

This was America's first experience with the little stamps that would eventually come to play a part in the purchase of everything from raisins to canned pineapple to steak. In December 1942, OPA informed the American public that point rationing of processed foods would begin in March 1943. In early March 1943, the agency announced plans for meat, fat, and oil rationing to begin at the end of the month. Everyday life for civilian Americans took on a new character as Uncle Sam placed new restrictions on people's ability to simply exchange currency for food products. In principle, point rationing allowed consumers more individual freedom than the more rigid certificate and coupon methods. Under the point system, each person received a book of stamps which could be used toward the purchase of newly rationed processed foods. Processed foods included "Canned, bottled and frozen fruits and vegetables, fruit and vegetable juices, dried fruit and all canned soups." OPA defined a processed food as "one that has been preserved so that it will keep as long as it stays in its processed condition. Canned foods, for example, keep as long as they remain sealed; frozen foods as long as they remain frozen." Items that were exempted included canned milk, jams and jellies.[28] Nielander described the strengths of this program:

The point system is very flexible from a consumer's point of view; it gives him a very wide freedom of choice. He may not be able to get a specific item, but he is given such a wide choice that he is likely to be able to find a passable substitute. It was obviously the only way in which to ration processed foods, since it was impracticable to divide the total supply of any processed food equally among all consumers. Furthermore, the package itself is often of such a nature that it cannot be divided. Consumer choice can be greatly liberalized by merging quite dissimilar items under a point system — as was evidenced by an extensive swapping of coffee for sugar by household consumers when these items were under unit systems. The point rationing plan also provides flexibility for regional, religious or racial tastes and requirements — something impossible under specific rationing.[29]

Regardless of its characteristics or its intentions, point rationing added a new dynamic to the homefront experience. Weekly grocery orders would now have to be accompanied by both American currency and valid ration stamps.

Within a year of Pearl Harbor, the exigencies of war had transformed the American economy from its ascent out of Depression and into wartime mobilization to one governed by new restraints and controls on purchasing power. By early 1943, stocking the pantry was no longer a simple matter of stopping at the corner store. American consumers learned quickly that sacrifices on the homefront included limitations on their ability to purchase goods. Today, more than a half-century removed from the World War II experience, many Americans view weekly excursions to the grocery store as the bane of their existence. Such unwelcome tasks as determining menus, clipping coupons, and comparing prices between various supermarket circulars necessitate the expenditure of time, energy, and planning — not to mention money. Yet these seem to be small inconveniences when compared to the situation during World War II.

Meet the Smiths

The Public Affairs Committee, an agency based in New York City, published a series of pamphlets throughout the war years. According to the agency's constitution, it strove "to make available in summary and inexpensive form the results of research on economic and social problems to aid in the understanding and development of American policy. The sole purpose of the Committee is educational. It has no economic or social program of its own to promote."[30] In Maxwell Stewart's pamphlet, *The Smiths and Their Wartime Budgets*, the author introduces his readers to the fictional Smith family:

> Like millions of other American housewives, Mrs. Smith has had a hard time making ends meet. When her husband, Jim, received his long-expected 10-per-cent raise back in the early winter of 1942, she had thought that the Smiths would be on Easy Street. She hadn't counted on prices going up. But now she finds that her food costs her nearly half as much again as it did at the beginning of the war, and it is hard to get what she wants. Clothing is also up, and the landlord boosted the rent a few weeks after Jim got his raise. Formerly they paid no income tax; now Jim has a good-sized chunk taken out of his wage for taxes.[31]

Throughout the pamphlet, Stewart employs the Smiths as an example of how the average American family dealt with wartime inflation and scarcity. He explains that some families (such as the Smiths' neighbors, the Coopers) benefited by having more than one wage-earner. In contrast, there were also those families (like that of Mrs. Smith's daughter) whose livelihoods decreased dramatically because the husband was a member in the military. Stewart tells readers that price increases during wartime are inevitable as the government purchases more goods to supply its military and the allies. But, he points out: "The worst part about rising prices in wartime is that they do not affect families fairly or equally."[32] He proceeds to comment on the varied reactions to rationing and the criticisms that many people leveled at OPA. According to Stewart: "None of them understands clearly that the government has had the interests of all the Smiths in mind in its efforts to prevent inflation."[33] Explaining the purpose and mechanics of rationing and defending the system against citizens' attacks and questions was an important undertaking and one that required the widespread dissemination of facts.

Keeping people like the Smiths happy and motivated to produce and sacrifice was the primary goal of wartime government planners in the Roosevelt administration. A common refrain in their campaigns was the idea that in spite of food shortages and rationing, it was possible for Americans to eat well. In fact, many pointed out that rationing would improve Americans' unbalanced diets by encouraging people to consume more fresh fruits and vegetables and less meat, fat, and sugar.

Plenty in the Pantry and Points in the Pocketbook:
The New York Times *Explains the Fine*
Points of Point Rationing

A 7 December 1942 *New York Times* column described the goal
of various government agencies as "providing an intellectual safety net
for the American woman who is forced to swing on the wartime mental trapeze of running a home." The article noted further that the
"broadest media of expression, newspaper, radio, motion picture, magazine, pamphlet, cartoon, poster, public address and personal inter-
view are being drafted by departments of the Federal Government and
newly established war agencies to interpret the war's effect on the
home."[34] This national coalition played on Americans' willingness to
sacrifice for the common good, and they reminded people that by doing
without, they were helping feed a soldier in the field or an Allied civilian in a bombed-out European city.

Amid all of the appeals to housewives to monitor their families'
health and nutrition came point rationing. As historians struggle to
understand the culture and society of wartime America, they search
for different windows through which to view the process of homefront
mobilization and the creation of political obligation.[35] In support of
that effort, such popular cultural media as newspaper reports and advice
columns can provide a useful lens for viewing the exchange of information and ideas between policy makers, social scientists, industry, and
the civilian population. Because there was no precedent for such widespread federal control of consumer activity in American history, it was
necessary to reassure people that their strict adherence to ration policy would, in fact, further the war effort. The popular media was one
medium used to reassure consumers. Their producers sought to alleviate the misunderstandings and fear generated by rationing. In addition, because the intended audience for much of this information was
the housewife, these print sources have much to say about gender relations during the war era. Although there was an influx of women into
the workforce to support the expanding war industries and to replace
men siphoned off for military duty, women retained the central responsibility for providing food for the family. For them, point rationing
was most significant because it altered the patterns of everyday life and
fostered a new sense of accountability and patriotism.

Suddenly, the provisioning of a household would require not only legal U.S. tender but also valid ration points. As Charles Egan of the *New York Times* stated:

> The average American housewife who shopped for canned goods last week was in much the same position as a tourist in a foreign land. She had not only to judge whether she could afford the dollars-and-cents value of the items she bought but also to weigh the desirability of one purchase against the amount of ration 'points' available for the current month.[36]

Or, as columnist Jane Holt insightfully observed: "Good Diet in 1943 Will Need More Than Fat Pocketbook and Interest in Nutrition." In her 30 December 1942 column, Holt revealed that according to the Bureau of Home Economics, diets were "better this year and last than they were from 1936 through 1940." Experts reasoned that factors including increased income, school lunches, and such advances as enriched bread had contributed to this steady improvement. Still, while shortages had not yet affected American diets in a negative fashion, the results of food rationing remained to be seen: "Housekeepers will be required to plan and scheme, to guard against waste, to know enough about food values to be able to cope intelligently with shortages. To take advantage of whatever is plentiful at the moment, they will have to overcome prejudices and superstitions."[37] Expert advice from members of the bureau and figures like columnist Holt would certainly be a significant factor in shaping housewives' attitudes toward the food situation and their role within it. When OPA announced plans for point rationing, the *New York Times* and other newspapers nationwide became important tools for publicizing the "wheres, hows, and whys" of the system. Beginning in December 1942, the *Times* provided readers with a steady stream of information regarding the basics of rationing.

On 2 December 1942, OPA confirmed that point rationing would be instituted in 1943. Initial reports were sketchy and somewhat confusing, but OPA endeavored to explain that point rationing was different from the coupon system already in effect for sugar, gasoline, and fuel oil "in that it is made to cover a group of related products rather than a single item."[38] Later in December, when OPA solidified its plans, Secretary of Agriculture Claude Wickard officially announced its rationing plans. His speech concentrated on stirring up patriotic enthusiasm and reassuring Americans that rationing would not prove detrimental to national health and well-being:

In spite of the tremendous demand for American food, the food available for civilian consumption in 1943 will more than meet the nutritive standards set up by the National Research Council and other groups composed of nutrition scientists.... Now I realize that this entire food program is something comparatively new to all of us. We never have fought a global war before, either. I am depending upon you to make the program a success. With your support I do not see how we can fail. For many of us here at home the battle of food offers our greatest opportunity to contribute most directly to winning the war. And I am confident that you will make the most of this opportunity.[39]

It is unclear exactly how many American citizens agreed with Wickard that food rationing was an "opportunity." Though some argued that it was an unnecessary governmental intrusion, most accepted it as a consequence of war.[40] At the time of the official announcement, OPA was criticized that advance notice of the rationing program would result in massive hoarding sprees. OPA officials had anticipated that hoarding was a possibility and thus attempted to "head hoarders off at the pass." Unfortunately, the success of their efforts was questionable.

Leon Henderson, administrator of the OPA, told Americans that the point system allowed them freedom of choice. He defended the advance notice given with the assertion that both retailers and the public needed time to understand the system before it began to operate.[41] Newspapers and other media outlets would perform a key task in distributing details and information about the program before it went into effect. Those who were critical of OPA's action noted that hoarding would be unavoidable. Donald E. Montgomery, a former consumer's council at the Department of Agriculture, commented: "To avoid tipping off trade speculators, pantry hoarders and pocketbook patriots, no rationing plan should be announced in advance."[42] Many people blamed the government and OPA for shortages and rationing. Information regarding the volume of supplies held by the government encouraged the spread of rumors that rationing was, in fact, an uncalled for infringement on the activities of the free market. One specific group of people were thought to benefit from the unfair distribution of scarce goods — those in Japanese American "war relocation camps." A California Representative stated that he had been told that local civilians were going without many products while camp residents received "huge shipments of scarce foods, including eggs, butter, sugar, coffee and meats." Such reports contributed to the growing black market and fed the suspicious natures of those so inclined.[43]

By late 1942 and early 1943, meat shortages were a particularly thorny issue for many civilians. New York Representative Donald O'Toole called for an investigation of OPA activity. He accused it of exacerbating supply difficulties by failing to establish ceiling prices for livestock in sufficient time to avoid fresh meat price elevation. He implied that OPA was aiding meat packers to the detriment of butchers and consumers.[44] Then, in January 1943, the Commodity Credit Corporation released figures that clearly illustrated the quantity of surplus goods maintained by the government. The government was shown to hold large stocks of wheat, tobacco, soybeans, imported fats and vegetable oils, and other foods designated for use in the Lend-Lease program.[45] When citizens thought that their government was hoarding without approbation, they grew in distrust and skepticism. Why, some people wondered, should they sacrifice through rationing when the government could alleviate the situation by releasing some of its surplus stocks? On a few occasions, the government did respond to the pressure of shortages by releasing supplies. For example, in December 1942, the Food Distribution Association attempted to remedy milk shortages by making available to consumers 2 million cases of evaporated milk from government coffers. This milk came out of a supply which was not intended for Lend-Lease "because these demands shifted to more concentrated forms of milk products on account of shipping shortages."[46]

Still, reports accusing the government and civilians of hoarding persisted. The American Institute of Food Distribution declared that food products packed in 1943 were sufficient to feed the nation. The institute also reported that the army and navy had already received their shares and that the government continued to hold large supplies in warehouses and canneries. It observed that in March 1943, canners were "still holding 40 per cent to more than 75 per cent of government purchases from 1942," an indication "that government took excessive quantities from 1942 packs, probably 25 to 30 per cent more than was needed." Furthermore, the Institute blamed meat shortages on the necessity of providing America's Allies with "immense quantities of meats."[47]

In their effort to encourage people's acceptance of equitable sacrifice, OPA attempted to limit hoarding by requiring all consumers to fill out a declaration form in order to receive Ration Book 2. This form, which appeared in newspapers across the nation, asked each consumer to list the number of "commercially processed fruits and vegetables in the individual's possession and stamps will be deducted accordingly before the ration book is issued. Heavy penalties are provided for any applicant who makes a false declaration of the amount of goods he has on hand."[48] When Book 2 registration began in late February 1943, OPA determined that consumers would have to list any canned goods in excess of five cans per person held as of 20 February 1943 and all coffee in their possession as of 28 November 1942.[49]

The declaration form was a source of considerable anguish for many persons with well-stocked larders. To begin, many people were uncertain exactly what goods they would have to declare. One woman commented: "All I have is five cans of soup. I don't know how this will work out. I have a teacher friend who has promised to help me make out my application."[50] Interesting stories of massive food stocks soon surfaced. A woman from Pittsfield, Massachusetts, declared 1,000 cans. Registration officials told her "that she would not be entitled to any more coupons until about 1960."[51] Other reports of unimaginable stashes included a Bryn Mawr, Pennsylvania, family with 4,502 cans, and Washington, D.C., woman with 1,219 cans.[52] In a reassuring measure, the OPA decided that rather than deducting the entire number of points from the first ration period, they would tailor the ration books to the family declaration by spreading the deductions out over several intervals.[53]

To see how this deduction might affect a person's allocation, it is useful to understand the construction and distribution of Ration Book 2.[54] To obtain a book, one member from every family reported to a local distribution center (typically a school, church, or community center) and presented both a completed declaration form and a valid Book 1 for each member of the family. Children and adults received the same number of points. This distribution was intended to lessen confusion and "red tape" inherent in systems based on age or other variables. The individual books contained both blue and red stamps. The blue stamps were used for processed foods, and the red stamps were reserved for meats and fats, which were rationed in late March 1943. The stamps were lettered to designate a specific validation period and were valued at eight, five, two, or one points. Each rationed food had a point value that was consistent across the country, although its retail price might vary. In addition, different grades, or qualities, of a certain commodity were also valued uniformly.

Under the dictates of Ration Book 2, each person was allotted forty-eight points per month. Although some members of retail associations suggested that uniform national allotments were impractical because "urban dwellers had more need for the canned items in short supply than 'Navajo Indians and hillbillies,'" OPA maintained that uniformity was necessary, and that adjustments would only be made at a later date.[55] Any declarations in excess of five cans per person were valued at eight points, but a total of twenty-four points was all that OPA would remove from any one person's book at a given time. Initially, a grocer could not give "change" in ration stamps, so shoppers had to engage in careful budgeting and calculations to avoid wasting points or coming up short.

During the week before the 1 March 1943 inception of point rationing, all retail sales of rationed goods were suspended to allow suppliers and retailers sufficient time to prepare for the change. As expected, it was during the last days before suspension that a frenzy of hoarding kicked in as consumers engaged in excessive buying and cleared grocers' shelves. Some New York City stores reported that sales were up by as much as 300 percent with "housewives wheeling precious purchases away in perambulators, children with toy wagons helping with the family marketing, many customers struggling homeward with purchases totaling as much as $50 and $60, and shelves in numerous cases stripped or almost bare of canned goods."[56] Clearly, such consumers were less concerned about declarations and points than of the effects of point rationing on their family's diet. OPA's Prentiss Brown attempted to quell these escapades by reminding people that "rush buying" only benefited the enemy. He declared that the rationing system was devised by the government with the civilian in mind, but pointed out that the success or failure of rationing depended in large measure on the cooperation and "intelligence of the American people to withstand any impulses to stampede as a result of baseless rumors. Wars must be won on the fields of battle, but they can be lost at home."[57]

Perhaps these hoarders had not heard about or simply chose to ignore potential penalties, but the government did not just rely on moral suasion. In December 1942, when the point system was still in developmental stages, OPA announced that it would prosecute hoarders under the terms of two federal statutes. First, any untrue declaration of food supplies would constitute falsifying federal records, which was a felony. Second, under the Second War Powers Act, any violation of rationing regulations could be prosecuted as a misdemeanor.[58] Once rationing began and OPA made its first attempt to bring violators to the bar of justice, protesters started to make their voices heard.

A heated controversy erupted in Baltimore in March 1943 when OPA officials entered a private home to inspect for hoarding. OPA had selected Baltimore as a test city to determine the extent of the hoarding problem. Investigators wanted to compare consumer declarations with actual holdings. To do so, they telephoned several homeowners and asked to view the contents of their larders. Baltimore officials selected sixty families and asked them to report to OPA headquarters to "explain their canned-food holdings and their declarations." Three individuals held out and refused to cooperate. Although the situation was eventually settled, OPA regional attorney Walter Gellhorn was forced to battle fierce rumors regarding unwarranted searches. He asserted that OPA recognized that its investigators had no authority "to enter homes to check canned-food hoards without the consent of the owners, and that they are not to resort to the use of search warrants except in extreme cases."[59] Gellhorn's statements did little to smooth the ruffled feathers of one New York City resident who declared that the United States was on the threshold of Hitlerism. In a letter to the editor of the *New York Times*, the author used the Baltimore incident as ammunition against what he viewed as the failure of the Roosevelt administration. He remarked that the New Deal had reigned for ten years, and he wondered: "How many similar Hitler-like acts have been perpetrated by the Washington bureaucrats in those years? Are we going to go on suffering these violations of rights and protection guaranteed to us in war and peace alike?"[60] Shortly after his letter appeared, an editorial in the same newspaper defended the administration, commenting that the actions taken in Baltimore were an aberration and that according to the Fourth Amendment: "an American's pantry is his castle.... The canned goods legitimately on our pantry shelves are safe, even under the emergency war powers. The hoarders can be got at by due process."[61]

Clearly, issues surrounding hoarding aroused the emotions and ire of many Americans. No one wanted to be accused of a lack of patriotism, but by the same token, few seemed willing to sacrifice their share either. One New York City housewife, A. Smith, expressed her dismay in a letter to the editor of the *New York Times*. In her estimation, hoarding was rampant: "How can we be patriotic when we see most of our community rushing to buy canned goods, knowing if we don't do it we will be left high and dry?" She lamented the advanced announcement of rationing, commenting: "This is a cockeyed way of doing things. If the government wants to ration anything, it can very easily let the retailers and wholesalers know about it quietly and make arrangements with them, and then when all is set the public would have a reasonable chance." In her final paragraph, Mrs. Smith revealed her disgust with the federal government and the rationing system: "I say either ration everything at once without preliminary warnings or stop fooling. A good many other people besides myself are getting pretty exasperated about a lot of things that are going on — especially in Washington and the various alphabetical bureaus."[62]

Jane Holt and the Creation of Allegiance to the Golden Rules of Food Rationing

A lion's share of the task of drawing women into a common, patriotic fold during the challenging and tumultuous war years fell to newspaper food writers like Jane Holt.[63] Her daily "News of Food" column became a forum for describing the best methods for dealing with limited supplies and coping with the restraints of rationing. She offered her readers recipes, menus, and advice and frequently included suggestions from the experts at the Bureau of Home Economics or the OPA. Beginning in late November 1942 through March 1943, much of the information in Holt's column focused on finding suitable substitutes for scarce or costly foods and explanations of the impending point rationing system.

During late November 1942 and the month of December, Holt guided her readers through holiday meal preparations under the constraints of rising prices and scarce goods. For New Yorkers, who faced shortages of meat and butter, Holt listed cuts of meat that were plentiful and economical. In spite of the price controls enacted to slow the spiraling cost of living, food prices continued to soar. In November 1942, a *New York Times* column compared the price of a typical family Thanksgiving dinner in 1942 to that of the same menu during the preceding year. The list, compiled by Mrs. Frances Gannon, a home economist with New York City's Department of Markets, confirmed that an average dinner would cost $10.44, or $2.46 more than it had one year earlier. The price of turkey, in particular, had risen dramatically. The columnist noted that turkey supply problems were a result of government purchases and reduced shipments to the East Coast due to higher consumer purchases near the turkey farms: "The springing up of war industries in those areas and greater purchasing power are held responsible for the greater demand in those areas."[64]

Surveying the situation, Holt remarked that if such high prices barred the family from the standard holiday bill of fare, alternatives such as chicken or duck could be equally festive, even if they did "fly in the face of tradition." She published three different menus, suited to different tastes and budgets. The first, which was estimated to cost $3.50 for six people, took "notice of good buys rather than, necessarily, the traditional trappings for the holiday dinner." The feast included broiled grapefruit, fowl fricassee, boiled brown rice, buttered kale, grape jelly, pumpkin pie, cheddar cheese, and small cups of coffee.[65] Although this hardly fits the image of a typical family Thanksgiving dinner, it suited the needs of the cautious cook who took availability and economy into account. It is interesting to note that with every menu Holt provided, she suggested "small" cups of coffee — a reminder that coffee rationing was set to begin on 29 November.

Through much of December, Holt focused on the meat shortage. Although in late 1942 the nation attempted to avert meat shortages through a voluntary Share the Meat program, it proved to be unsuccessful as prices continued to rise and supplies continued to shrink.[66] To help consumers through this difficult time, Holt offered ideas for meat substitutes such as beans and unusual meat cuts: "There is only one favorable comment to make on the meat situation — pork feet and knuckles are fairly plentiful and comparatively cheap. All other meats are scarcer than ever, and cost the same as they did last week."[67] On 24 December, she surveyed the situation and found that it was much the same as it had been at Thanksgiving. Prices remained high and supplies were low. In light of this situation, she proposed an economy Christmas dinner that would cost a family of six $6.80: roast turkey, bread crumb stuffing, giblet gravy, cranberry sauce, mashed white potatoes, baked squash, boiled snap beans (buttered), hot steamed molasses pudding, custard sauce, fresh apples and tangerines, small cups of coffee.[68] For Holt, shortages did not have to prevent a family from eating well, but they did necessitate paying higher prices or accepting nontraditional cuts and protein substitutes.

A striking characteristic of this Christmas menu is the absence of elaborate desserts, cakes, and cookies. The combined effects of sugar rationing, which began in May 1942, and butter shortages meant that many housewives had to curtail holiday baking. For these reasons, Holt mentioned several local bakeries that specialized in certain holiday confections. Still, she discouraged housewives from forgoing all holiday baking if it was an important part of their seasonal rituals:

> It is the little things that make Christmas merry and it's not too early to think about them. You can evoke the spirit of bygone holidays in small ways, duplicating the traditional celebrations in mood if not in detail.
>
> You bake just one batch of cookies, for example, a fraction of what your great-grandmother prepared, but each wafer as delicious as those that scented her kitchen with their warm fragrance for weeks ahead of the great day.[69]

She clearly recognized the fact that maintaining any sense of tradition in the inverted atmosphere of war was a significant factor in keeping up homefront morale.

Holt also made suggestions for those women who might engage in special baking projects to send treats to the members of the armed forces. She published ideas and recipes prepared by the Bureau of Home Economics for "goodies that travel well" and informed her readers of the most efficient methods of packing them for shipment: "There are service men who like to eat, who even say — when you ask them what they want — that a dozen brownies or a layer cake is the kind of present they like to receive." Holt included one "ingenious woman's" creative solution to sending fudge cakes to her son in Iceland. She simply baked the cake in a coffee can, "the kind left over from a happier era," frosted it in the container, packed it in a box, and sent it on its way. In the same column, under the heading "Good Travelers," she published a recipe for Chocolate Drop Cookies. This recipe, although very much like one of our modern standbys, Toll House Chocolate Chip Cookies, differed in one significant way. Because of the effects of sugar rationing, rather than using white or brown sugar, the recipe called for honey and maple syrup.[70]

After the Christmas holiday passed, Holt turned her attention to the coming of point rationing in 1943. She endeavored to reassure her readers that while point rationing would not mean bare cupboards, it would involve more planning and attention to food preparation. In an article called "The Cook's New Leaf," Holt gave her readers ideas about conserving food and preparing meals under wartime constraints. She opened with the following appeal:

> Resolve to be a patriotic cook next year. Decide to be the kind of cook, in fact, who is completely attuned to the times. Make up your mind to adapt your art to the changes that the war will work along the food front in 1943. And determine to do it so well that the meals you serve will not only be nourishing but thrifty, not only thrifty, but appetizing.[71]

The new year was to bring many changes to homefront menus. Throughout January and February, Holt strove to prepare her readers for the effects of a limited supply of canned goods:

> Spur-of-the-moment cookery — an art that depends on tinned and bottled and frozen foods — is about to enter an eclipse. For next month the plan for rationing processed goods goes into effect. And the reliance you once put on a can opener will then be placed on other things. Most especially, perhaps, it will be placed on a knowledge of how to buy, store and prepare fresh vegetables.[72]

She repeatedly reminded housewives of the importance of fresh fruits and vegetables and continued to survey local markets and publish prevailing prices for fresh produce and meat. When a certain product was abundant and cheap, Holt gave a recipe or idea for its use. For example, in early January, when cabbage was in ample supply she highlighted the vegetable in her column. In her estimation, the main problem for many cooks was that of the "ugly ducklings." These were the often overlooked and shunned foods that many people found unappetizing simply because they were unaccustomed to them: "All your life you do your best to ignore them, but now, what with high prices and shortages and rationing, you have no choice. You're compelled to conquer your prejudices, to consider the commonplace, to buy what is available and cheap." Americans would be forced to consume foods like parsnips, turnips, and liver without relying vast quantities of scarce butter and cream to disguise their natural flavors.[73] Along with a graphic representation of the 1943 food supply which included those foods that might be considered "good, variable, and scarce," Holt commented that rationing would mean more substitutes and "more honest-to-goodness cooking ... Menus will be devoid of richness, but if the cook is canny, they will still be balanced, appetizing, satisfying."[74]

Holt continued to rely heavily on information provided by home

economists at the Department of Agriculture. She even offered readers who wrote to her office a complimentary copy of the Bureau of
Home Economics pamphlet *Ninety-nine Ways to Share the Meat*, which
she described as prepared by "experts."[75] Because meat shortages continued, she turned to these other experts for ideas about cooking unfamiliar cuts and new substitutes. One of their principal solutions to the
meat shortage was to encourage people to eat more of the foods that
were in abundance. For example, in January the Department of Agriculture called for the increased consumption of cereals and grains,
which were inexpensive and plentiful. In response, Holt gave her readers new recipes for using such grains as oatmeal and shredded bran.
Her Hearty Chowder recipe combined oatmeal with vegetables for a
main dish, while Honey Bran Pudding was a novel dessert created from
milk and bran.[76]

Throughout February, Holt used her column to reinforce notions
of economy and thrift in food conservation and preparation. Rising
food prices remained an important consideration for many people. On
10 February, she printed figures from the Department of Labor that
detailed the effects of recent price increases. During November and
December 1942, the cost of food "rose an average of 1.2 per cent — that
is, those under ceiling increased 0.5 per cent; those not under ceiling,
7 per cent. Incidentally, in December food cost city wage earners and
clerical workers about the same as it did in 1929. Compared with the
1935–39 average, it was about a third higher."[77] Clearly, despite wage
increases and a booming wartime economy, high food prices meant
that average families still had to be cautious in their food purchases.
As in previous months, Holt offered budget menus for families concerned with their finances. In planning one such menu, she consulted
with a student in an advanced nutrition class at Columbia University.
The resulting menu for a family of four including a husband who
worked in an office, a mother who led a "moderately active life," a
fourteen-year-old son, and a ten-year-old daughter, would cost the
family $1.43 per day. A sample menu from day one offered such dishes
as lima bean casserole, meat loaf with gravy, and spice cake with prune
sauce.[78] Far from elegant or complicated fare, this menu provided the
necessary amount of calories and nutrients without excessive cost.

Once a family had expended valuable currency, and soon, ration
points for food, it was necessary for the housewife to make sure that
she extracted every bit of value she could from her purchases. When

the New York State College of Home Economics held a conference in February 1943, one of the main discussion topics was food conservation. Holt reported that for the city women who attended the conference, the questions that rural women asked at first seemed strange. These "country" women wondered about conservation through dehydration and "whether meat that was frozen in home-units lost nutritive value." Clearly, the concerns of rural and urban women differed, but Holt remarked that in the end "it was plain" that both groups' concerns were essentially the same: "For what these women wanted to learn more about was the art of conservation — how to plan and prepare and present wartime meals so that not a scrap of food goes to waste." In keeping with that theme, experts at the conference spoke about how to market intelligently based on changing local conditions. One important piece of advice was that shoppers remain flexible and open to the possibility of substituting an abundant food for one that was scarce. Other speakers reminded women to pay attention to all of the available information regarding new scientific cooking practices. Recent research about nutrients had resulted in new beliefs regarding proper cooking methods. Especially in preparing meats, research showed that lower cooking temperatures resulted in less reduction in the weight of the meat. At a session titled "Science Helps the Cook to Conserve," the presenter "exploded that sentimental theory — 'the recipe that worked for my grandmother is good enough for me.' Stuff and nonsense, she said in effect; careful research has led us to abandon many of the cooking practices that were dear to the hearts of housekeepers a couple of generations ago."[79]

As the reality of point rationing drew closer, Holt offered hints for dealing successfully with the specifics of point rationing. She asked various home economists to lend their expertise to planning nutritious menus under the new constraints. They reminded women to consider the food groups, to be familiar with substitutes for scarce goods, and to be flexible as to the time of their shopping and the choices they made.[80] Holt endeavored to allay fears and misconceptions by answering basic questions such as "Why are processed foods being rationed?" For Holt, the new regime was necessary:

> Because the demand for them — our armed forces and Allies require 50 per cent of the 1943 pack of canned fruits and vegetables — exceeds the supply. Rationing insures a fair share of these scarce but essential foods for every one and prevents chislers from getting more than their por-

tion. The point system gives civilians a certain freedom of choice in their shopping; it is the nearest thing to unrestricted buying that is possible under wartime rationing.[81]

In response to the question: "Why must I report my household stocks of processed foods and coffee?" she returned to the "fair share" refrain:

> Because the government is eager to "even things up." Those who have more than their share of rationed goods will be deprived of some of their points. This prevents hoarders from benefiting because they bought excess amounts of canned foods and coffee. (The government recognizes, of course, that some householders ordinarily purchase canned goods in large amounts, and that not all who have more than the allowance are necessarily unpatriotic hoarders.)[82]

Rationed Reality

With such ringing endorsements of the point ration plan, Holt led her readers through the difficult preration and initial ration period. By March 1943 she had turned to the "nuts and bolts" information necessary for shopping with ration points. She published a list of the point values for processed foods and printed several suggestions for getting as many servings as possible from a can or bottle. After point rationing began in March, the "News of Food" column changed little. Although points introduced a new dimension, Holt continued to focus on economy and thrift in purchases and preparation. Now, when Holt published her budget menus for a family of four, she considered both cost and point values. In addition to the menu, she provided a shopping list for the rationed commodities. When meat and fat rationing went into effect, she came to the housewife's aid by explaining the best ways to spend their red points for such goods. Throughout the entire period from the announcement of point rationing to its inception, Holt consistently supported the government, the OPA, and various nutritionists, home economists, and other assorted experts. Her column was a bulwark against hoarders and black marketers who threatened the integrity of the entire system. Through her explanations of the necessity of the system, definitions of new terms and policies, and of course recipes, she armed women with information to help them cope successfully with point rationing. Throughout, Holt reinforced the important role that the housewife played in making rationing work.

Clearly, point rationing demanded more of a woman's time and attention in planning menus and preparing meals. Because housewives were the principal agents of food purchase and preparation, their understanding and support of the system was of vital importance. One *New York Times* editorial noted that the coming of point rationing would result in increased equality between men and women:

> Women in the home will have come closer than at any time in the past to achieving equality with men, in the sense that they will now have to master an intricate rationing system, roughly equivalent to their spouses' income tax returns. We can, in fact, already visualize a living room scene in which the husband struggles under the lamp with the new tax law covering his March 15 return while the woman of the house masters the Wickard coupon plan. This may not make for amusement so wildly exciting as to require a sedative to induce sleep. But it's about the best we have to offer for early 1943 homework, and the American home will patriotically do what's expected of it of course.[83]

Such assertions of women's significance in the war effort aimed to temper their tendency to hoard or support the black market. In addition, they helped make women feel that they could play an important role in the national effort from their own kitchens. The *New York Times* reported Food Administrator Wickard's summary of the housewife's part wherein he expressed his hope that "we can keep not only producers, processors and distributors of food well-informed concerning the current food situation but that we can keep housewives better informed. I'd like to make that kind of pledge to the housewives." Wickard highlighted the significance of housewives to the entire war effort, stating that they would "have a very important part to play in this new program in making the best of what they will have."[84]

4

Sharing in the Sisterhood of Sacrifice: The Recipe for a "Homogenized" Homefront Housewife

During World War II, two radically different propaganda campaigns converged on one common subject: American women. Some wartime slogans encouraged women to keep both feet firmly planted in the domestic sphere while others asked them to emulate the sacrifice of Rosie the Riveter by participating in war industry "for the duration." Those women who sought employment outside of the home, whether as volunteers or industrial laborers, found glorification in their contribution to the national war effort but also faced criticism for their lack of time and energy to devote to family well-being. They found themselves burdened with reconciling both the time constraints of being working wives and mothers and the supply constraints imposed by rationing. While many people accepted changing women's roles as necessary for the duration of the war, still others remained ambivalent to any radical departures from women's traditional place in the home.[1]

Although women entered the workforce in record numbers during the war, they were accepted only out of necessity, not due to a radical reversal in attitudes about women's place in society. Americans modified their definition of women's proper sphere to fit wartime needs, yet expected working women to maintain high standards in caring for their families; it was commonly thought that after the war women would resume their traditional roles. Even in the midst of war, conceptions of proper behavior defining femininity continued to affect women's lives.

The crucible of war provided home economists and other assorted experts the opportunity to celebrate the honor and value of housewifery. Even while wartime campaigns to encourage women to enter the market of paid labor outside the home continued, other voices reinforced the notion that women could engage in political and social activities of national importance while neither threatening the quality of family life nor challenging the traditional sphere of feminine activity. As cogs in the machinery of food rationing, women played a vital role in the success or failure of controlled consumption. Indeed, a woman's most significant contribution to the war might come in the conscientious planning and serving of meals. By practicing conservation and thrift and rejecting hoarding, women would renew a bond with their sturdy, patriotic forebears who had successfully defended their homefronts during past wars.[2]

The effort to constitute the ideal wartime consumer became a quest for the ideal woman — the patriotic, consuming housewife. As far back as the American Revolution, the ideology of republican motherhood had emphasized the female's significance in creating the moral atmosphere of the home. Beginning in the late nineteenth century, however, Americans' perceptions of the home and women's roles within it began to change. Historians of women's experience in the United States have demonstrated how industrialization redefined the sexual division of labor that had previously served to separate men's and women's roles within families. Industrialization and commercialization removed men's work from the home and gave it potent meaning through its cash valuation. In contrast, the labor associated with running a household remained largely outside the market economy and hence devalued because it remained mostly unremunerated. In this environment, women's connection to the national economy was increasingly channeled through the activity of consumption, a wholly appropriate female activity.[3] Not surprisingly, for middle- and upper-class women at least, domesticity came to represent a training ground for not just morals but also appropriate consumer behavior.[4]

Historically, domestic treatises, household advice manuals, and cookbooks have played an important role in advancing the precepts of female propriety. From the early Republic through the nineteenth century, authors like Amelia Simmons, Catharine Beecher, and Harriet Beecher Stowe used this genre to combat the various threats to women's traditional roles posed by changing social, economic, and political patterns in American life. Prescriptive literature attempted to ensure that regardless of whether or not they internalized standards of female conduct, women would be made aware of their transgressions when acting counter to the socially acceptable image. Likewise, the domestic science or home economics movement of the late nineteenth and early twentieth centuries instigated an effort to recast the value of women's roles within the home. This movement played a vital role in forging and strengthening the links between women and consumer culture. Proponents of the movement attempted to dignify housework with the cachet of a scientific endeavor. Through their efforts to validate women's position in the home by emphasizing efficiency and the science of homemaking, leaders such as Ellen Richards and Christine Frederick simply reinforced cultural values that placed women firmly in the domestic realm. As national spokeswomen, they and others directed housewives about how best to consume, and thus they were valuable assets to industries marketing to women. These women utilized their influence to create powerful, nationally recognized personalities who could relate to the housewife's challenges and suggest ways to overcome them. Betty Crocker, for example, was the persona created by Marjorie Husted, an employee of General Mills who believed that women wanted domestic advice from someone they could relate to, someone who seemed to be knowledgeable but was also approachable.[5] Through such advice and prescriptions, Betty Crocker and other prominent home economists and spokeswomen helped define the traits and behaviors of the ideal, modern American housewife.[6] Although the domestic science movement made significant strides for many women, it also had profound consequences, and in many cases, it served only to undermine further women's status. In some ways, the home economics movement sold women out as it resulted in both increased trivialization of housework and the professionalization of a class of expert home economists, who often acted merely as a tool of the wider commercial culture.[7]

During World War II, the reality of global conflict and the mobilization of large numbers of women into the war industries did not alter the fact that an ideal family had a woman who remained in the home, just as women had done in the past. Although working women faced special challenges as they juggled conflicted status and broke old roles, all women needed to be included in the war effort. The authors of prescriptive literature such as newspaper advice columns and cookbooks attempted to bridge the chasm between ideal and reality and validate the housewife's role in the face of changing circumstances. Ultimately, these home economists and their supporters in government, media, and industry were among the most successful "colonizers" of the American kitchen. The invasiveness of food rationing legitimated their efforts and resulted in the increased homogenization of the American diet and an effort to cast all women into an idealized, common, national mold — the "homogenized housewife."

Margot Murphy: Also Known as Jane Holt

The Monday through Saturday daily editions of the *New York Times* carried Jane Holt's "News of Food" column. In addition, Holt wrote a column for the Sunday *New York Times Magazine*. Jane Holt was actually a pen name for Margot Murphy McConnell. She was born in Detroit in 1906. Before relocating to New York City, she worked for a time as a newspaper reporter for the *Detroit News*. Although Holt's educational background or professional training is not listed, her obituary, which appeared in the *New York Times* on 8 July 1976, credits her with beginning the newspaper's food column in 1941. After leaving the *New York Times* in 1943, she became general services editor of the women's magazine, *The Woman's Home Companion*, a position she held until 1957.

In 1942, Jane Holt stepped away from her *New York Times* persona to publish *Wartime Meals: How to Plan Them, How to Buy Them, How to Cook Them* under her given name, Margot Murphy — even though she was already married to James V. McConnell, an executive at NBC by this time. Although she chose to publish under the name Murphy, she included a parenthetical reference to her more widely recognized identity (Jane Holt) on the title page, and listed her position as "Food Editor of the *New York Times*" beneath that name. Drawing on her connection with the *New York Times* was a way of utilizing the institutional support attached to the name of the paper and capitalizing upon her already established reading audience. In the text of the book, she referred to her work there: "In the *Times*, I give more space to reporting what is in market and what it costs than to any other panel of the whole food picture. If there is a food column in your city which gives such information, follow it with dog-like devotion. And if your local paper hasn't such a column, write a beseeching letter to the editor, asking for it."[8]

A consultation with *The National Union Catalog* reveals that *Wartime Meals* appeared in only one edition. An excerpt from the *New York Times* book review of Holt's book reveals that she was awarded the status of an "expert": "From the Bureau of Home Economics of the Department of Agriculture market lists for the family are quoted before this expert goes on to suggest menus, tell what to do with leftovers, and set forth detailed information about marketing for fresh meat, fish, vegetables and fruits, and canned goods."[9] In his review, "Cookery Books of 1942," Helmut Ripperger, cookbook critic for *Publishers Weekly*, commented briefly on Murphy's book, noting: "Margot Murphy, widely known as the 'Jane Holt' of the *New York Times*, has gathered much of the advice she dispenses daily in her capacity as food editor into 'Wartime Meals,' how to plan them, how to buy them, how to cook them. It is indeed a useful book."[10] Ripperger provided readers with a checklist of the cookbooks published in 1942, including facts of publication and cost. Murphy's book retailed at $2. Most other books were priced in a range from $0.25 to $3, so her work would appear to have fallen in the moderate price category.

Murphy divided *Wartime Meals* into six parts, each having a different theme related to the wartime food situation. Much of the work is devoted to text, with only the final section comprised of actual recipes. It is important to note that this book appeared in 1942, the same year that sugar and coffee rationing began, but one year prior to point rationing for canned goods and other processed foods. It seems that Murphy's timing for publication was rather unfortunate. Point rationing caused dramatic alterations in Americans' consumption patterns that her work simply did not address. After 1942, readers of wartime cookery books would almost certainly have looked for a work that helped explain and untangle the complex web of rules and regulations involved with point rationing.

Despite its publication early in the war, however, Murphy predicted that shortages and inflation would affect the way that American families purchased and consumed their meals. Her opening chapter, "Get It Down on Paper," begins with the assertion: "One shortage is always oppressively present for most of us during a war. That is a shortage of money.... The grocery budget of most families will definitely have to take a cut, if it hasn't already done so." She continued by noting that food was as essential to the homefront as it was to the battlefield because undernourished people are less productive. Her solution was planning: "Pencils and paper are our primary weapons as we wage our kitchen battles." According to Murphy, a woman could perform a vital national service simply by being a good planner, a conscientious consumer, and a careful cook.[11]

Throughout the work, Murphy used a very conversational tone that is at times almost dialogic. She spoke directly to her readers in a way that engaged them personally with the work. In addressing her audience personally as "you" and including herself in the mix as "we," Murphy utilized two literary tropes that make readers feel personally involved in the book. For example, in discussing how a woman could stretch her budget by purchasing day-old bread, she noted that women should overcome the "poverty-stricken connotation to this practice which will make many turn up their noses in scorn." She continued, noting that most people would not "be able to tell the difference. After all, you don't — I hope — throw out a loaf of bread just because it has been in your bread box for more than twenty-four hours. So why scorn to buy one? Even though your palate is delicate, it will surely be deceived if such bread is toasted."[12]

In the above passage, it is clear that Murphy was addressing a certain type of reader, one who was accustomed to purchasing store-bought bread and had the economic means to take advantage of commercially canned ready-to-serve foods such as pork and beans, spaghetti, and soups. Coming out of the Depression years, not everyone would have had the resources to purchase such commodities. Yet throughout her work, Murphy endeavored to level differences among women by constructing a national reader who was sacrificing under the same circumstances and experiencing the same things as her fellow housewives of all classes and geographic regions. Unlike the Depression, which affected different regions and classes to varying degrees, the war promised to bring about a more universal alteration in national consumption patterns. Murphy reminded her readers, therefore: "In total war, all of us — men as they go about unspectacular civilian jobs,

women, older folk, even children — have a part to play." She endeavored to create a spirit of camaraderie between herself and her readers
through appeals to the universal experience of the wartime food situation: "One good at least stems from the dreadful situation in which
we find ourselves. With fewer tires available for retail deliveries, we'll
have to go back to the sound practice of doing our marketing in person, not by telephone. This is a cardinal rule to follow if you want to
buy at the lowest possible cost the meals you have planned."[13]

As author Susan J. Leonardi argues, recipes are a form of "embedded discourse." Leonardi describes the ritual of recipe sharing among
women as a gendered act that places the giver and the receiver in a
special relationship. She believes, furthermore, that cookbooks, like
actual social interaction among women, can serve as a mechanism to
re-create the "social context of recipe sharing" and overcome "the social
barriers of class, race, and generation."[14] In Murphy's case, the cookbook became a tool for constituting "the American woman." Murphy
tried to overcome regionalism and class differences and move toward
in essence, the unification of women. Yet in her efforts to infuse American women with a sense of "sisterhood," she continued to assume that
her readers were white, middle-class housewives with a significant level
of literacy. She did not apparently consider the special circumstances
of different racial and ethnic minorities, nor did she comment on
the plight of the growing population of women involved in industrial
or other war work — the Rosie the Riveters. In Murphy's eyes,
all women were linked through the activity of consumption, a role
transformed into an even more common experience by the reality of
rationing.

Indeed, Murphy made it quite clear that the most important aspect
of the housewife's wartime job was to be a savvy consumer who could
find the most nutritious, tasty foods at the best possible prices. Still,
she could not avoid the fact that variations in family income would
continue to exist and that women had to learn how to accommodate
the nutritional needs of their families to their personal budgets as well
as the wartime situation. She looked to the Bureau of Home Economics in the Department of Agriculture for assistance. This government
agency had established a series of three different meal plans based on
family income that would provide adequate nutrition for each member. They ranged from "low cost" to "moderate" to "liberal." Murphy
included all three plans in her work with the assertion that by

using them, you have the comforting assurance that you are giving your family a perfectly balanced diet which provides all the vitamins, proteins, minerals and calories which will keep them well and strong. The moderate-cost and liberal-cost diets, however, naturally provide greater variety and somewhat higher nutritive value than the basic minimum.

According to these guidelines, a woman should sit down with the meal plan, record the names of each person in her family, and construct a menu based on the quantities of various foods necessary for each individual in her family. Murphy concluded that ultimately the cost of the meals depends on "the canny thriftiness of the woman who buys and prepares the meals." By following the formula provided, however, a woman could plan her "ideal market order" based on her economic situation without the risk of sacrificing her family's health.[15]

In chapter 3, "Meals from the Model," Murphy provided her readers with a series of menus for summer and winter meals built from the requirements of the "moderate diet." She commented that this plan is "the one towards which most of us are likely to gravitate." Still, she appeared apologetic to those who might have consumed at a higher level prior to the onset of the war. Nevertheless, she defended the simplicity of the dishes included:

> I do not point to them as a gourmet's delight. Were I to set about planning menus with nary a thought as to their cost, the result would be quite different. Many inexpensive puddings are included, since they provide a means of using part of the large amount of milk which we need to keep us in fighting form, while choice cuts of meat are among the missing. Although not the sort of gastronomical adventure for which people used to journey to Europe in happier days — and which they struggled to duplicate when they got back — I think these are good meals. Perhaps their greatest recommendation is that my husband thinks so, too.

Murphy advised her readers that they did not need to adhere to the menus slavishly to maintain their integrity. For example, she noted that substitutions according to a family's tastes and market fluctuations were perfectly acceptable. She described a scenario where a woman had planned to serve peas for dinner but found that they were expensive due to poor weather conditions in Florida. Murphy's solution was to look for another inexpensive green vegetable, while cautioning not to "switch to an altogether different sort — say, a tomato — which has quite another role to play in the diet."[16]

Murphy presented in her work seven summer menus and seven winter menus. A sample menu for a summer Tuesday, for instance, includes:

> Breakfast: Tomato juice; Poached eggs on rye toast; Milk for children; coffee for adults
> Lunch: Fruit salad with whipped dressing*; Wholewheat muffins,* split, toasted, and buttered; Honey cookies*; Cold chocolate milk
> Dinner: Pea soup; crackers; Sliced cold tongue; Creamed onions; Raw grated cabbage with french dressing; Rye bread and butter; milk; Victory cake* with cocoa-flavored whipped evaporated milk; Demitasse

The asterisks denote the fact that recipes or instructions for that item appear in the final section of the book.

An interesting element of the above menu is the inclusion of tongue for dinner. This item fell into the category Murphy labeled "little-known cuts." She encouraged her readers to gain a full knowledge of these meat products because they tended to be less expensive, but "every bit as delicious" as the standard chops and steaks. She proceeded with a description of the various well-known and lesser-known cuts of beef, pork, lamb, and veal. She then described each cut and how best to prepare it. Many of the more unusual items such as beef kidney and heart, lamb neck, or veal tongue appeared with the asterisk denoting that recipes are provided. Similarly, she advised increased acquaintance with the possibilities for fish cookery. In a reference to the Catholic religious practice of consuming fish on Fridays, Murphy quoted a former New York Commissioner of Markets who had said that fish "don't swim in the sea just to be eaten on Friday."[17]

Murphy's instructions for overcoming food "prejudices" were not limited to meats and fish. She also advised women that condensed and evaporated milk were equally as nutritious as fresh milk and less expensive. In addition, she reminded her readers that cheaper skim milk "may do the full job" of whole milk when it was balanced in the diet with an adequate amount of butter fat. Further, Murphy encouraged her audience to make smart choices when buying eggs, urging them to consider price, quality, and intended use before making a purchase.[18]

With regard to fruits and vegetables, Murphy asserted that women needed to investigate options outside "the old, familiar standbys," which she argued based "on the law of supply and demand ... are likely to be the most costly." In these sections, Murphy spoke to regional and ethnic differences by advising the purchase of a wide range of unfamiliar products, including dandelion and mustard greens, a variety of South American squash known as chayote, and Italian summer squash, or zucchini.

> Not nearly all of these vegetables are, of course, in season all the time. That's the point. One must have a big list in mind so that there will always be a bargain on it. Nor are all of them sold in every neighborhood. Some are found only in stores catering to a foreign clientele. I strongly recommend exploring such stores, not only for the bargains which may be found in them, but for the variety and adventure they will lend your meals.[19]

Murphy sang the praises of Southern foods such as collard and poke greens. She noted that "the collard green is the most important green vegetable in Southern gardens during the winter months." Although these greens made their way to the North, she observed that they were rarely consumed by people other than "transplanted Southerners." For Murphy, however, they had a "delicious flavor" and "are to be cooked in much the same way as spinach — boiled and served with butter, or creamed. They are especially good when boiled with salt pork." As for the shoots of the pokeberry plant, "popular in the Southland," Murphy advised boiling and presentation with melted butter or hollandaise sauce. If nothing else, the war might serve as an opportunity to expand Americans' culinary repertoire.[20]

An important aspect of the war program was national nutrition. Recent scientific advances had resulted in an increased understanding of the role of vitamins and minerals in the diet. The poor state of health of many of the first draftees caused more people to pay attention to the importance of balanced diets. Murphy did not overlook this issue in her work. She commented that milled wheat and the replacement of fresh with processed foods had rendered Americans' diets deficient. She demanded that readers take notice of the situation:

> You may well be thinking that most of us get along all right, in spite of the starvation diet to which we have reduced ourselves. That we really have succeeded in making a fine mess of things is clearly attested by the fact that of the young men in the very prime of life who were called in the first draft, 40% were rejected for physical defects, a great number of which were directly related to poor nutrition. That's a state of affairs which would never be found in one of those backward middle–European countries toward which we feel so superior, and whose peasants we have pitied for the simple — and vitamin-rich diet — of soup, black bread, cabbage, cheese, a little meat, and milk, on which they raised strong sons.

By calling her readers' attention to this problem, however, she did not encourage women to become experts in the field of nutrition. Quite in contrast, she claimed that well before the discovery of vitamins and minerals, people understood that what they ate affected how they felt: "Proof of the fact that vitamins have been on the job ever since man began to eat — which it may be supposed was about an hour or two after he was created — is the fact that in 1500 B.C. the Egyptians were eating animal livers to improve their eyesight. It took us 3500 years to find out that liver contains A, which affects the eyes." Although she placated those with an interest in such scientific matters by providing an elementary run-down of basic facts about vitamins and minerals and the particular foods where one might find them, she stated that eating well is much the same as following a doctor's prescription. It was not so important to know what the remedies would do as to follow the directions for their ingestion. Women did not need to concern themselves with the technicalities; as long as they knew how to buy the right foods, their families would be fit and healthy.[21]

In addition to encouraging the planning of well-balanced menus that suited diverse family budgets, Murphy advocated a "War on Waste" through responsible consumption, but no hoarding. She spoke sternly to those women who did not plan effectively and ended up with leftovers, which were far too frequently discarded. She quoted the "old adage:" "A woman ... can throw out with a teaspoon more than a man can bring in with a shovel." Although perhaps "exaggerated to prove its point," Murphy commented that it is "based on fact. Now that our farmers are straining every effort to fulfill the Food for Freedom program, now that the transportation systems are laboring under unheard-of loads, and our allies are pleading for food with which to sustain themselves for our common battle, waste is the unforgivable kitchen sin." In her estimation, one thing that women could do to support the war effort was to purchase foods that required the least amount of transportation from field to table because "foods which come from near-by are usually and naturally inexpensive, following this patriotic practice is not incompatible with thriftiness."[22]

Another way to demonstrate patriotism was to avoid the temptation to stock an emergency shelf or hoard commodities. Murphy endeavored to assure readers that there would not be famine in the land of plenty. She observed that the nation's first worry was feeding the military, the Allies, and finally, the civilian population. She echoed

Secretary of Agriculture Claude Wickard's sentiments in his slogan "Food will win the war and write the peace." Using sugar rationing as an example, she reminded women that "there is a vast and agreeable difference between being limited in the amount of a particular food we may use, and having none of it at all." She made an eloquent case for careful use of food:

> One sure way to hasten rationing of any food is to hoard it, or to waste it. In fact, if every one of us could really learn to conserve what we have, rationing in many cases would not be necessary at all. Edwin P. Geauque, executive director of the National Grocers Institute, has made the amazing estimate that about 25% of all the food our hard-pressed transportation systems carry is thrown away, both in stores and homes, through ignorance of how to handle and use it.[23]

Similarly, she inveighed against those who might tend toward hoarding food products. Murphy observed that unlike Europe, the United States was not likely to face extended periods of closed stores and disabled transportation systems. She informed her readers that even keeping a few extra cans for an emergency could pose a problem of national scope. For example, if everyone engages in "laying in" extra cans of milk or soup, the result might be shortages, higher prices, and ultimately increased rationing. Murphy was quite adamant in her stand against such activities, and told her readers that during the Civil War, hoarding was "the unforgivable crime in the South" and that "among the old families, the descendants of those who committed it are often to this day unkindly reminded of their forebears' treachery. The shame of such criminal rocking of the boat during an emergency should, indeed, live on for generations." This vignette from the American past provided a good argument for careful planning and purchasing. No patriotic woman would want to run the risk of being labeled a hoarder.[24]

Clearly, the war demanded sacrifices from civilians on many levels. In Murphy's model, one way to cope with the situation was to resurrect sound practices from previous generations. She looked to the "simpler ways" of the past for guidance. She held up the recent past as evidence of extravagant and irresponsible spending.[25] For example, she commented that much of the food problem was one of packaging shortages rather than of an actual lack of food itself. Murphy observed that there

> will be no more cunningly shaped little jars of delicacies, adorably done up in colored cellophane and gaily beribboned. Some experts even believe that we will go back to the "cracker barrell" days, by which they

mean that we will buy our staples — flour, sugar, rice and the like — in bulk out of a big container, to conserve precious packaging materials.

Further, she noted that as a result of this situation, women would have to do more food preparation in the home rather than relying on ready-to-serve meals from the grocer's shelf. While she alluded to the fact that there was a shortage of men to work in the factories, she did not broach the question of women working outside the home but simply assumed that they would remain the ones responsible for households:

> Therefore, I believe that we will find ourselves doing more and more of the preparation at home, and increasingly using the basic, essential foods in their natural states. I don't believe that man-power or materials will be expanded on stuffed olives, pate de fois gras, or mushrooms in wine! — or that any American woman wants them to be so used while her country fights for its very existence.[26]

Among the practices that Murphy predicted would come back into vogue as a result of the war were home bread baking; "old fashioned" sweeteners such as molasses, honey, and maple syrup; increased use of herbs and the consumption of herbal teas such as sassafras; home rendering of fat; and home canning. The reasoning for resurrecting these vestiges of the past was that they were sound economically in time of shortage and inflation. Still, Murphy acknowledged that some readers might resist such ideas: "I hesitate even to mention one of the best ways of all to reduce the bread bill. It is to make it yourself, which, I well know, is just as old hat as camisoles and curio cabinets. Nevertheless, the sad truth is that the cost of its actual ingredients is naturally less than the price of a loaf of 'boughten' bread."[27]

Murphy also encouraged readers to emulate the women of the past: "Our grandmothers knew a lot more about thrift than we ever thought would be necessary for us."[28] Her ideal reader was a woman straight from the mythical "golden age" of the American past — wherever that might be. While historians today dispute the perpetuation of a "golden age myth," her work was clearly a call for a return to the "simpler days."[29] Her vision of American womanhood equated frugality and efficiency with "old fashioned" practices and in turn with patriotism. In the recipe section of the book, Murphy included three recipes that were throwbacks to the World War I era. In a footnote, she told her readers that the recipes for War Cake, Oatmeal Macaroons, and Popcorn (made into a "sweet" in the form of popcorn balls), were "honorable veterans of the First World War and were advocated by the

United States Food Administration in its leaflets on economy and conservation."[30]

For Murphy, the power of womanhood lay in the activity of consumption. Although the exigencies of war called for a return to some less extravagant methods in the kitchen, women were still defined by their activity as consumers and housewives. In Murphy's construction, ideal women remained in the home and did not engage work outside the household — an interesting point of view coming from a woman who was employed as a food editor. The author made clear that in spite of the obstacles of shortages and rationing, a woman's most important job was the provisioning of her household. Toward that end, she directed her readers to plan, purchase, and prepare their foods with responsibility and care. Along with the calls for Rosie the Riveter, there was an equally potent effort to keep women in the home. Murphy continued the tradition, stretching back to Catharine Beecher and other female writers of the nineteenth century, of attempting to increase the respect given to a woman's duties in the home.

Reading *Wartime Meals* today, more than sixty years removed from the experience of rationing and wartime shortages, is almost like having a first-person encounter with the past. Wartime housewifery comes to life through detailed descriptions of how to market and how to prepare common foods. Murphy's recipes are embedded in a discourse rich with social and economic implications. In a sense, this book was a narrative of her perceptions of women's proper role in society. It encouraged readers to follow its prescriptions so that the nation might emerge victorious and the individual woman's family be taken down the path to health and happiness. The *New York Times* book review described the work as "an inclusively helpful aid to the wartime housewife" and one of "well-met purpose of complete and practical usefulness."[31] While Murphy's work may not speak to modern women in the same voice as to its contemporaries, it remains a book of "practical usefulness" as historians attempt to uncover the many intricacies of the female experience on the U.S. homefront.

"A Wonderful Lunch in a Box": Prescriptions from Cookbooks and Magazines

The historiography of women's roles in World War II is heavily weighted toward studies of Rosie the Riveter and her fellow female

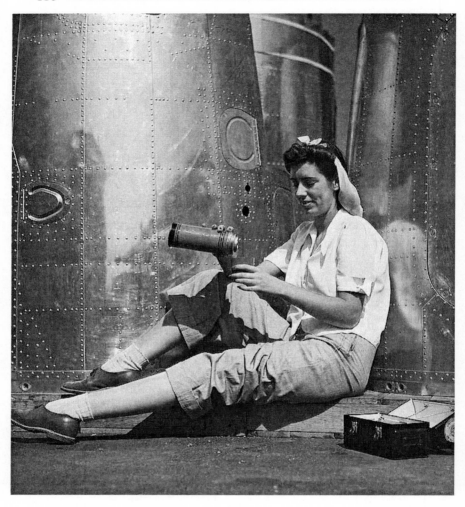

A worker at the Douglas Aircraft Company in Long Beach, California, this woman (name unknown) enjoys a respite during her lunch break, October 1942 (Library of Congress, Prints and Photographs Division, FSA-OWI Collection, LC-USW36-112).

workers.[32] An examination of Murphy's work provides a glimpse of another powerful propaganda campaign directed toward women — one that focused on creating a "happy homefront housewife." *Wartime Meals*, like many other World War II–era cookbooks, highlights the patriotic role that an American woman could play without leaving the confines of her kitchen. Other cookbooks, like Alice Winn Smith's *Thrifty Cooking for Wartime*, also encouraged women to see their wartime roles as "no less important than that of the worker in the munitions plant or the soldier advancing with the tanks. But in order to do her part the housewife, like the soldier, needs a new set of rules." Betty Crocker used the General Mills 1943 publication *Your Share: How to Prepare Appetizing, Healthful Meals with Foods Available Today* to rally readers with the assertion that "whatever else you do — you are first and foremost, homemakers — women with the welfare of your families deepest in your hearts." She continued, telling women to "heed the government request to increase the use of available food, and save those that are scarce — and, at the same time, safeguard your family's nutrition." Finally, Crocker told her readers: "Never has there been such a need, for what American women can contribute. So to you women behind the men, behind the guns, we offer this little book... And we salute you all!"[33]

Because the majority of cookbook authors concentrated on women who maintained traditional roles, direct references to women working outside the home are sparse. Nevertheless, some authors did attempt to help women reconcile their roles as housewives and mothers with their roles as volunteers or war workers while maintaining that feeding their families remained their fundamental responsibility. Authors played on women's sense of self-sacrifice to further a moral cause. In references to women's work outside the home, however, the common theme was that despite her other activities, her main responsibility was to care for her family. American women were the generals of the household. Approaching the employment of women in war industry as a temporary aberration necessary only for the duration of the war, these authors advocated methods for conserving time and energy to allow women to focus on other tasks that might contribute to victory. In the introduction to *Cook It in a Casserole*, Florence Brobeck advised her readers to take advantage of leftovers, casserole recipes, and other time- and labor-saving techniques because so many women were involved with "war relief service or are employed, either because the men-folk are with the fighting forces and it is necessary to earn, or because, following a patriotic urge, the woman of the house has decided to help the labor shortage in a near-by munitions, airplane, or machine plant."[34]

The author of *The Working Girl Must Eat*, Hazel Young, laid out menus and work plans in a step-by-step fashion to help the young, inexperienced, working girl:

> "Out of the kitchen" and "in the defense plant" are taken for granted these days and young girls and old, from Sister Sue to Grandma, are working from morning till night and even from night till morning. That makes meal getting a bit incidental and certainly rather haphazard. This we know is a pity, for "Food must fight for Freedom," and good meals, well planned and cooked with care, play no small part in keeping the family fit and efficient.[35]

Interestingly, although Young claimed that her book was intended to assist working women by providing them with 100 menu suggestions, including detailed instructions for preparation and serving, many of the time-saving hints labeled "preparations for the future" required readers to engage in rather time-consuming projects. Obviously, standards for housekeeping and cookery were not being adjusted for working women. Many of Young's bits of advice described tasks that could be completed ahead of time for a future dinner or dessert or reminded the reader to complete certain housekeeping chores on a regular basis, thereby increasing efficiency: "Check to see if your linen is crisp and fresh and your silver bright and shining. If not, we're afraid you'll have to get busy. Boil 3 or 4 medium sweet potatoes in their jackets. See if you have plenty of French Dressing."[36] For Young, business-like household management was the key to balancing domestic duties and war work.

Other authors broached the subject of women working outside the home by examining the situation of women participating in less radical capacities. For instance, voluntary war-related work in soldiers' canteens might require recipes and tips for preparing large quantities of food for a crowd. The 1943 edition of *The Good Housekeeping Cookbook* included a special "wartime supplement" in the middle of the book because the original contents had been planned before the United States entered the war. Under the section titled "Canteen Work," the supplement's authors directed the housewife to turn to the instructions for buying and cooking for a crowd. There she would find information to help her estimate the quantities of food needed to serve a large group of hungry servicemen.[37]

Any work outside the home reduced the amount of time that women could devote to food preparation. Meeting the varied needs of men working the night shift, of schoolchildren, and of a woman's responsibilities outside the home called for foods that were quick, easy to prepare, and might perhaps be cooked ahead of time so that they could be "popped into an oven or onto a range as soon as the cook has finished her day of making parachutes."[38] Another way authors provided assistance to harried women was by including recipes for "busy day" meals and menus. Under the chapter "Busy-Day Meals," one author offered her readers recipes for casserole of canned corn and spaghetti and five-minute steak sandwiches. She also included a week's worth of sample menus for quick meals. Monday's menu, for example, called for barbecued hamburgers, creamed leftover potatoes, apple celery and nut salad, peach and banana cocktail, milk, coffee, and tea.[39] Clearly, with the help of a cookbook, even a busy woman could continue to provide her family with a well-planned meal.

An especially important part of any housewife's caring duties involved preparing meals for the lunch boxes of children and spouses employed in war production industries. This particular role was highlighted in both cookbooks and magazines. According to the authors of *What Do We Eat Now? A Guide for Wartime Housekeeping*, the lunch box was of vital importance to the maintenance of home front morale:

> The lunch box is a part of the war program, and an important part. It carries sustenance and mealtime enjoyment that promotes good spirits, good health, and good work.
>
> Menus for it must be planned as carefully as those for the family, in fact more so, since they are harder to vary and keep interesting. They should, of course, correlate with the meals of the family to save time, to prevent the buying of extra foods, and to include the good things that are served at the table. And they must carry their share of the foods needed for the day.[40]

Presenting a clean, well-appointed lunch box involved much planning and creative cookery on the part of the housewife. For both children and adults, the recommended box lunch included a "substantial" food such as a sandwich, fruit or vegetables, a sweet, and if possible, something hot, such as a beverage or soup. Lunches that contained such foods helped a housewife ensure that she was providing her family with a balanced diet, and one that, according to the Basic Seven recommended by government nutritionists, included elements from each of the essential food categories.[41]

The authors of *What Do We Eat Now?* offered recipes and ideas for foods to include in the lunch box. Among their ideas were variations on sandwich fillings and beverages. They suggested several types of sandwich fillings, including meat, egg, cheese, vegetable, and fruit. Since eggs and meat were in the same category in the Basic Seven, egg fillings were a good replacement when meat ran short. Harriet Hester, author of *300 Sugar Saving Recipes,* included five sample school lunch box menus:

1. Split Pea Soup (vacuum),[42] Honey and date sandwich on whole wheat bread, Peanut cookies, Apple juice
2. Spinach au gratin (casserole), Peanut butter and onion sandwich, Cottage Cheese cookies, Orange egg milk shake
3. Baked beans, lettuce and tomato sandwich, Oatmeal cookies, Canned peaches, Banana milk shake
4. Green salad, Meat-filled sandwich, Baked apple, Ginger cookies, Chilled milk
5. Hot vegetable soup, Cheese and banana filling on nut bread, Maple custard, Fruit juice.[43]

Though most people agreed that the school lunch was important, the war worker's lunch was equated with the quest for victory. Frequently, authors advised women on how to provide their husbands with nutritious, filling lunches for the workday. Florence Laganke Harris urged women to "Do yourself proud in the lunch box you pack. Don't make the man ashamed when he opens his box in front of other workers."[44] The appearance of the box was equally as important as its contents: "That it be neat and trim of appearance is even more important than for the dining table at home to be so. The dining table has the warmth and cheer of the room to enhance its appearance, while the box has nothing save itself and its packings to make it inviting."[45] The woman's task was to ensure that the box she packed was attractive and full of nutritious foods calculated to make her husband proud. For women whose husbands worked on the night shift and returned home with a ravenous appetite, Harris had a cautionary note, however. Getting up in the middle of the night to prepare a meal would deprive women of necessary sleep. Instead, she suggested that they set aside a shelf in the refrigerator with foods that their husbands could easily prepare for themselves. She also suggested that women "clip colored illustrations of the food which he is to prepare.... Their very attractive coloring may induce him to prepare a really adequate meal.... Many a man will fry hamburgers. Have the meat cakes flat and waiting in the refrigerator.... Don't expect a tired man to enjoy foods which are hard to eat."[46]

Similar to the cookbooks' prescriptions for appropriately balanced menus for the boxed lunch, women's magazines engaged their readers in an effort to follow the plans set out for them by home economists and editors. A January 1943 *Good Housekeeping* article, "A Wonderful Lunch in a Box," provided readers with menus for lunches that had been developed in the test kitchens of the Good Housekeeping Institute. The author told her readers that lunch box packing was vital to the productivity of war workers and that it was "a challenge that you can't ignore." The article also provided a forum for telling women about "the interesting activities, all designed to help homemakers plan and prepare meals that meet the needs of sound nutrition." Toward this end, the author mentioned the efforts of gas and electric companies to organize local meetings and "advisory services" for women: "Homemakers who are doubling as war workers should find these activities helpful in meeting their special needs for menus that are easily and quickly prepared."[47] An October 1943 *Good Housekeeping* article, "Nothing Fancy about These Box Lunches," included a "Daily Lunch Box Guide" that listed the five categories of foods that should be included in every lunch every day: meat, poultry, fish, eggs, or cheese; vegetables; fruit; bread; and milk. The author of this article commented that the recipes had also taken rationing "into account, for they use foods that are widely available."[48]

A constant theme in the events and literature aimed at the lunch-packing women of America was the significance of their attentive planning and careful packing of lunch boxes. Packing lunch boxes or seeing to the proper nutrition of their families through other means was increasingly viewed as a part of women's civic and moral duty. It was not simply a matter of tossing food into containers or onto the table, but rather a public display of a woman's competency as a wife and mother. Murphy, along with her fellow cookbook authors and magazine writers, assured readers that through planning, conservation, and thrift, they could provide nutritious, tasty meals that would help keep their families (especially husbands employed in vital war jobs) healthy and productive citizens. Thus, for Murphy and her colleagues, a woman's most significant contribution to war work was by being a conscientious consumer and cook. *Wartime Meals* and works similar to it provided a recipe for the ideal American housewife—a savvy shopper and willing producer of a fit family. Clearly, patriotism began at home—whether from a home-packed lunch box, in the kitchen, or around the dining room table.

5

A Nutrition Victory:
World War II and the Noon Meal

The dawn of the twentieth century ushered in a new era in food consumption and nutritional science. During the latter part of the nineteenth century, many Americans welcomed the dramatic dietary effects of processed foods. In this period, entrepreneurs like Gail Borden, Gustauvus Swift, Philip Armour, and Clarence Birdseye developed the scientific and technological knowledge necessary for processes such as condensing milk, canning meats, and freezing vegetables. As a result of their efforts in commercial food processing and concurrent developments in national transportation systems, Americans experienced a virtual revolution in their eating habits.[1] The ability to obtain milk, meat, and vegetables from their pantry liberated many people from the arduous tasks of procuring food and keeping it safe. They were no longer forced to rely on their own farm productivity or on the success of their neighbors' crops as they were assured of the availability of food from sources other than their own labor. Breakfast was a meal that underwent significant change as commercially processed cereals like Kellogg's Corn Flakes replaced the more traditional meat and potatoes fare of the earlier nineteenth century. Industry leaders like Kellogg and Post championed their products' nutritional value and made claims for the superiority of a scientifically balanced diet.[2]

The next major food-related advancement was an increased understanding of the role vitamins and minerals played in maintaining good health. Scientists in the early twentieth century discovered vitamins and their importance in nutrition, but methods for isolating the compounds in tablet form remained primitive. Therefore, nutrition advocates argued that the only way to ensure that one received a healthful amount of these nutrients was to consume foods rich in key vitamins and minerals.[3]

Not until after World War I, however, did the emerging data on vitamins and minerals in human diets gain the approval of scientists, and soon, the endorsement of the federal government. For the United States, it was the health of the first class of World War II draftees that served as a wake-up call. The nation's leaders heard an alarm sound when the military rejected for physical defects 40 percent of the first million men drafted.[4] Brigadier General Lewis B. Hershey, addressing the National Nutrition Conference in 1941, stated:

> America must be strong, but she cannot be strong when one-half of her sons are substandard physically. America needs whole men, not half men. She must develop vigorous and healthy youths; she must prehabilitate those whose defects are slight; she must rehabilitate those examined and found deficient. The task before us, like all tasks in a democracy, is the duty and responsibility of each and every citizen. The Selective Service by its very nature will play a vital part in the solution of this all important problem. It dedicates itself to a participation in the movement for better and healthier bodies for all the citizens of America.[5]

For one group of Americans during World War II, the understanding and appropriate use of vitamins and minerals partially defined patriotic wartime activity. The rejection of so many of the first draftees brought American mothers to the front lines of the nutrition battle. Shortly thereafter, widespread campaigns for national nutrition spread across the nation. Critics had long held mothers responsible for the health (or lack thereof) of America's children. Unwilling to have their own children deemed undernourished or vitamin deficient, many women were prone to accept the science of nutrition as the gospel according to "Dr. Win-the-War." Clearly, something had to be done to ensure that American citizens and soldiers were physically capable of fulfilling their duties overseas and to energize the homefront as it began vital war production.

In 1940, the government took the first step by appointing a committee of the National Research Council to make recommendations to boost the nation's nutritional status. The lasting result of its efforts was a scale of recommended daily allowances of vitamins and minerals necessary for good health. These daily allowances became known as the nutritional yardstick — an objective way to ensure that all Americans consumed a diet that "measured up" to federal standards.[6] In her 6 March 1943 "News of Food" column in the *New York Times*, Jane Holt enumerated the elements of the Basic Seven: "Milk; Tomatoes, citrus fruit or other Vitamin-C-rich food; Leafy, green or yellow vegetables; Other vegetables or fruit; Meat, poultry, fish, eggs, sometimes dried beans or peas, soy beans, cheese, nuts; Cereals and bread, Fats." She described it as a "yardstick of good nutrition," as "a translation into kitchen language of the daily dietary allowances recommended by the National Research Council." She noted that it had "been revised in keeping with the recent revolutions occurring along the food front." According to Holt, the new guidelines were "a simple but scientific guide for women who must prepare meals under growing wartime restrictions."[7] Such a campaign to equalize nutrition across the board meant the creation of a more homogenous national diet.

Spreading the Word: Uncle Sam's Nutrition Plan

During the war, there was considerable discussion of the status of the American diet with regard to nutrition. Most experts agreed that Americans were not eating enough of the right foods. In November 1942, Dr. Clive McCay, a professor of nutrition at the State College of Agriculture at Cornell, was pleased to report that because of the war, Americans were eating less sugar. He described sugar as "the poorest food you can eat" and noted: "In the past fifty years we have traded our diets, and in the process we have made what amounts to a poor horse swap. We have let our taste for sweets dictate to us." The *New York Times* reported Dr. McCay's survey of the food situation. He stated that although shortages might develop in various foods, that there was "no need for panic." McCay "cited experiments showing that animals could live a full life span on a diet of whole wheat and milk." He noted that Americans, would "never be reduced to such a diet, but it shows diet changes can and should mean an improvement in health."[8]

The economics of homefront mobilization worked in such a way that many people who did not previously have the means to purchase their fair share could now do so through increased income. By the same token, many members of economic groups who had possessed a vast amount of purchasing power in the prewar era saw their ability to purchase dwindle as the economics of wartime scarcity came into play. During the war years, therefore, some members of the middle and upper classes consumed lesser amounts of certain commodities while members of the working and lower classes may have enjoyed an increased ability to purchase these same commodities. For this reason, some historians have argued that the war helped close the dietary gap between the classes by artificially leveling the purchasing power of all Americans.[9]

Studies of consumer behavior under the constraints of controlled consumption have shown that many people increase their consumption of nutritious foods because such items are more readily available to all classes.[10] Nielander has pointed out that rationing causes many shoppers to purchase better grades of products than they had hitherto. Whereas they might have bought two pounds of an inferior quality product before, when limited by rationing to only one pound, they were more likely to purchase the superior grade available at the same price point. This process was evident in the changing consumption patterns of coffee during the war. Although wartime shortages taught many people to be more frugal in their consumption of coffee, they also helped increase consumer preference for better quality products. Advertising also figured into the equation as "new consumer preferences were strengthened by distributor advertising of higher-priced coffee, emphasizing the fact that more cups per pound could be obtained from better coffee."[11]

Still, however, a rising tide did not raise all boats, and many people faced supply constraints not only from rationing but from low incomes and lack of access to higher quality food products. Even before food rationing began, President Roosevelt sensed the gravity of the national nutrition situation and called for a National Nutrition Conference, to be held in Washington, D.C., from 26–28 May 1941. The conference was chaired by Paul V. McNutt, whose résumé included a single term as governor of Indiana before becoming the administrator of the Federal Security Agency in 1937, a position he maintained when he was later named chairman of the War Manpower Commission.[12] McNutt kicked off the conference by reading a letter from the president to the delegates:

The White House
May 23, 1941.

MY DEAR GOVERNOR: I am highly gratified to learn that invitations to the National Nutrition Conference for Defense met with such generous response. It demonstrates the eager interest of the public, of educational and research centers, of medical and social sciences alike. I only regret that because of the pressure of these critical days I shall be unable to meet with you.

The Conference has significant responsibilities — to explore and define our nutrition problems, and to map out recommendations for an immediate program of action. This is vital. During these days of stress the health problems of the military and civilian population are inseparable. Total defense demands manpower. The full energy of every American is necessary. Medical authorities recognize completely that efficiency and stamina depend on proper food. Fighting men of our Armed Forces, workers in industry, the families of these workers, every man and woman in America, must have nourishing food. If people are undernourished, they cannot be efficient in producing what we need in our unified drive for dynamic strength.

In recent years scientists have made outstanding discoveries as to the amounts and kinds of foods needed for maximum health and vigor. Yet every survey of nutrition, by whatever methods conducted, shows that here in the United States undernourishment is widespread and serious. The Department of Agriculture has estimated that many millions of men, women, and children do not get the foods which science considers essential. We do not lack and we will not lack the means of producing food in abundance and variety. Our task is to translate this abundance into reality for every American family.

I shall follow the work of the Conference with deep interest and expectantly await its recommendations.

Very sincerely yours,

FRANKLIN D. ROOSEVELT[13]

So charged by their president, the conference delegates went forth to discuss, deliberate, and develop plans. One committee, headed by Lucy H. Gillet, the Director of Nutritional Work for the Community Service Society of New York City, and Hazel Kyrk, a consulting specialist to the Bureau of Home Economics of the Department of Agriculture, discussed the economic policy and social responsibility inherent in the planning to improve national nutrition. The committee ultimately recommended the intervention of government and industry. First, it encouraged greater government regulation of salaries and more equitable taxation policies. Next, it advocated the "increased supply of protective foods and reduced costs of processing and distribution." Among its suggestions for realizing this goal were the creation of more federal programs for government subsidies and price supports in agricultural production along with more efficient processing and distribution of surplus commodities. An important element of this step included enhanced government incentives to industry so that low-cost and nutritious products such as soybean, peanut, and milk products "in forms acceptable to consumers" would be readily available, and additional "fortification" of processed foods with vitamins and minerals "to the extent that scientific research indicates that such practice is in the public interest and provides an economical method of improving nutrition." Other recommendations for industry included more adequate grade labeling of fresh produce and a simplification of product packaging to allow consumers greater ease of comparison. Further, the committee suggested a standardization of food labels, and "the provision of more information in advertising to facilitate the identification and comparison of the quality of food and the size of the container." The committee also expressed strong support for the extension of food stamp eligibility, penny and nickel milk programs, and endorsed the school lunch program: "Wherever free school lunches are provided they should be selected on the basis of the nutritive needs of the children and the educational opportunity thereby offered for the formation of sound food habits to be fully utilized." In general, the committee agreed that poor nutrition was not the exclusive problem of low-income groups and contended that "high food expenditures alone will not guarantee adequate nutrition. Education is needed not only in the choice and preparation of food but also in food buying and home production."[14]

For this wartime nutrition education campaign to be successful, it was necessary for the government to enlist the assistance of a civilian army comprised of physicians, nutritionists, and home economists. When he addressed the National Nutrition Conference on the subject of Nutrition and National Defense, Vice President Henry A. Wallace stated:

> I am confident that this National Nutrition Conference can produce results which will affect nearly every man, woman, and child in the United States during the next 20 years. Because the knowledge of food has been growing so fast in recent years and because this knowledge has such unusual importance to everyone, there have been invited to this

Conference many kinds of people. First come the experts — the doctors, dentists, nurses, home economists, social workers, the professional nutritionists, and those who have an especial interest in feeding our armed forces well. Then there are representatives of the great farm organizations, because we know that the men who produce the food are as important as those who serve and eat it. The millers, the packers, the canners, the dairymen, and all the varied wholesale and retail food concerns are represented, because they are the channels through which food flows on its way from the farmer to the table. Land grant college professors, who live continually with the farmers and the food trades, are here. So, also, are representatives of the great national consumer organizations, such as union labor, women's clubs, Negro organizations, etc. Dozens of Federal Government agencies are represented as well as a number of State and local agencies.

The doctors and nutritionists are here to tell us what they have learned, which will help us to build up and maintain our health and strength during these days when we shall put forth the utmost national effort. The farm people are here to tell us just what we have in the way of food resources and how we can change, if need be, our methods of working the land in order to get the products which will best meet the needs as the experts see them. All of us at this Conference will focus on the most important job of all, which is the development of plans for action to put our modern knowledge of nutrition to practical use serving our 130 million citizens as soon as possible.[15]

And so the experts moved forward to victory on the national nutritional battlefront — beginning in American kitchens.

Improving American Diets: The Committee Approach

In the latter months of 1940, President Franklin Roosevelt had appointed a Committee on Food Habits under the direction of anthropologist Margaret Mead to study American eating habits and propose methods to reconcile food shortages with traditional eating patterns. Mead and her colleagues knew that the process of altering food habits was not a simple one. As social scientists, they were well aware of the relationship between food and culture and of the danger posed to national morale by dramatic, government-mandated shifts in the food supply. Studies of eating habits by modern historians, psychologists, sociologists, and anthropologists have demonstrated that consumption habits tend to be conservative and are influenced by factors such as ethnicity, gender, age, and class.[16] Generally, people resist rapid changes in food unless they are prompted by personal choice or economic necessity.

In *The Problem of Changing Food Habits*, published in 1943, members of the Committee on Food Habits acknowledged this difficulty by choosing women, particularly "wives and mothers," as prime targets for their initial attempts at altering consumption patterns, citing them as contributors to the "weaknesses and deficiencies in our national dietary habits."[17] "On the women," concluded the Committee, "more than on any one else, depends, in the short run and in the long run, the family's diet, both as to choice of food and as to preparation thereof."[18] While they chastised women for failing to provide adequate nutrition, they turned those shortcomings into an appeal for action. The findings of the Committee revealed that the relationship between health and patriotism was a powerful one: "Greater potency was given to the health area by linking health with patriotism. This was accomplished by the explanation of the government's concern over the number of young men rejected by the army on grounds which might be related to nutrition."[19] The Committee observed that women could be drafted into the ranks of kitchen commandos if pride in their family's health, nutritious meals, and the national defense were equated.

The Committee also quickly recognized the potential influence of the professional class of home economists that peppered the country. Mead noted that "wartime conditions have made it necessary to resort to special measures to accomplish immediate changes and adjustments to shortages and substitutes." She pointed out that "the Committee was confronted with an already established program of directed social change" that was led by the nation's home economists. In Mead's estimation, these home economists were in "a key position, whether to give food demonstrations, calculate new menus to fit shortages, set up new methods of food preservation, direct the professional propagandist of newspaper or radio, or train the neighborhood leader to carry the word of mouth messages into homes not reached by other media." She concluded, stating that the preparation of materials "in a form which could be used by home economists and experiments in procedures which would facilitate their tasks have therefore been an essential part of the Committee's work."[20]

Beyond that, the Committee saw the most important aspect of modifying the national food habits involved a "basic alteration in the culturally defined style of what is a meal and what is food." To accomplish this task, the members knew that they needed to address the cultural and social factors that influenced food selection and meal patterns. Toward that end, they focused their inquiries on the national "folkways" related to food rather than on diet and nutrition. This method allowed them to make informed "recommendations upon the use or misuse of the forces which affect changes in food habits."[21]

In "Forces Behind Food Habits and Methods of Change," a study sponsored by the Committee and headed by Kurt Lewin and the Child Welfare Research Station of the State University of Iowa, researchers sought to understand how cultural and psychological factors affected food habits. These social scientists discovered, first of all, that to answer the question, "Why do people eat what they eat?" they had to determine how various foods made their way from the marketplace or garden to the dining table. The Channel Theory, developed by Lewin, helped explain the factors that were involved in food selections. This theory begins from the assertion that "once food is on the table, most of it is eaten by someone in the family."[22] For food to arrive on the table, it had first to enter one of the many channels that led into the household. Among these were the grocery store, the garden, delivery services, direct purchase from producers (farmers), or home processes such as baking or canning. What was of concern to these researchers, as well as to the government, was the fact that during wartime, some of these channels could become blocked, therefore forcing a family to search for alternatives that might either be less nutritious or might lead the family to the black market. Lewin observed that whether or not a food entered into a particular channel was controlled by a "gatekeeper." Most often, the gatekeeper was the woman of the family. Thus, women were the prime targets for campaigns related to rationing, food preparation, and nutrition.

Lewin's study included housewives belonging to five different groups: "(high, medium and low income levels) of White American stock, and two subcultural groups, Czech and Negro."[23] He and his team of researchers interviewed these women during May and June 1942. The interviews focused on women's attitudes and values toward food and meals. When the researchers inquired about meal patterns, they found that lunch was the meal with the greatest flexibility. The women were asked: "In what terms do you think of the meal: what goes into breakfast? lunch? dinner?"[24] The various foods that women mentioned were tabulated and analyzed. The researchers found that there was a fairly high degree of homogeneity across the groups with regard to food habits. Lunch, however, presented some interesting variations on this theme. Members of the "high group" were the most likely to list certain specific foods as characteristic of lunch. Women in the remaining groups saw lunch as a less structured, informal, "pick-up" meal.

When the researchers questioned women about the motivations and values that affected their food choices, the most common responses fell into one of four categories: money, health, taste, and status. Under the imperatives of the wartime economy, the desire to fulfill these aspirations sometimes resulted in conflict for the gatekeeper. Lewin discovered that the middle income group was the one most often faced with conflict between rising prices and consumption desires. Members of this group felt that their financial and social position was tenuous. They wanted to maintain the aura of prosperity, and yet they had a nagging fear of falling back into the "poor" category. Lewin wrote that "in the effort to resist lowering their social status they might economize first in those areas which are socially least prominent, such as food, thus keeping up appearances."[25] For the scientists and officials interested in improving food habits, this observation proved to be most troubling as it might induce people to consume less nutritious diets out of a desire to maintain their social status. The only way to avert this potential hazard was to change the way people thought about food and mealtime. This might best be accomplished by making "a food that had been considered *food for others, but not for us*' into a '*food for us.*" Lewin continued: "In the American culture the 'food basket' has three distinct parts assigned to breakfast, lunch, dinner; many foods are considered fit for only one part. In case of food shortage this might change. Since lunch is the least structured of these meals there might be a greater readiness to change the content of the 'lunch' than of the other meals."[26]

The nature of wartime production meant that many more industries operated on a twenty-four-hour clock. To keep up with the demand, some workers found themselves working "midnights," which meant that they had to adapt the traditional schedule of meals to suit their working hours. Lewin observed an interesting phenomenon related to how these people organized their dining experiences. He asserted that "regardless of working hours, people eat according to the clock." By the American cultural pattern, one eats breakfast as the first meal of the day. What Lewin found, however, was that a person who awoke at noon would eat a "lunch meal rather than a breakfast." The problem, as Lewin saw it, was not so much that a person deviated from the standard meal order but that his diet would suffer as a result of losing the "nutritional elements which he normally obtained through breakfast foods."[27] Mead made similar observations on the issue of meal schedules:

> Meal patterns are equally arbitrary and important, and alterations in the time or designation of a meal may mean severe nutritional dislocations, as when some Eastern Europeans, upon immigrating to America, dropped the second breakfast, or when odd-shift workers eat three meals, none of which is breakfast; and so the foods which customarily appear only at a breakfast table, fruit juice, cereal with milk, and eggs, tend to disappear from the diet.[28]

Fortunately, Lewin noted, "since the results indicate that the lunches of all but the high group are the least 'structured' of the three meals, it would follow that other foods might be fitted most easily into the lunch pattern."[29]

While Lewin, Mead, and the other members of the Committee were concerned that the food habits of individuals and families were not measuring up to the yardstick of good nutrition, they also realized that to instigate rapid, broad-based cultural change in eating habits, it would not suffice to target selected people or families. Mead called for a balanced approach to reform whereby the experts in "applied science" maintained cognizance of and respect for certain subcultural patterns and habits, while simultaneously trying to find ways of "controlling a social process in such a way that the desired changes will occur."[30]

After identifying the cultural and social patterns of specific subcultures such as "second generation Americans of Polish, or Italian, or Hungarian extraction, where both men and women work in the mills and the average grade completed is the fifth," or "southern sharecroppers whose food habits are tied to a one crop method of production," the next step was to uncover the most direct avenue by which to gain access to these communities without provoking unnecessary alarm or resistance to the suggested changes. Lewin experimented with two different methods of inducing behavior modifications: group decision and lecture. His test group consisted of the residents of eight men's dormitories at the University of Iowa and approximately 120 Iowa women from diverse economic situations.

In the dormitory experiment, the male students were divided into several small groups. Some of the groups received letters that asked them to discuss the possibility of increasing their consumption of wheat bread over white. Other groups were given letters that simply asked them outright to make the change from wheat to white bread. The experiment showed that the men who arrived at a group decision to change their eating habits were more likely to succeed than their counterparts who attempted to make changes based on the petition of an outside entity. Interestingly, in the groups who received only the request for change, their degree of success in doing so and overall desire for group success was tied directly to their personal preferences. In contrast, among the group decision subjects, the desire for group success proved to be independent of individual tastes. Except in cases where the majority of the group voting for the change was too marginal, the group decision method showed more positive outcomes than the request approach.

Among the women, a similar experiment was carried out. One group of women met with a nutritionist and discussed the possibility of using kidneys, brains, and hearts as main-dish meats for family meals. These particular cuts were selected because of the "known resistance" that existed among the subjects. The results of the study were predictable — the women who interacted with the nutritionist and other participants made more significant efforts to change than those who simply attended the lecture and received the recipes. For the women in the discussion group, the decision to change was not imposed on them, nor was it contractual with other people. It was "made by the individual concerning her own action — the housewife decides what she will do at home. The group setting gives the incentive for the decision, and facilitates and reinforces it."[31]

Lewin's experiments made clear the function of a group experience in altering foodways. The nature of the eating situation, be it in a restaurant or cafeteria, with other people or in solitude, had a tremendous impact on mealtime actions and attitudes. Lewin commented:

> The psychological meaning of eating is closely tied to group situations. Eating with co-workers in a factory is something different from eating at the family table or eating in a restaurant. The "eating group" influences greatly the eating conduct and the eating ideology of the individual. One can say that every eating group has a specific eating culture.[32]

The goal shared by Committee members and the government was to target these specific eating cultures in such a way as to institute changes that would result in improved nutrition. Their biggest challenge came in determining how best to frame the information so that it would be acceptable and inoffensive to the intended audience, the gatekeepers of the family table: American women.

Studies regarding the dissemination of nutritional information demonstrated that women often resisted sullying the bonds of friendship with morally framed attempts to alter their friends' food habits. One study of women from southern Illinois concluded that the sharing of recipes for special occasion dishes served as the only exchange of food-related data among friends.[33] A method that seemed to work better was the "block plan, which invests a neighbor with a governmental sanction of patriotism and patriotic license for intrusion into domestic affairs ... here also nutrition information can be discussed more efficiently if the emphasis is on adjustment of meals to wartime conditions rather than upon eating correctly, upon helping a woman to adjust a process rather than urging her to be good." This plan, too, might suffer if the block leader felt that the tone of her efforts was "cast in terms which suggest that she is trying to reform her neighbor."[34] Thus, a tactic that was patriotic yet free of moralism appeared to harbor the greatest potential for success. In Mead's estimation, the best way to present nutritional information to the public was from the innocuous and disinterested perspective of science. She cautioned that nutritional reform not be linked in people's minds with the shortages and hardships of wartime and therefore deemed to be one of the many temporary accommodations to the war situation. She articulated a long-term goal of transforming food habits so that they would be "based upon tradition which embodies science and to do so in such a way that food habits at any period are sufficiently flexible to yield readily to new scientific findings."

Mead closed with the admonition that "the food habits of the future will have to be sanctioned not by authoritarian statements which breed rigid conformity, but by a sense of responsibility on the part of those who plan meals for others to eat."[35] In this way, Mead expressed the commitment of the scientific community to the progressive improvement of the nation's food habits. By adopting a scientifically precise yet broad appeal to the betterment of the human condition, and an attitude respectful of individual and cultural variations, experts might be able to bring about a steady improvement in all Americans' diets. The most significant element of Mead's philosophy, however, was her use of the word *responsibility*. Beyond that, a new group of people, scientists affiliated with and endorsed by the federal government, would now play a key role in shaping national eating habits. The changes in the wartime food supply caused by shortages and rationing provided the rationale. The real challenge was in finding ways to link the national needs, scientific data, and individual practices in such a way as to produce the most healthy and happy citizens possible. In Bridgeport, Connecticut, a locally planned and administered program for improving war workers' nutrition brought these various interests into harmony.

"Pack a Lunch a Man Can Work On"

Improving the nutrition of war workers was a proposition that could transform a whole community. In spite of wartime labor demands on men and women, the fact remained that on women fell the bulk of responsibility for providing all family meals. When such meals were inadequate nutritionally, the result was a less efficient workforce — a danger to workers, industry, and the nation during wartime. A survey of lunches in Bridgeport showed that the majority of the 75,000 industrial workers carried their lunches to work. The most commonly carried items included sandwiches, coffee, soft drinks, candy, and pastries. The Bridgeport Gas Light Company, whose home economists presented cooking demonstrations throughout the community, launched the campaign for improving the lunches of the city's workers. The home economist–demonstrators, because of their relationship with the wives and mothers who were "responsible for workers' lunches," did not hesitate to include nutrition education in their presentations.[36] Eventually, the Bridgeport Plan united local officials, industrial and commercial leaders, and the women of Bridgeport toward a common goal.

Changing people's food habits, as demonstrated in the studies conducted by Lewin and Mead, involves a delicate balance between respecting traditional ways and advocating change without making moral condemnations. As Lewin and Mead found, lunch was the meal most open to alterations. Although Bridgeport's initial goal was simply to energize workers for optimal productivity, the possibility that the improvements to workers' eating habits might carry over to family meals was always present. After all, the same women who packed the lunches also prepared the breakfasts and evening meals for the entire family.

Those involved in the effort to reform Bridgeport factory workers knew that for the plan to be successful, they had first and foremost to be assured of support from the women of the community. A diversity of ethnic backgrounds, to say nothing of individual personalities and tastes, made selling the plan to Bridgeport women a challenge. Leaders were successful only when they played up the patriotic aspect of nutritional changes and received the endorsement of religious and secular officials. Robert A. Crosby, the executive secretary of the Bridgeport Chamber of Commerce, summarized the main motivations for implementing the plan:

> *For the worker*: Better health, joy of living, more money — money otherwise lost through absences from work because of illness, for drugs, for medical bills, etc.
> *For industry*: A reduction in the huge bill, including $450,000,000 for colds alone, which industry now must pay because of workers' illnesses.
> *For the public*: Uninterrupted production of bombers, tanks, guns. That means fewer sons, husbands, and brothers lost on battlefields, a speedier victory, and return to normal family life.
> No one, as we have said, can therefore question the desirability of improving the nutrition of all people, and, in particular, of war workers. But how are these aims to be accomplished, showing tangible results in terms of improved health and faster production?
> An answer to this vital question has been found in the "Bridgeport Plan." In harmony with the wishes of government officials, who realize that the success of the national nutrition program must lie, finally, with the actions of communities themselves, Bridgeport Conn., has evolved a plan whereby women will be encouraged to pack nutritious lunches for the workers in their families. The slogan of the "Plan" led by the Civilian Defense Committee is "Pack a Lunch a Man Can Work On."
> Simple, isn't it? And that, we feel is the signal advantage of this plan. Emphasis on one meal. It is believed that, having mastered the fundamental rules of nutrition for lunches, women will automatically then apply what they have learned to other meals for the entire family.[37]

A writer for the journal *Hygeia*, Helen Morgan Hall, began her article on Bridgeport with a brief critique of the quality of foods consumed by the industrial workforce. She described their meals as "sorry affairs, both nutritionally and esthetically." She attributed the statistics on absenteeism to the quantity of ill-fed "men drawn from relief rolls" and "others rejected for physical reasons by the selective service" who had poured in to meet the demands of wartime production. She warned: "Statistics show that two thirds of the American people are inadequately fed, and it seems safe to assume that a goodly proportion of this group are men turning out weapons for war." "Since this is a democratic country," Hall added, "the most obvious tool appears to be education — not regimentation, not force, but enlightenment regarding the right kinds of foods coupled with creation of a desire to eat those foods."[38]

In Hall's estimation, Bridgeport served as a model for the power of education to reform the eating habits of a diverse population. A "factory city of foreigners," Bridgeport numbered 80 percent of its population of 180,000 as "foreign born or of foreign parentage." Among the many nationalities represented were Hungarian, Polish, Lithuanian, Ukrainian, Swedish, Italian, Russian, and Slovakian. Hall held Bridgeport up for emulation by other similar cities: "Experience in this city shows that what has happened in Bridgeport can happen anywhere in America if the citizens originating such programs understand and keep faith with the people." These leaders who were so attuned to the needs of the people were primarily leading male citizens. Hall noted that the "active leadership" was shared by the chairman of the Health Division of the Civilian Defense Council (Dr. Joseph H. Howard), an executive of a local gas company, and the associate editor of the city newspaper.[39] These leaders met early on with some opposition from women who believed that they were being robbed of their individual prerogative to pack lunches as they so desired. Leaders drummed up support with a letter from Eleanor Roosevelt sounding praises of the plan as a way for women to contribute to the war effort. Later, Dr. Howard issued the following motivational statement:

> This is America. Any individual here has the right to remain below par physically if he wants to, providing that, in doing so, he does not jeopardize the lives of others. But the man next door has a right, too. He is entitled to use the knowledge which brilliant scientists have got together for the sole purpose of making him a healthier and therefore happier person. This is the man we want to help through the Plan.[40]

One of the methods of instituting change in eating habits was begun with a survey of workers' lunch boxes. On the Sunday prior to the Monday when the survey was to commence, the pastors of local churches announced the details to their congregations, thus, "in Hungarian, Swedish, Ukrainian, the word went out to women from men they trusted." At the same time, the local newspaper launched a new feature called the "Kitchen Soldier." Each week in this column, a different woman would share her experiences in lunch packing: "The Kitchen Soldier, who might be Polish or Hungarian, or Italian, would agree only to modify the lunches she packed to include every day milk, meat (or eggs, fish or cheese), bread (whole wheat or enriched), vegetables, fruit." Each of the menus was then evaluated by the chair of the Committee on Nutrition, who also happened to be a woman.

Dr. Howard described the plan's benefits: "This Plan becomes your Plan. All of you — once you have agreed that the men who are turning out war weapons deserve the best food that can be given them — will help each other with suggestions for packing better lunches." After some initial resistance to the plan, women were later described as inviting surveyors into their homes with greetings such as: "'We're expecting you,' or 'Oh, yes! This is what Mrs. Roosevelt said we should do.'"

Many women in Bridgeport also participated in classes conducted by the instructor of the nutrition subcommittee of the Civilian Defense Council or another volunteer who was a graduate of a Red Cross or Civilian Defense nutrition class. Hall described the content of the classes:

> Here the spirit of the Plan is sustained; demagoguery is out, and emphasis is on helping women solve practical problems like: "What shall we put in the lunch boxes?" and "How can we save time?" Instructors launch quickly into such hints, unsnapping a lunch box and showing neat paper containers filled with intriguing foods packed inside.... Invariably such hints get women into what educators call a "learning mood." In a moment, women are buzzing experiences to neighbors, pelting instructors with questions. This response pattern is the same whether the instructor's remarks are being translated into Yiddish, Ukrainian, or Hungarian.[41]

One of the underlying goals of this nutritional education campaign was the creation of a sense of unity and common purpose. For the diverse population of Bridgeport, this meant conformity to a new way of planning meals and eating centered less around individual tastes and desires and more around the information and advice provided by experts. Although experts acknowledged that the "packaged lunch" continued to "hold the spotlight" for many people because of its "human, personal appeal," increasingly, new parties assumed responsibility for providing lunches that would meet standards of nutrition set by scientists and enforced by the government.[42] The homefront wartime environment provided the conditions necessary for individual nutrition to become a part of the national interest.

Government, Industry, and Community Cooperation

The interplay among the causes of war production, national nutrition, and corporate America formed a complex web of mutual support toward achieving what were sometimes very different goals. As the agency overseeing food provisions in the workplace, the War Food Administration (WFA) was motivated by the goal of keeping national productivity levels high for the war effort. At the outset of the war, the WFA focused its efforts on improving the contents of workers' lunch boxes through education aimed at getting "something more than a sandwich, a piece of pie, and a bottle of coffee into the lunch box." Later, when the agency was better established and had a greater amount of money and supplies to distribute, it honed in on the need to make meals available in the workplace. By 1944, for example, the WFA had "industrial feeding specialists whose services, for surveys and recommendations," could be "requisitioned without charge by management or by governmental production and procurement agencies" who believed that "production could be improved by better food facilities."[43]

Although the WFA maintained that the "main responsibility for adequate meals" rested with "management," the agency started its efforts by converting the laborers because they were the consumers. Eventually, many labor unions became supportive of the in-plant feeding program. With labor on its side, the WFA then had to make its case with management. Gradually, it brought many plants to its side by promising higher worker morale, fewer requests for a transfer, fewer employees leaving the job, and better productivity. Once a company agreed to open a plant cafeteria, it became eligible for assistance from the federal government. This assistance came in the form of extra ration points for food, access to equipment and supplies necessary for the operation of a cafeteria, and help with the construction of additional buildings to provide space for food service.

At the local level, other American communities launched programs similar to that in Bridgeport. As had been demonstrated in
Bridgeport, through the cooperation of industry and community, both
could benefit. General Electric distributed bulletins to each of its plants
across the country and employed a staff of home economists in plant
nutrition centers. When the General Electric home economists made
recommendations on what to include in workers' lunches, "the planners kept in mind the subject's taste buds and limitless variety was
introduced through the use of paper containers — an angle that was
assiduously promoted by the Cup and Container Institute, Inc.," a
trade association for the manufacture of such products.

Westinghouse, a peacetime manufacturer of household appliances,
had shifted to war production, therefore forcing many appliance salesmen out of a job. It found that it could remedy this unemployment
problem by shifting salesmen to jobs with the Health for Victory Clubs.
These Clubs promoted good nutrition through balanced meals "for
every day in the month, including box lunches" for a family of five on
a budget of $14 a week. Although "Westinghouse equipment" was not
"mentioned," the company still benefited from "plenty of goodwill
through contacts with consumers, utility companies, distributors."[44]

There were other ways for nongovernmental agencies and commercial enterprises to get into the act of promoting better nutrition.
One of these was the "lunch box derby." These events were public ways
for businesses and agencies to publicize their commitment to the war
effort. In 1942, a Los Angeles food store, Barker Brothers, sponsored
a contest whereby twelve different workers' lunches, submitted by home
economists who were selected by newspaper food editors, were judged
by a committee of aircraft workers' wives. This was an interesting turn
of events. Here, the wives judged the home economists' selections based
on the following criteria: nutritional balance, appetite appeal, attrac-
tiveness, and variety. The result was a lunch box show that was viewed
by 10,000 women over a two-day period. Later, the ideas generated by
this event were shared with 268 other Barker Brothers stores across the
country. A *Business Week* summary of the derby concluded: "The lunch

Opposite: **Cover of the Westinghouse Electric** *Health for Victory Meal
Planning Guide* **for December 1943. Notice the dome-shaped lunchbox
and classic thermos bottle (reproduced with permission of Westinghouse
Electric Corporation).**

HEALTH FOR VICTORY
MEAL PLANNING GUIDE

CONTAINS MENUS AND RECIPES
for EVERY MEAL IN THE MONTH OF

December

1943

Featured in this Issue:

**MEETING
MEAT PROBLEMS**

●

92 Recipes not in the
November issue

15¢

Contributed in the Interest of the National Wartime Nutrition Program
PREPARED BY HOME ECONOMICS INSTITUTE
Westinghouse Electric & Manufacturing Co. ● Mansfield, Ohio

box has become a definite food merchandising unit."[45] Barker Brothers both provided a service to its customers by helping solve the dilemma of what to put into lunch boxes while at the same time generating goodwill with its customers.

A somewhat less commercialized lunch box derby was sponsored in the fall of 1942 by San Francisco's branch of the American Red Cross and the local Nutrition Council, with assistance from the California Dietetic Association, the Home Economics Women in Business organization, the Parent-Teacher Association, and the American Women's Voluntary Services group. Together, they aimed to provide a "practical contribution to the educational campaign to improve box lunches for industrial workers." According to a May 1943 *Journal of Home Economics* report by Gertrude York Christy, a member of the San Francisco Red Cross, the derby was held in the auditorium of a local department store and included over 100 displays of lunches for industrial workers as well as children's lunches and "well-selected school cafeteria trays." There was also a "special display of lunches for career girls and attractive, disguised lunch carriers. One group of girls sent in beautiful lunch containers made of round rolled-oats boxes, covered with wallpapers, shellacked and equipped with a gay cord for carrying. They looked like expensive knitting boxes."

Christy reported further that the California State Board of Health had a "fine exhibit" that included a map of California on which the locations of various industries were labeled with ribbons. These ribbons "led from the map to the tables" where specific lunches suited to the needs of the workers in each of the different industries were on display: "There were lunches for the redwood workers, the Sierra miner, the city office worker, the ship-builder, the agricultural worker in the hot valleys, and the Mexican laborer."[46]

The Red Cross had its own exhibition space where it featured lunches planned for "different nationality groups in San Francisco: British, Dutch, Russian, South American, Mexican, Chinese." At yet another Red Cross table was a display that contrasted a "well-planned lunch" for an industrial worker with one that consisted of "just whatever Mamma had in the house." Through the aid of a chart that broke down the nutritional values of each lunch and a nutritionist stationed nearby, the Red Cross demonstrated how a well-planned lunch would improve a worker's mental attitude and physical stamina. The well-planned lunch included "three hearty sandwiches of meat, cheese, and peanut butter on whole-wheat and rye bread; a cole slaw salad; a large orange; a big square of gingerbread; and a pint of milk." The "poorly planned lunch," that was "really one purchased near a shipyard," included "two thin sandwiches of white bread with a spoonful of liverwurst, a paper-thin slice of bologna, a small apricot turnover, a very small piece of fruit, and a chocolate mint." The most incriminating facts about the purchased lunch were its lack of adequate calories, vitamins, and minerals. When a man who passed by the booth commented that the poor lunch resembled one that he might carry, a nutritionist cautioned: "That's pretty low in vitamin B-1. Hope you don't get into any fights with the boss or the little woman at home. If you have a low-calorie breakfast such as a doughnut and coffee and then a lunch of only 700 calories you'd soon be cross enough for most any kind of argument."[47]

One of the main attractions at the derby was a contest to evaluate the nutritional and "appetite appeal" of various lunches and to award prizes to the winners. The judges for the contest came from local "CIO and AFL auxiliaries, women who put up lunches every day," as well as a "jury of nutritionists" who checked the ladies' selections to see if they were nutritionally sound. Prizes were awarded by type of lunch: a midday snack, a snack for the late afternoon shift, and an afternoon "wake-up snack" for the worker on the midnight shift.

Winning the Nutrition War

Clearly, lunch was defined in many different ways by ethnic and regional groups, industrial and salaried workers, shift workers, men, women, and children. Still, the one thing that united all of these diverse lunch experiences was the fact that they occurred outside the home in an environment that was often beyond the control of the individual lunch eater. Events such as the lunch box derbies drew public attention and support for the promotion of better nutrition. These events created a group experience that encouraged people to make alterations in their food habits. As Lewin and Mead demonstrated in their studies of foodways, people are more likely to accept dietary change when it is framed with patriotism and science and is a part of a unified effort toward some common goal — in this case winning the war with the support of the homefront. Efforts such as the Bridgeport Plan, the

General Electric pamphlets, the Westinghouse Health for Victory Clubs, and the lunch box derbies each presented nutritional change in a tone that was enriched by the cachet of science and the endorsement of the federal government. While nutritional reformers might have seen their subjects' ethnic, regional, or personal foodways as inadequate and irrational, they had to take care in addressing their audience without moralistic judgment. They did this by recognizing some diversity in the lunch tailored to a specific ethnic group and also by enlisting leaders of these groups to appeal to other members. Although the various individuals, businesses, and the federal agencies each had different motivations and reaped different benefits from the crusade to alter Americans' eating habits, the exigencies of war covered seams that might have divided their efforts and rendered them ineffective. Ultimately, however, the effort to improve nutrition led Americans down a path toward increased dietary homogeneity.

6

Staking a Claim on Lunch: Eating on the Job after World War II

When the United States emerged from World War II, the home-front experienced a period of readjustment. Women who had secured employment in war industries found themselves pushed out in favor of the returning soldiers who were seeking jobs. An ideology exalting domesticity was highly visible in American life as men and women of the war generation looked ahead to a future that, for many, included a home and a family.[1]

As food rationing came to an end and industrial production turned away from military preparedness, the eyes of the government officials and reformers turned away from lunches provided to workers as their focus shifted to the implementation and direction of the National School Lunch Program.[2] As had been the case in the early twentieth century, the worker's lunch, while still a subject of conversation and concern, was once again to be seen as more of a personal, not a national responsibility. Nevertheless, the effects of the wartime intervention of reformers, employers, and the government in worker lunches did not evaporate entirely. Many workers had internalized an understanding of the relationship among good nutrition, well-being, and productivity.

Lunch Time Is My Time

The modern lunch might be thought of as resulting from the automation of daily life initiated by the industrialization and urbanization that took root in nineteenth-century America. Issues of monetary compensation for time spent on the job have a different resonance when a laborer is working for someone else rather than for himself. In addition, work is oriented less to the natural rhythms of the day and more to the values of productivity and efficiency, time loses its neutral status and becomes either friend or foe. British historian Edward P. Thompson describes the phenomenon thusly: "Those who are employed experience a distinction between their employer's time and their 'own' time. And the employer must *use* the time of his labour, and see it is not wasted: not the task but the value of time when reduced to money is dominant. Time is now currency: it is not passed but spent."[3]

Not incidentally, he notes that there was a "general diffusion of clocks and watches ... at the exact moment when the industrial revolution demanded a greater synchronization of labour."[4] Thompson enumerates three stages in the process of industrialization and the development of time awareness. The first stage is marked by resistance on the part of workers. Preindustrial laborers, who were accustomed to rising and retiring on their own schedule, had a difficult time adapting to the discipline of quantified time. The shift to the second stage was characterized by a growing acceptance of the time-management system as it became more internalized and widespread. An indication of the advent of this stage was the fact that workers soon began to fight "not against time, but about it."[5] This bargaining over time included efforts to control the number of hours worked in a single day. In the third and final stage, workers have become so adept with time categories that they are able to use them as negotiating tools with their employers to ensure that the number of hours worked and the amount of pay received are in appropriate balance.

Thompson's theory seems applicable to the United States. As mass production became more common and merchant capitalists reorganized the structure of the workplace, the conditions of labor changed. Workers in various crafts and industries came from a wide variety of occupational and social experiences and responded in different ways to changes in their work environment. Some workers felt a loss of independence as the result of constant supervision or machine-regulated production while others resented the reduction or elimination of breaks caused by the continuous production. Although American workers began the struggle for the ten-hour day at a later period than workers in England and other European nations, when the concept of time as a divisible commodity gained preeminence in the nation's factories and trades, workers asserted their own interpretations of the time-work exchange and began to agitate for change. As time went on, such workers became more aware of the fact that their time was, in fact, a commodity. Workers' calls for shorter hours involved a desire both to reclaim possession of their time for use both in bargaining with their employers and for marking out the boundaries between "labor" time and "personal time."

The mechanization of production has generally resulted in a marginalized role for the worker. Rather than being important for his humanity and uniqueness, he is significant only for his role in the productive process. It is a disconcerting prospect for humans to be reduced to such an easily replaceable status. To reclaim some vestige of individuality in the face of tremendous pressure toward uniformity and efficiency, American workers since the early years of industrialization have clung to their breaks and mealtimes during working hours as a reminder of their humanity.

The interlude of early twentieth-century progressive reform helped secure better dining environments, and increased attention to workers' meals during World War II resulted in significant changes, but after the close of World War II, workplace dining conditions and content of workers' meals faded from the docket of reform issues. Although no longer the center of national attention, workers' meals remained a significant element of personal identity and a central item in negotiations between workers and their employers. The government was less involved in workplace dining issues than it had been during the war, but it maintained an influence through judicial and legislative decisions.

Where Have All the Reformers Gone?

Cartoonist Frank Adams attempted to draw attention back to the worker's meal with his 1951 book, *Then Ya Just Untwist*. The book con-

"You don't get this kind of comfort in the cafeteria."

Cartoon from Frank Adams' *Then Ya Just Untwist* (1951).

sists of a series of cartoon illustrations that depict the lives of everyday working-class Americans. What is particularly interesting about these simple and often humorous cartoons is that, with only a few exceptions, every one of them contains a lunch box. In Adams's work, the lunch box acts as a symbol of the paucity of suitable dining conditions, poor pay, and lack of respect from employers, family, and the culture at large that culminated in a sense of disenchantment for many working Americans. Adams dedicated his work to "those valiant men and women who miss their rides, punch time clocks, pay the taxes ... and carry battered lunch pails."[6] In this world of long hours and lunch boxes, leisure and enjoyment are uncommon.

Among the cartoons in the book are several that parody the conditions of dining in factories. One illustration shows two men, sandwiches in hand and an open lunch box beside them. One sits with his

"Well ... Saturday is her birthday ... Sunday is our anniversary ... Monday is Christmas ... and I could use a new lunch pail ..."

Cartoon from Frank Adams' *Then Ya Just Untwist* (1951).

feet resting on the back of a third man, who is in the middle of scrubbing the floor of the work station. He looks at his lunch partner and says: "You don't get this kind of comfort in the cafeteria."

There is one image that best summarizes the tone and message of Adams's work. It depicts a tired-looking man standing in front of the desk of a rather disinterested loan officer. The man's dented lunch box is on the floor beside him. He pours out his request to the officer: "Well ... Saturday is her birthday ... Sunday is our anniversary ... Monday is Christmas ... and I could use a new lunch pail." In this image and text, more than any other, Adams makes clear the disenchantment of working people in postwar America. It emphasizes the industrial and manual workers' sense of invisibility to their employers and to the broader public. Further, it epitomizes the growth of a consumer culture marked by the celebration of birthdays, anniversaries, and holidays. The struggle to reach the level at which the basic needs of food, clothing, transportation, and shelter could be met was such that for many, the durable goods and consumer luxuries that pervaded imagery of the American good life were all but unattainable. In Adams's work, the lunch box is the symbol of that continuous effort. It is a material representation of unity among men and women working to achieve the accoutrements of a better life — a life where lunch did not always have to come out of a box.

Observations from the Real World

While Adams's cartoons highlighted the difficulties encountered by working people, Ida Bailey Allen, a nutritionist and cookbook author, made investigations into the actual lunches and dining environments common in American factories. Allen stepped into the reformers' role that had been vacated after the war and attempted to revive interest in workplace dining conditions and concern for the nutrition provided to American workers. Many of her observations reinforce points made in the Adams's book.

Allen, born in Connecticut in 1885, graduated from the New York Metropolitan Hospital as a dietician. Her career spanned a broad spectrum of contemporary media. Having already published several works by 1918, during World War I, she published two cookbooks related to the wartime food situation: *Mrs. Allen's Book of Sugar Substitutes* and *Mrs. Allen's Book of Wheat Substitutes.*[7] Thereafter, she directed and spoke at cooking schools, and wrote for several periodicals, including *Ladies Home Journal*, and she was the food editor for *Good Housekeeping*, *Family Circle*, and *Parade*. She wrote a syndicated food column from 1946 to 1968, was a featured guest on many radio and television programs, and served as a consultant to the food and household industries. The author of more than fifty books, Allen was in the world of food and nutrition something of a celebrity, with an estimated 20 million books sold by the time of her death in 1973. Not surprisingly, she was a vocal advocate of the importance of good food and nutrition, and her obituary in the *New York Times* (which also included one of her favorite recipes for Boston baked beans) stated her belief that "good home cooking was an antidote to a rising divorce rate."[8]

In the September 1955 issue of *Today's Health*, Allen dispensed some of her culinary advice and wisdom. She declared that lunch boxes were neither "old-fashioned nor "declassé," and they were not carried only by the "underprivileged." Allen cited recent surveys that had shown lunch boxes being carried by "more than half out of the nation's 60 million city men and women workers of all classes." Allen discovered that in "addition, millions of workers in suburban and country districts, where restaurant facilities are often unavailable and workers do not have time to go home for lunch, carry a lunch box." She noted that even though many factories had facilities that served hot lunches, in a survey of "365 manufacturing plants of all types in the 48 states," each with cafeteria, more than 50 percent of the men and women employed still chose to carry a lunch box. Allen wondered: "Why should these workers prefer to carry their lunch?" She proposed that the answers were obvious: "In many cases the time factor is important. In others the majority of both city and country workers cannot afford to buy adequate lunches in a restaurant or cafeteria. Some supplement their lunch with coffee, a soft drink, milk, candy or peanuts from vending machines."

Allen asked other significant questions about the consumption of lunch in America. Her research revealed that for the majority of American workers, lunch was not eaten in the "charmingly decorated, peaceful environment advocated by dieticians, nutritionists, doctors and psychiatrists, but in any place available." Among the locations in which Allen observed workers eating were rest areas and lounge rooms, office desks, "by the worker's machine; outside with lumber and crates for tables and seats; outdoors at shipbuilding plants; amid the noises and smells of processing plants.... Occasionally in small plants women workers get permission to fix an unused section of the building for lunching." She saw that in good weather, rural workers often ate outside, while their city counterparts sometimes dined at the local park.

In an effort to determine what kinds of foods American workers were carrying to work, Allen sent out questionnaires to workers in various locations across the nation. One response from a "manual worker" described his lunchtime observations:

> The dreary pattern is not unique with me. Few of the men carry lunch boxes; mostly they bring sandwiches and a cookie in a paper bag. Then they buy coffee. The sandwiches are generally peanut butter, peanut butter and jelly or some kind of luncheon meat. The women carry more complicated sandwiches: sometimes cheese spreads with olive and

pimiento. The bread is usually white, but sometimes you see a dark loaf.

There is a smaller group, mostly older workers, who carry lunch boxes.

I know one man who has two thermos bottles, one for a hearty soup every day — even in the summer — the other for coffee. With this he has a few good meat sandwiches and a piece of pie or cake.

Allen's informant went on to state that in his estimation, the addition of some type of fruit would be the best improvement to workers' lunches: "If the guys have fruit they eat it." He further commented on the commonness of "plain and simple malnutrition, due partly to poor planning and education." His solution was to instigate change at the source of the lunch — the women who packed them.

Allen seems to have supported this position on the need to encourage women to pack better lunches. She observed that the three main reasons that women packed insufficient lunches were cost, lack of information, and time. Allen noted that there were 12 million working mothers nationwide who had to rush off to work themselves, and as a result, often left their husbands and children to prepare their own lunches. She concluded that in the end, no matter what her employment status outside the home, the woman was responsible for lunch:

> For a man to bring home a well-filled pay envelope every payday he must be in good health. Proper nutrition plays an important part, not only in helping avert absenteeism due to sickness, with consequent loss of pay, but in promoting physiological well-being and maintaining the alert mental attitude necessary to achieving success. For purely selfish reasons, if for no other, it pays to pack a good lunch for the family provider.

Allen went on to give box packers advice about "what belongs in a lunch box." She concluded with the assertion: "Success depends on the realization that the lunch box must contain the equivalent of a regular meal and the desire of the homemaker to prepare the food with intelligent and loving care."[9] The lunch was a clear reflection of domesticity and an extension of the home.

Both Adams and Allen used print media to focus renewed attention on the quality of workers' meals and dining areas. To them, it appeared that these issues had receded from the general public's awareness. For the workers themselves, however, the challenges of obtaining adequate nutrition during the workday had never disappeared.

Claiming Lunch: Workers, Management, and the Law

As Nelson Lichtenstein demonstrates in his essay "Conflict over Workers' Control: The Automobile Industry in World War II," wartime changes in the economy and the composition of the labor force contributed to a workplace climate that was not conducive to organized union efforts. Although worker militancy did not disappear during the war, the influx of new workers diluted the old nucleus of radical union activists to a point where they became relatively ineffective at gaining power over the productive process. The exigencies of war meant that labor was in demand and prices were high, and companies such as General Motors were able to take advantage of the changing labor force to reassert managerial control over the shop floor. After the war, unions, under the leadership of strong figures such as United Auto Workers President Walter Reuther, focused more on issues of pay and subsistence than on questions of shop discipline or productivity standards.[10] In such an environment, lunch breaks became an important source of conflict between workers and management.

For some workers, meals available in the factory were a benefit of wartime mobilization, and one that they proved unwilling to relinquish. As had been the case during the earliest years of industrialization in the United States, after World War II, the worker's lunch returned to its status as a bargaining chip between employers and employees. Most workers refused to give up their lunch break as a concession to productivity or other goals of management, believing that lunch was a necessary break in the day. It provided a time for refueling and socializing with their fellow workers that helped underscore the necessary separation between humans and machines.

An article in *Business Week* on 1 September 1945 predicted that there was "no likelihood that either workers or management" would "be willing to see on-the-job meals suspended and industry return to the days of the dinner pail." The same article cited evidence of workers striking to protest cancellation of factory-feeding programs and warned that demands for such programs would only increase the "reshuffling of workers in the transition from war." Those who were "accustomed to hot meals at 35c to 50c a day may prove unwilling to go back to lunchboxes in plants which serve no meals."[11]

The 1950s proved some of the prognosticators to be correct. In

1953, the employees of Northwestern Bell Telephone Company demanded that their concerns over their lunches be heard. The impetus for their actions was a new contract between the Communications Workers of America (CWA) and Northwestern. A clause in the contract stipulated that the company would provide workers with funds for "additional expenses" incurred when the employee was required to attend to a job out of town. The workers believed that this phrase obligated the company to pay for their lunches. Predictably, Northwestern's executives disagreed. They "contended that packing a lunch for out-of-town assignments doesn't mean any additional expense, because workers usually eat at home anyway; what they eat from a plate at home they eat from a lunchbox when out of town." The union "agreed that workers normally go home for lunch — but for spaghetti, goulash, stew, and other leftovers that can be heated easily and put on a plate. You can't make sandwiches out of leftovers," said CWA, asking: "Who ever heard of a spaghetti or goulash sandwich?" The lawyers for the union "backed their case with workers' home lunch menus and lists of what they usually take with them on out-of-town jobs — mostly meat sandwiches packed at what CWA called 'strictly an additional expense.'"[12]

Clearly, in the estimation of these workers, the lunch break was an important part of the day. The nature of the foods described indicates that many of them were probably members of ethnic groups that valued traditional foods. When the company mandated that they break with their habits and consume their meal away from home, the workers deemed it appropriate for the company to make a sacrifice as well, in the form of compensation. Two years earlier, in 1951, the U.S. District Court ruled that if an employer required an employee to perform any job-related task during his lunch break, that worker had to be paid for his time.[13] Both of these cases show how workers used the leverage of lunch to gain what they believed were their rights as employees. They also emphasize the fact that many workers thought that their time and humanity were undervalued by their employers.

Throughout the later decades of the twentieth century, food-related issues continued to be prominent in bargaining between employers and employees. In an important Supreme Court case in 1979, the high court ruled that food prices and services inside plants were subject to collective bargaining. The case came about after employees of a Ford plant had staged a three-month-long strike against the company cafeteria because of its high prices. Justice Byron White wrote:

The availability of food during working hours and the conditions under which it is to be consumed are matters of deep concern to workers, and one need not strain to consider them to be among those "conditions" of employment that should be subject to the mutual duty to bargain. By the same token, where the employer has chosen, apparently in his own interest, to make available a system of in-plant feeding facilities for his employees, the prices at which food is offered and other aspects of this service may reasonably be considered among those subjects about which management and the union must bargain.[14]

This ruling made clear that debate over workplace food provision or dining facilities was legitimate and would not fade away. It did not, however, resolve the issue.

The "Lunch Crunch": Transforming the Three-Martini Lunch

Americans today, both workers and to a lesser extent students, have a wide array of options when it comes to procuring a noon meal. For the majority of these two groups, some type of on-site food service is available; they may be able to leave and purchase food at a near by fast-food outlet or restaurant; or, as always, they may carry their lunches to work with them. According to a January 2001 survey conducted by research firm Datamonitor, 20 percent of office workers bring their lunch to work every day and 45 percent carry a meal from home at least once a week. One reason some workers gave for carrying their lunch was that it was easier for them to monitor the fat, sodium, and calories in their diets. Some were trying to lose weight or needed a special diet for health reasons and did not want to have to rely on the selections in the cafeteria.[15]

Dietary concerns alone certainly cannot account for the recent resurgence in the number of people carrying lunch. Something else is at work in this equation — the lunch crunch. This phrase appears with some frequency in newspaper articles related to the subject of lunch. The "crunch" refers to a decrease in the amount of time available for the noon meal as well as for personal tasks in general. According to the author of the Datamonitor report: "People are really feeling that time is at a premium and that they don't want to waste it eating." The report revealed that time was the most important variable in determining whether an employee ate or did not eat lunch. Many felt peer pressure if co-workers were either eating at their desks or skipping lunch altogether. The study broke down as follows:

> Overall, 40 percent of workers do not feel that they are taking a proper lunch break. Employees aged 55 to 64 are even less likely to take a leisurely lunch — 47 percent claim not to take their full allotted time. And while their younger counterparts, workers aged 18 to 34, are more likely to take their break — just 39 percent say that they shortened the lunch hour — they are more likely than other age groups to use the time for activities other than eating. Fifty-five percent of that group admits that they shop, run errands, or exercise during lunch.[16]

Another concern for some people resurrects past fears of the status attached to lunch carrying. Over time, the lunch box has continued to be identified with blue-collar and factory workers — an indication of vocational rather than professional work. Escaping from these socially constructed categories requires the ability to subvert them in creative ways. In 1985, journalist Anne Lear wrote "The Great Lunch Box Caper" for the magazine *Gourmet*. In this article, Lear explains how she empowered her husband to carry his lunch box with pride among the status-conscious membership of the Washington press corps. Lear notes that reporters who

> "have arrived" do not carry lunch boxes, or at least not plebian ones. Dear me, no. They carry paper bags, at worst, and damn the leakages, or, better, they hide their sandwiches in (often otherwise empty) briefcases. Best of all is to carry a briefcase so expensively slim that the absence of a sandwich may be clearly noted and the inference drawn that the carrier invariably eats out at Lion d'Or, the White House mess, or someone else's expense.

Anne's husband, Gil, however, liked to carry his lunch. Anne prepared meals that suited his individual taste, and the extra time he saved by not leaving the office he was able to devote to pleasure reading. When the bureau chief walked by Gil's desk one day, and commented: "Ah, I see you carry a lunch box," Anne decided to "retaliate." She said to herself: "Lunch box, eh? Wait 'til they see what I can put into that too, too proletarian bucket!"[17] Anne's plan involved preparing and packing elaborate meals, complete with utensils, for Gil to consume as conspicuously as possible in front of his colleagues. Her entrees ranged from fettuccine Alfredo to rock Cornish game hen to a whole lobster. Each meal was complemented by an appropriate wine. Eventually, Gil's office mates and the bureau chief heard Anne's message — as broadcast through Gil's lunch box. Like the old adage, "you can't judge a book by its cover," you should not judge a person by his lunch box.

Bigger workloads and increased personal and employer demands make desktop dining a frequent occurrence for many workers. Gone are the days of the three-martini lunch. The phrase "three-martini lunch" was a sort of short-hand code that referred to the extended lunches, frequently with large quantities of alcohol being consumed, that were common when employers could deduct such meals as a business expense. Although there is certainly much to be said for the business transactions that may take place over a leisurely meal, such lunches were extravagant wastes of time and money that served to enhance a sense of division among employers and employees. Changes in corporate tax laws in the late 1980s and early 1990s reduced the amount of the deduction allowed for the business lunch resulting in a corresponding decrease in the number of three-martini affairs. Time and money increased in value when the possibility for large deductions fell.

Although rules regarding personal deductions for the so-called three-martini lunch have tightened in recent years, deductions for employers providing employee meals have been enhanced. Beginning on 1 January 1998, business owners could deduct 100 percent rather than the previous 50 percent of the cost of employee meals provided free of charge or at below market value. Another tax law change allowed workers whose hours were regulated by the Department of Transportation (commercial pilots, truck drivers, and merchant mariners, for example) to deduct a higher percentage of the cost of meals consumed on the job. The amount of the deduction is slated to continue to rise until 2008, when it will reach 80 percent. The increased deductions were described by a legislative representative of the National Restaurant Association as a boon both for employees and America's restaurants.[18]

Not only did changes in tax code affect the three-martini lunch, but in some workplaces, it also affected the use of on-site dining space. The three-martini lunch often took place in an executive dining room reserved for high-ranking employees only. Segregated dining facilities for workers and management, particularly in factory settings, had been normal. Tighter budgets and criticism from staff has resulted in some companies abandoning the idea of separate eating areas. A common reason for the separation in early factory cafeterias was that workers were dirty from their jobs and managers did not want to risk disheveling

Workers having lunch at the Joseph Teshon textile plant in Paterson, New Jersey, in August 1994. Left to right: Teresa Maturano, Cindy Fanslau, Carmen Ortiz, Gladys Ortiz (*Working in Paterson: Occupational Heritage in an Urban Setting.* American Folklife Center, Library of Congress).

their business attire. Increasingly, however, as technology has removed the messier aspects of factory work, managers have found that their interaction with employees as well as employees' interaction with one another can be a valuable tool for building better working relationships and generating new ideas. Kraft Foods Company, for example, in the early 1990s opened up its executive dining rooms to any employees who wanted to hold a "special-occasion lunch" or "reception." According to the Director of Corporate Affairs: "The executives were not using these rooms as much as they used to, and we thought it would be a good idea to make them available to everyone." Although executives retain some scheduling privileges, the "democratized" dining room has been well accepted by all: "The employees enjoy it, and if you want to look at it from a productivity angle, it is much better having them in the building than getting in their cars and driving somewhere for a celebration lunch."[19]

In a bit of a renaissance of the early twentieth-century paternalistic attitudes toward employee meals, some employers encourage their

Workers at the Watson machine plant in Paterson, New Jersey, making selections from a lunch wagon in August 1994 (*Working in Paterson: Occupational Heritage in an Urban Setting.* American Folklife Center, Library of Congress).

staffs to eat "on campus" rather than run the risk of having them leave for lunch only to buy alcohol and unhealthy foods and return intoxicated and late for the afternoon hours. The health of the employees is important for productivity and costs. Unhealthy employees are a drag on the daily operations and potentially on health insurance as well.

Restaurants that once relied on lunch trade for both executive three-martini afternoons as well as quick-service establishments have found that they must compete with both the corporate cafeterias and the carried lunch. The shortage of noontime diners in many of America's biggest restaurants has resulted in recent talk in Congress to consider restoring the meal deductions as a support to the hospitality industry and a way to provide tax assistance to businesses.[20] In summer 1999, Lespinasse, a pricey New York City eatery, advertised: "In the 70s you had lunch. In the 80s you did lunch. In the 90s you skipped lunch. Perhaps it's time you redefined lunch." The creative marketing strategy was crafted to promote a special one-hour-long, three-course meal for the fixed price of $36 (apparently reasonable in relation to other New York hot spots). According to a 1999 article in the *New York Times*: "As lunch has come under increasing pressures of time, budgets, and health concerns, many restaurants have realized that they must adapt, or face empty tables. They have chosen to give customers what they want, like two appetizers and a beverage in 45 minutes, or a meal ready to go in a container."[21] Some restaurants, such as Morrison's near New York City's Wall Street, will prepare a "brown bag" lunch for workers to carry back to the office.[22] Other popular stops for early morning coffee have found that their customers appreciate being able to buy a ready-to-go brown bag lunch for the day's noon meal.

Reclaiming Lunch

Employer, government, and public attention to the lunch habits of workers in the post–World War II era has included periods of both intensification and abatement in the conflicts regarding the over an employee's work time. Although many workers have continued to believe that the lunch break is a right owed to them as human beings, many employers have acquiesced through the provision of, at the very least, a time and a place for employee meals: a significant acknowledgment of the difference between man and machine. Still, as a 1994 dispute between the LTV Steel Company and members of the United Steel Workers Union demonstrates, the negotiation of these boundaries has not vanished. During this struggle, thirty workers were sent home when they refused to obey a supervisor's command to return to their work stations when they had begun their lunch breaks only five minutes earlier. The company wanted to maintain continuous production — even at the expense of the workers' meal time. Union negotiators asserted that the workers required twenty minutes of labor-free time as well as a clean and safe place to refuel themselves for the remainder of their shifts.[23] In the eyes of the corporation, the value of these employees' productive work time trumped their need for personal time.

For manufacturers and marketers of convenience food products and quick-service food establishments, the reality of these continued tensions among employers and employees and the slippery issues of productivity, time, and money mean open territory for their efforts to influence workers' lunch habits. The upshot of all of this debate about worker lunches is that although both the players and the conflicts have changed, the colonization of worker lunches and lunch times continues.

7

Carrying Lunch to School: Players in the Institutionalization of Students' Noon Meals

When it comes to debates over the quality of lunch and the environment in which it is consumed, no arena provides more examples of the colonizing process than the school lunch. This meal has been hotly contested by a plethora of special interests, including parents, educators, bureaucrats, scientists, members of the media, farmers and other agricultural interests, and the food service industry. By examining the carving up and distribution of responsibility for the school lunch among all of these colonizing groups, it is possible to trace their legacy from the first penny lunches in the late nineteenth century, through the increasing federal and commercial interventions in the twentieth century, to current debates over the attribution of rising rates of childhood diabetes and obesity to poor nutritional habits.

Making School Lunch Permanent

On 4 June 1946, President Harry S Truman signed into law the bill making school lunches a permanent feature of the national budget. Truman's statement revealed his hope for the program and the nation:

Today, as I sign the National School Lunch Act, I feel that the Congress has acted with great wisdom in providing the basis for strengthening the nation through better nutrition for our school children. In my message to Congress last January, I pointed out that we have the technical knowledge to provide plenty of good food for every man, woman, and child in this country, but that despite our capacity to produce food, we have often failed to distribute it as well as we should. This action by Congress represents a basic forward step toward correcting that failure.

In the long view, no nation is any healthier than its children or more prosperous than its farmers; and in the National School Lunch Act, the Congress has contributed immeasurably both to the welfare to our farmers and the health of our children.[1]

In the years leading up to the 1946 National School Lunch Act, legislators and assorted interest groups, including those representing home economists, agriculture, and children, began positioning themselves for a permanent federally supported school lunch program. School lunches held the promise of acting as a homogenizing influence that could help level differences across geographic regions, races, classes, and ethnic groups. Some observers went so far as to call school lunches "truant officers." According to a February 1941 article in *Reader's Digest*, school lunches helped encourage attendance and attentiveness in students. Particularly in Southern areas with high rates of poverty, teachers reported being pleased at seeing an end to the "slow death in lunch pails: corn bread spread with lard; flour-and-water biscuit and a slice of sweet potato; hoecake smeared with molasses." Some of these teachers commented that they had "seen children bring empty lunch pails and go off alone at lunch time so that others wouldn't witness their poverty." One author credited school lunches with "winning a new generation away from the meal, meat, and molasses — the deadly 3-M diet on which millions have slowly starved." The educational value of the lunch helped create in these students an "appetite for protective foods — fruits and vegetables." Without the vital nutritional elements found in such balanced school lunches, the author feared that the nation ran the risk of becoming overrun with "sickly, dispirited wrecks who might have been useful citizens."[2]

The Roots of Federal Assistance

The Depression of the early 1930s had tested the nation's private charities and state budgets. Historian Ronald Edsforth has noted that the tradition of "local responsibility for poor relief" dated to the colonial era, "but had never been tested in an urban mass-consumer society."[3] As more families experienced the stress of unemployment and other financial losses, it soon became apparent that the many individuals, school boards and associations, and other private philanthropic organizations could no longer maintain adequate school feeding programs without increased public assistance. Slowly, more responsibility for school food distribution fell under the purview of municipalities and states, and eventually the federal government.[4] President Franklin Roosevelt responded to the crisis with New Deal social measures that shifted some of the burden for social welfare from the private sector to the government. Roosevelt believed that the government had a responsibility to see to the creation of an economic and humanitarian safety net for those in need.

By the early 1930s, the federal government had instituted relief measures designed to help both individuals and businesses cope with economic pressures. A bulletin on school lunches published by the Bureau of Agricultural Economics (a part of the Department of Agriculture) in 1942 noted that during the Depression, the government had acted to "bridge the gap between unused abundance and those in need."[5] Thanks to the support of the Works Progress Administration (WPA) and the National Youth Administration, "thousands of country and city children who had not been reached by the scattered earlier attempts now for the first time had a chance at the lunches."[6] WPA lunch projects employed people and fed children. One observer reported:

> Reports show that before the establishment of the WPA projects, the food brought to school by many of the children in the rural sections of South Carolina consisted of such items as a sweet potato or a poorly cooked biscuit spread with fat. In Georgia, the mid-day meal of many of the children now fed on WPA projects was often nothing more than a piece of cold bread — occasionally supplemented by a piece of fried fish. The usual lunch brought to school by under-privileged children in Vermont was bread — sometimes spread with butter. Some of the poorer children in Minnesota are reported to have come to school empty-handed, while many others brought such unappetizing lunches as a pickle and a piece of soggy bread — packed hastily by an over-worked mother.[7]

Under the Reconstruction Finance Corporation, in 1932 and 1933 some Missouri towns received funds to support the labor needed to prepare and serve school lunches. By 1934, the program of relief had expanded to other states under the Civil Works Administration and the Federal Emergency Relief Administration; ultimately, it involved thirty-nine states and employed 7,442 women. In 1935, Public Law 320 provided for the distribution of excess agricultural commodities to poor families and school lunch programs. The purpose behind this legislation was twofold. First, it provided assistance to families and individuals in financial distress. Second, it alleviated the market pressures caused by surplus food in a manner that did not inhibit normal distribution. By 1940, each state had a representative on the Federal Surplus Commodities Commission who coordinated relations between the state and the various organizations responsible for school lunch programs.[8]

The WPA was another federal organization that lent support to school lunch programs. Under the umbrella of the WPA, schools received funds to pay salaries for cafeteria employees, and the WPA saw to it that the supervisor in each school was qualified "by training and experience to arrange menus and direct personnel in this work." Although participating schools benefited from federal involvement, the initiative for lunch programs had to begin first at a local level. WPA Assistant Administrator Ellen S. Woodward noted that a board of education often took the lead in establishing a program and remained as its official sponsor, although many programs also relied on additional support from Parent-Teacher Associations, local civic groups, and other interested individuals. Woodward also commented on the proliferation of such programs in regions of unstable and stable economic circumstances. Most programs were begun in response to the needs of families on relief, but lunch providers soon realized that "growing children" needed a hot meal "irrespective of their financial condition." It became the policy of many school districts to provide lunches for all students who wanted them.

The happy result of New Deal–era lunch programs was an overall improvement in the health of many children. Still, as the World War II Selective Service rejections would demonstrate, a national nutrition deficiency persisted. In its 1942 pamphlet on school lunches, the Department of Agriculture summarized the desperate need for a strong commitment to a national lunch program. The Department pointed to successful programs in Europe and Latin America and decried the lack of progress in the United States: "No one even knows with certainty how many children in this country are malnourished, but experts have abundant evidence that malnutrition, especially among children is a serious problem." Further, nutrition science cautioned that good nutrition had less to do with the quantity of food than the quality. A national survey conducted by the Bureau of Home Economics concluded that only one-fourth of American diets were "good," while another fourth were "fair," and "far more than one-fourth were downright poor." The study demonstrated that although the situation was "most acute among families with low incomes," malnutrition was not confined to "those who cannot afford to pay for good diets. Because they do not know the principles of nutrition, or are indifferent, malnutrition is found in many families that do not have thin pocketbooks." In spite of such dismal facts and figures, there was some room for optimism. As the authors of the Bureau of Agricultural Economics' school lunch bulletin noted, the information "on what makes a good balanced diet" was constantly improving. Furthermore, the country was

> now engaged in a vigorous campaign to make known to people generally these newer facts regarding vitamins, nutrients, and protective foods. Now, more than ever, there is an urgent need for getting this information to even the most remote citizens as rapidly as practicable, for improved nutrition and improved health are fundamental in adequate national defense.[9]

Although World War II strained the national coffers with expenditures for the military and aid to allied nations, through annually renewable congressional allocations, the school lunch commitment weathered the hardships intact. Support came in the form of cash subsidies payable to the sponsors of local lunch programs. A stipulation for the use of these funds was that they be used only toward the purchase of food supplies and not for payment of the salaries for foodservice staff or for procuring equipment. Surplus commodities were also available, albeit in reduced quantities. According to one historian, in addition to the shrinking potential workforce as a result of higher employment rates, the foods available for distribution to the school food program fell from a high of 454 million pounds in 1942 to 93 million pounds by 1944. Perhaps even more telling, in February 1942, there were 92,916 schools involved in the school lunch program. These schools served a population of 6 million children. In contrast, by April 1944, only 34,064 schools were participating, and the numbers of students served had fallen to approximately 5 million.

These cash allotments carried the nation through the difficult war years, but in postwar America, the lunch program faced new challenges. Congress had continually supported the lunch program, but it had never made any provision for establishing its permanent budgetary status. Renewal of support was made on a year-by-year basis and was contingent on the availability of funds. This fact made some school systems cautious about undertaking a lunch program as funding might not prove to be consistent.

1946: A Benchmark for School Lunches and Child Nutrition

It was not until the 79th Congress met in 1946 that legislators set about the task of instituting a stable formula for the continual support of school lunch programs. The debates leading up to the approval of the National School Lunch Act in the Senate and the House highlighted long-held concerns over issues such as state's rights and racial and economic discrimination.

Some members of Congress questioned whether the school lunch program should be supported by the federal government at all. The proposal encountered its most serious opposition in the House, which witnessed the revival of old sectional enmities and the creation some interesting new political alliances. New York Republican Representative James Wadsworth called it "another step calculated slowly but surely to transfer responsibility from the states." A Democrat from Texas, Hattan W. Summers, told the House: "If you pass this bill, you will be inculcating in little children at the most impressionable period of their lives, the idea that they can get something for nothing from Uncle Sam."[10] When the bill finally passed the House in February 1946, the *New York Times* reported that the program differed little from the one in place for nearly ten years, except that it was permanent. The newspaper noted that "Republicans and Democrats alike joined in approval of the programs but divided sharply on the issue, now presented for the first time, that the Federal Government should assume responsibility permanently." According to this report, members "on both sides contended that the States could and should bear the responsibility." Those in support of federal backing argued that while "the treasuries of most of the States were just now in a better financial condition than that of the Federal Government," there were still states "and communities where continuation of the programs would depend upon Federal aid."[11]

Specific parts of the bill were hotly contested prior to passage. The House rejected the inclusion of funding for nutrition education and training programs. On this issue: "Democrats opposed even more strenuously than Republicans what they argued was a move in the direction of Federal control of the State school system."[12] When the bill moved to the Senate for debate, however, Ohio Republican Senator Robert A. Taft was defeated in his proposal to follow the House in rejecting the nutrition education allocation. In opposition to another of Taft's ideas, the Senate approved an increase in the House's approved spending limit for school lunch programs.[13]

A proposal by New York Democrat Adam Clayton Powell to deny aid to any school that discriminated on the basis of race, creed, color, or national origin also caused a stir. Some members interpreted Powell's idea as a way to ensure "proportionately as much money for lunches for Negro children as for white children." Texas Democrat Representative William Robert Poage, however, voiced another possibility, declaring that the amendment meant that any state with a segregated school system would be ineligible for federal aid:

> He said that it would result in having a Government official declare that States with separate schools for the different races could not benefit from the Federal funds. The majority leader, Representative McCormack, and Mr. Tarver declared that the racial issue had been raised by opponents of the lunch program in order to alienate Southern support."[14]

Despite the opposition that the race provision generated, it was retained in the bill that passed the House in February 1946.

In Section 2 of the Act, titled the "Declaration of Policy," Congress made a clear statement of goals:

> It is hereby declared to be the policy of Congress, as a measure of national security, to safeguard the health and well-being of the Nation's children and to encourage the domestic consumption of nutritious agricultural commodities and other food, by assisting the States, through grants-in-aid and other means, in providing an adequate supply of foods and other facilities for the establishment, maintenance, operation, and expansion of non profit school-lunch programs.[15]

The legislation stipulated that the states were to be given funds based on two factors: first, the number of schoolchildren between the ages of five and seventeen in the state; and second, the need for federal assistance, which was determined through the use of a formula for comparing the per capita income in the state with the per capita income of the nation. Individual school districts were to determine which children needed a free or reduced price meal, but the text of the act stated specifically: "No physical segregation or other discrimination against any child shall be made by the school because of his inability to pay."

The Persistent Problem of Discrimination

From its inception in 1946, the National School Lunch Program (NSLP) has not been without its critics. Throughout the decades since NSLP began, Congress has authorized amendments to the original legislation in the hope of silencing controversy arising out of the determination of which children are eligible for free or reduced price lunches and how to distribute national funds most equitably among the states.

One of the biggest problems that schools face is finding a way to provide assistance to children who cannot afford to pay without creating an obvious separation among free, reduced, and full-cost lunches. Until 1970, the standards used to make such judgments were left up to the states and individual districts. Prior to congressional action to standardize such practices, one critic complained that in Chicago, for example, among children from one family, one student might qualify for a free lunch because of his age and the fact that he was in school all day, while a younger sibling attending kindergarten for a half day would not. This writer for *Parents* magazine, who was also a substitute teacher, had been involved in a study of the Chicago school lunch situation that called on a variety of community leaders including "doctors, nurses, nutritionists, legislators, and journalists." They uncovered what the writer described as the "shocking failure of the school lunch act" brought about by "bureaucratic red tape and callous indifference." In the opinions of these citizens, Congress had never authorized enough federal funding to make NSLP self-supporting. The requirement that states match each federal dollar with three state dollars had resulted in a system of passing the buck that left parents footing the bill. In many cases, where states or municipalities refused to use tax money to augment NSLP, the costs fell on poorer parents, who might not be able to afford even the few cents necessary to bridge the difference between the federal allotment and the actual price of meals.

The ultimate cost came in the hunger and shame suffered by the children who could not pay for their meals. Even though the original act had specified that children should in no way be segregated based on their ability or inability to pay, it appeared to the Chicago investigators that discrimination still flourished at the hands of "some unsympathetic school administrators" who "insisted on" such "humiliating practices" as requiring students to wear red tags around their necks that said "Free Lunch," making these students work for their food, or placing them at the end of the cafeteria line. The writer commented on a proposal made by Michigan Representative Martha W. Griffiths in 1969, which called for the passage of a bill guaranteeing three meals a day to all children under the age of sixteen whose families were on welfare or had an income that fell below a specified poverty level. Although the writer did not endorse this proposal outright, her closing commentary on the dangers of hunger revived arguments reminiscent of those made by earlier reformers:

> The Griffiths proposal may seem too expensive until one compares it with the cost of not feeding our nation's children, of not caring, of not sharing. That price is truly astronomical, computed as it must be in terms of crime, correction, hospitalization, early death. Since we cannot and do not wish to assume such high costs, let us instead pay the costs we should to underwrite school lunch programs that work.[16]

In 1970, Congress responded by amending the act by establishing national criteria for the eligibility of children for free and reduced price meal which would be adjusted annually in accordance with federal income poverty guidelines. School districts were still allowed some flexibility in using welfare income, family size, and the number of children attending school as additional ways for establishing eligibility. The federal poverty income was to serve as a baseline. Participating schools now had to draft a statement including details as to their policies regarding the determination of need for aid and their proposed method for collecting payment. In addition, schools were required to inform parents about the eligibility standards and commit to a policy of nonsegregation of children based on ability to pay. No longer would schools be allowed to publish or distribute the names of children receiving assistance, and these children "would not be required, as a condition of receiving such meals, to use a separate lunchroom, go through a separate serving line, enter the lunchroom through a separate entrance, eat lunch at a different time from paying children, work for their meals, use a different medium of exchange than paying children, or be offered a different meal than the paying children."[17]

Among the other important changes brought about by the 1970 legislation was the creation of a National Nutrition Advisory Council. This body was to be comprised of thirteen members appointed to service by the Secretary of Agriculture and composed of various experts in the field of child nutrition: a representative from a state school lunch program, a school administrator and a school board member or teacher, a child welfare worker, a representative of vocational education, a nutrition expert, a school food service expert, a state superintendent of schools, and four people from the Department of Agriculture with "training experience and knowledge relating to child food programs."[18] The purpose of the council was — and remains — to conduct studies regarding school lunches and make recommendations for change based on their observations.

Commodities Distribution: Are Schools a Convenient Dumping Ground?

Another of the major battles over the school lunch bill centered around the degree to which lunch programs should be used as an outlet for surplus agricultural produce commodities. This aspect of school lunches dated back to the New Deal–era federal food purchase and distribution programs. In 1945, when the Chairman of the House Agricultural Committee, John W. Flanagan, a Virginia Democrat, introduced a bill to make school lunches permanent, he called for its approval "as a measure of national security and as a means of encouraging the domestic consumption of agricultural commodities." The *New York Times* reported that while Flanagan made his presentation to the House there were "representatives of the American Association of Home Economics, the National Education Association, and The National Congress of Parents and Teachers" waiting to express their opinion "that the school luncheon program should be primarily for the benefit of children rather than for eating up agricultural surpluses," and they favored "having it keyed with the educational system of the country.[19] Other critics of the commodity distribution plank of the school lunch program charged that the prime motivation for lunches seemed to be one of an economic rather than a humanitarian nature. Some people believed that the schools were but dumping grounds for excess commodities not salable on the open market. Defendants of the commodity distribution plan maintained that the products were helpful to school cafeterias that struggled to remain out of debt. In early 1944, the U.S. Office of Education weighed in on the matter. It proposed a plan under which the school lunch program, then under the supervision of the War Food Administration, would be turned over to "State and local educational authorities, on the ground that school lunches are primarily an educational rather than a war food matter."[20]

Support for the linking of food service and the Office of Education came from predictable corners — home economists, education experts, and parents. Ultimately, the educational and agricultural interests reached a compromise whereby the program remained under the umbrella of the Agriculture Department, but the funds would be spent by state governments, often through the state educational systems. Congress required that the lunch programs be operated on a nonprofit basis and that the funds distributed to the states through the act be matched by the states. A special formula allowed poorer states with large numbers of students to "receive a higher proportionate share."[21] The 1946 act stated that during the first year of the program, states could match federal dollars on a one-to-one basis; from 1951 to 1955, however, they would have to match $1.50 to each federal dollar, and for 1956 and after, they would be required to pay out $3 for each federal dollar they received. The states were allowed to consider the lunch payments made by children, the cost of labor, and the value of donated commodities and equipment as part of their matching funds.

From the standpoint of child nutrition reformers and other experts, the School Lunch Act was a great leap forward. Not only did it guarantee that the federal government would remain committed to the program, it also established a national standard for minimum nutritional requirements in school lunches. For a school to qualify for federal assistance, the lunches had to meet certain criteria "prescribed by the Secretary on the basis of tested nutritional research." These lunches were labeled Types A, B, and C. A Type A lunch was intended to fulfill one-third to one-half of the minimum daily nutritional needs of a child between the ages of ten and twelve, but the meal pattern could be adjusted to suit the needs of children of any age. A Type B lunch was essentially a supplement to carried lunches, mainly served in schools where facilities were inadequate for the provision of a more complete meal. Finally, a Type C lunch consisted of simply one-half pint of whole milk served as a beverage. The amount of money that a school received per lunch was based on the type of lunch it served. If a school failed to provide milk when it was easily obtainable, the reimbursement was reduced by 2 cents per lunch.[22]

Of course, because the program drew its lifeblood from the Department of Agriculture, schools received indirect pressure from the Department to support agriculture by purchasing local products and surplus commodities. Over the years, commodities provided to schools free of charge or at minimal cost have included cheese, butter, beef, and other high-fat products, as well as such items as figs, potatoes, and peanuts. While these "bargains" have certainly helped provide financially strapped schools with food for their lunches, the unpredictable nature of the commodities market has made the nutritionist's job of menu planning a challenge. The task is further complicated by the fact that foods like figs are often not popular among schoolchildren. Most important, the commodity foods are not always the most nutritious and healthful foods necessary for young minds and bodies.

Recently, in renewed recognition of the increasingly poor physical health of American children, including higher rates of childhood obesity and diabetes, the federal government, via the Department of Agriculture, has embarked on a broad effort to reform school food service, known as the School Meals Initiative for Healthy Children. This program, established through federal legislation amending the School Lunch Program in 1994 and 1996, marked the first significant alteration in nutritional standards and requirements since 1946. According to the new legislation, schools that receive federal assistance must now meet certain nutritional guidelines over each one-week period. For example, the meals served in the cafeteria must have, on average, no more than 30 percent of their calories from fat, and must provide one-third of the government's recommended daily allowance of protein, calories, and certain vitamins and minerals. To continue to receive aid under the National School Lunch program, schools had to institute these changes by the 1996–1997 academic year. Such menu restraints may render the use of commodity foods more difficult in the years to come.

What's Wrong with the School Lunch?

In spite of amendments to the National School Lunch Act and attempts to improve and strengthen NSLP, the school lunch that once held the promise of reforming eating habits, of helping produce children imbued with health and well-being, and of leveling economic differences through the provision of quality meals for those who could not otherwise afford them, has received a failing grade from many critics, parents, and children. A 1994 article in *Redbook* that asked: "Who's to blame?" posited that the system broke down around issues of cost and children's changing eating preferences. Financially, providing lunches that are high quality and low cost has proved to be an increasingly difficult endeavor. Schools that suffer under budget restraints find that they must use free government commodities as the framework for menu planning. These products are not always the most nutritious or desirable foods. Another major difficulty for school food service directors is that children often want high-fat and high-salt foods and refuse more nutritious fare. They want the fast-food, commercial products that they are familiar with from life outside school. According to *Redbook*'s survey of school food service directors, many see the cafeteria as a business and students as customers whom they must entice — regardless of whether they reinforce their poor eating habits. The directors contend that children's tastes are formed before they come to school as a result of three factors: parents who are too busy to cook and hence rely on takeout and fast food; the advertising industry that encourages children to view fast food as "cool"; and the prevalence of microwave ovens that allow even the youngest children to " 'cook,' so that their idea of a meal is something that comes prepared in a box."[23]

For schools with tight budgets, the acceptance of commodities is often a necessity, not a choice. Their only other option is to opt out of the federal system entirely by inviting in vendors, a private contractor, or other food service company to provide meals. Doing so creates another set of nutritional and educational concerns, however, for allowing these entities access to school cafeterias revives a debate regarding commercialism and its relationship to education.

Carrying Commercials to School: Character Lunch Boxes Open the Door

Each year, along with the paper, pencils, and pens that appear magically in store aisles even as families continue to enjoy leisurely days of summer vacation, lunch box displays multiply and signal the coming of the fall season. If a lunch box is to be a part of a child's back-to-school ensemble, the selection process can be an important opportunity for self-expression through a mass-market product.

A significant innovation in lunch box manufacturing was the successful addition of colored lithographs to the outside of the containers. Although there had been some earlier attempts to place lithographs on the surface of metal containers, the true dawn of lunch box art did not break until 1935. In that year, Mickey Mouse became the first cartoon character to grace a child's lunch container. The Disney brothers contracted with the Milwaukee-based Geuder, Paeschke, and Frey Company, a manufacturer of tin trays and toys, to produce an oval-shaped carry-all sporting images of that spunky mouse. Later, the same company manufactured similar boxes carrying images from *Snow White* and *Pinocchio*. According to Scott Bruce, a lunch box aficionado, collector, and historian: "By today's standards, these relics look like glorified canned ham tins, but they revolutionized the schoolroom. Kids discovered that their social standing, if not graces, improved when a Disney pal joined them at the lunch table."[24]

Although the lunch box industry slowed during the 1940s due to wartime mobilization and production, by the early 1950s, the market for metal lunch boxes was well established and fueled by an explosion of American cultural icons that resulted from the new media sensation — television. Indeed for Bruce: "In addition to the postwar affluence that enabled decorated kits to fit the family budget as well as a brown paper bag, the key to the spectacular boom was the television."[25]

The first of the TV character lunch boxes was manufactured in the fall of 1950 by Aladdin Industries, a manufacturer of vacuum bottles. The box featured Hopalong Cassidy, a popular children's hero of the day. Bruce quoted an Aladdin executive who described the phenomena of the "Hoppy" box: "Overnight, the mundane, boring lunch box trade became Big Business.... We sold a staggering six hundred thousand *Hoppy* kits the first year."[26] From that moment forward, the latest TV characters and series logos were carried into schools nation-wide via children's lunch boxes. This metal box inaugurated a new era in the history of American lunch culture. Ultimately, box manufactur-ers added characters from live-action TV shows such as *Lost in Space* and *The Brady Bunch*, and later, movies such as *Star Wars*. These boxes were bright, colorful, and overall visually stimulating. Many included coordinating, decorated thermoses. The illustrations often appeared on the front and back and sometimes around the "band" or outer edge of the box. A few manufacturers made attempts at producing different shapes that mimicked the dome of workmen's style boxes. One promi-nent example of this was the Disney School Bus design, which was immensely popular and sold from 1961 to 1973.

While many TV and popular culture icons appealed to both boys and girls, box designers made a concerted effort to capitalize on gen-der distinctions. Until Barbie hit the "tween" girl scene in the early 1960s, box designers had a difficult time targeting this group. Then around 1962, companies like Aladdin hit on the vinyl lunch carrier as a way to reach the audience of girls who believed themselves to be too old or too sophisticated to carry a simple lunch box. Because of their lightweight construction, these bags were often less durable than other types of lunch containers. Sporting such images as a picture of the pop-ular musical group The Beatles, or the TV series *The Flying Nun*, the bags were appealing for the weight and ability to mimic a purse, although they rarely survived the rigors of a daily trip to and from school for a very long period of time.

Box iconography was a literal method of marketing in the schools. In the opinions of many social critics, members of the educational sys-tem, and parents, TV was a threat to its institutional authority, and they worked to discourage its ascendancy. Ironically, the very structure of the lunch box resembled a television set. In fact, the original box decals often measured four inches, which was approximately the same size as the screens of the first TV sets. Teachers and other educational experts might have been able to avoid the use of TV in their classrooms, "but those thirty small sets on the coatrack shelf never stopped broadcasting."[27]

"McCafeterias": Fast Food Infiltrates the Schools

Although the commercial imagery on lunch boxes and their con-nection to television and other media was disturbing to social critics, educational experts, and parents, more upsetting were the pervasive corporate influences that came in the form of partnerships between corporations and schools toward the end of providing a school lunch. As early as the 1950s, the Gorton's Fish Company developed fish sticks that would obviate the difficulties involved in serving fish to students in the conventional format. In addition, according to the company, their "Perchies" were easy to prepare and store and were proportioned to suit the protein requirements of the Type A school lunch.[28]

An outcome of the 1990s-era legislation to amend the National School Lunch Act has been an increased degree of cooperation among schools, the government, and private industry. Under the rubric of Team Nutrition, the government unveiled a new program that was intended to help schools initiate, publicize, and popularize new school lunch nutritional guidelines. According to the U.S. Department of Agriculture (USDA) journal *Food Review*, "Team Nutrition was created to be the implementation tool for USDA's 'School Meals Initiative for Healthy Children,'" by providing technical assistance, training, and nutrition education. As a part of this effort, USDA established "public and private partnerships that promote food choices for a healthy life." A major corporate partnership in this endeavor was formed with the Walt Disney Company. Disney contributed through the production of thirty-second public service announcements that featured characters from the popular animated movie *The Lion King*. The company also distributed posters for use in the schools. The Scholastic Company, in association with Team Nutrition, helped by developing a nutrition education program for use with a standard school curriculum.[29]

Perhaps the most controversial example of cooperation among the government, the schools, and private industry has been the growth in the number of schools contracting their food service out to management groups and even fast food chains. Companies such as McDonald's, Taco Bell, Pizza Hut, and others have become key players in the effort to bring corporate America into school cafeterias. While these endeavors are generally met with accolades from the student population, (hamburgers and pizza continue to top the list of favorite student meals), the nutritional value of these lunches is subject to question. The fast-food chains answer the nutritional debate with the often valid assertion that their menu items can be adapted to meet new federal nutritional requirements. Taco Bell, for example, has formulated a special low-fat menu for use in schools. Some schools have found that the participation rates in the lunch program are much higher when such foods are a part of the regular meals. A sort of compromise measure adopted by some schools is to follow a regular cycle of "brand days" where fast-food meals are featured.

Fast-food chains have a more difficult time silencing critics who say that their involvement is evidence of the creeping commercialism infiltrating the nation's schools. In an exposé in the September 1998 issue of *Consumer Reports,* the magazine noted that the 1990s had witnessed an incredible growth in the amount of corporate sponsorship visible in the schools. From free book covers provided by Kellogg's to a Pizza Hut reading program that rewarded successful students with a coupon for a free Personal Pan Pizza, commercialism seems to have become a typical feature of school life in America. Critics of mass commercialism in the schools contend that when commercial entities such as McDonald's enter the lunchroom scene, "they are selling more than today's lunch; they are creating tomorrow's consumer habits." Further, critics argue that by providing schools with their products and sponsoring the production and distribution of educational materials, corporations erode the ability of schools to teach children to engage in independent thinking and analysis. A representative for the Center for Science in the Public Interest commented that brand-name products are, for the most part, "not particularly nutritious. Yet, when schools sell fast foods in their cafeterias, they are sending a message that the foods are A-OK."[30]

The Consequences of "Junking" Junk Food in Lean Economic Times

In early 2002, legislators in the Commonwealth of Virginia introduced a proposal to require public schools to eliminate so-called junk food from vending machines on grounds. The impetus for their action was the claim that such poor quality foods contributed to a rising rate of childhood obesity and general poor health. Although schools that participate in NSLP must turn off the machines during hours when the cafeteria is serving, they are free to have them on at other times. The problem is that the schools reap tremendous financial rewards from the sale of such items before, during, and after school hours. The Newport News City Schools, for example, during the 2000–2001 academic year made a profit of $153,191 from vending machine sales to students and staff. The money was then used to cover costs ranging from field trips to general supplies. Many supporters of school vending contend that students should be allowed to make their own judgments about what they should and should not eat. They back up their stand with the argument that if the students cannot obtain the sodas and snacks they want at school, they will bring them from home.[31] In this situation, the schools end up locked in a battle between access to much-needed extra funds and questions about student health and welfare.

At the root, the debate over commercialism in the schools revolves around the question of who is responsible for controlling the curriculum taught in our nation's schools. It involves a sense that schools should be a commercial-free zone where students learn to make judgments without being influenced by outside advertising. Advertisers and corporations that step into this zone are motivated by the need to sell their products and create a bond of goodwill with a captive audience of future consumers.

Defending and Debating the School Lunch

During the twentieth century, the United States shifted away from a system of local and private philanthropy in providing school lunches toward a national effort to feed children as a measure of national defense. Federal assistance was intended to ensure that America's children had the health and strength to win battles of both a literal and figurative nature. Theoretically, a well-fed child would be more apt to absorb learning, and hence better equipped to be a productive citizen.

The national school lunch was a centerpiece of both the New Deal and the Great Society because of its proponents' assertion that it would help "even up the starting line" for children of differing economic and social backgrounds. It appealed to people across the political spectrum because it was neither a conservative nor a socialistic proposal, but an idea grounded in the core belief in equality of opportunity.

Although the initial program acknowledged a dual benefit to both agricultural interests and students, neither the early proponents of child feeding programs nor their successors were prepared to reconcile the often dissonant economic needs of the agricultural community with the nutritional needs of growing children. Nor were advocates equipped to provide accommodations for or barriers against the other coloniz-ing interests — food manufacturers, advertisers, and the media, when they entered into the forum of the school cafeteria.

Over time, various groups of educators, legislators, scientists, busi-nesspeople, and others enamored with the use of statistics as indica-tors of social progress, have entered into the debate over school lunch. The result of their intervention has been the conversion of the school cafeteria and lunch box into a battleground in a series of turf wars, the prize being control over the school lunch.

8

Lunch Ladies: Magazines, Advertising, and the Construction of Women as Lunch Box Packers

American anthropologist Anne Allison spent just over a year conducting fieldwork in Japan. One of the central subjects of her study involved the experiences that she and her nursery school–aged son had as participants in the culture and rituals of the Japanese educational system. Much as in the United States, the school lunch is an important part of both the educational and nutritional goals of Japanese school curricula. Japanese preschools require their students to carry lunches to school with them. These lunches, packed by the children's mothers, are placed in special containers called *obentos*. As a part of learning to obey authority and follow directions, teachers inspect students' boxes to ensure that each student consumes all of the food in his obento every day. Japanese women expend a great deal of time, energy, and money trying to make the contents of the obento box as appealing as possible for their children. There exists in Japan an entire body of cookbook advice literature devoted to the preparation of obentos. In addition, many Japanese companies manufacture obento kits and specialized packing products.

For Japanese mothers, the obento box is a highly public statement of their commitment to their children. The obento production process is inscribed as exclusively female, and it thereby enhances the gendered division of labor in Japanese society. Further, Allison asserts, the obento is a manipulative tool employed by state-sponsored schools "not only to code a natural order, but also to socialize children and mothers into the gendered roles and subjectivities they are expected to assume in a political order desired and directed by the state."[1] She concludes that in Japan, the ritual preparation and consumption of the obento is one element of the ideological indoctrination process that begins for both mother and child once the child enters the public educational system. Through the complex interplay of mothers, children, schools, and the state, the obento becomes a tool by which "mother and child are being watched, judged, and constructed; and it is only through their joint effort that the goal can be accomplished."[2] Important, however, is the fact that although this message is manipulated and sometimes masked by the ideological apparatus, it can also fall victim to subversion by nonconforming subjects. Ultimately, Allison concludes, the "manipulation is neither total not totally coercive" and often it is a source of "pleasure and creativity for both mother and child."[3]

Children's school lunch boxes in the United States, though in a somewhat less structured and organized fashion than their Japanese counterparts, often serve a similar ideological function in perpetuating traditional gender roles and visions of idealized motherhood. Mirroring the obento from another angle, the American school lunch box, its "packers," and "carriers" also benefit or suffer from (depending on one's perspective) similar types of masking, manipulation, and subversion.

The American child's school lunch box also serves as the entry point for commerce. Although various commercial elements have been involved in lunch since the early days of lunch wagons, automats, and diners, the insidious nature of the commercial colonization of school lunches has exploded in recent decades. These individuals and organizations, following the trails set down by earlier reformers, center their efforts on the gatekeepers of the family table — American women and more specifically, mothers. These colonizers cull from the methods and successes of previous reformers and utilize the established channels to sell their products. The result is an increasingly complicated relationship among families, educational institutions, the state, and the marketplace.

Setting the Table: Women and the Responsibility for Lunch

At the April 1944 meeting of the General Federation of Women's Clubs in St. Louis, Missouri, Mrs. Florence Kerr, a representative of the Federal Works Agency spoke regarding the positive effects of child care and recreation centers for working mothers. She noted that more of these centers would be constructed "if suitable locations near the working place of the mothers could be obtained." Later at the meeting, when the new officers of the Federation were introduced, the new president, Mrs. LaFell Dickinson, "advocated that women turn their attention more closely to the task of homemaking in the years to come." She asserted: "Let us have one dynamic cause for our permanent goal, the career of homemaking."[4] In their own fashions, both of these women gave voice to the tension experienced by many American women; the difficulty of balancing between a career and one's family life.

According to a historian of household technology, Ruth Schwartz Cowan, although there have been numerous opportunities for moving more labor outside the home, thus freeing women for paid labor outside the domestic realm (public kitchens and laundries, for example), as a whole Americans have rejected these options out of a desire to preserve the autonomy of the individual, private family unit. The persistence of the autonomous tradition with regard to lunch has meant an incomplete shift of responsibility from mothers to restaurants, the workplace, or school. Regardless of other duties within or outside the home, women have historically carried primary responsibility for the procurement, preparation, and serving of family food. This phenomenon continues to define everyday home life for many American families whether "Mom" is a fulltime homemaker or a career woman.[5]

Although in economic terms, this work is both invisible and undervalued, feeding the family is the core of what is culturally considered to be "women's work."[6] Over the years, attempts to delineate women's place in the American republic have led popular writers and historians to use such terms as "separate spheres," "republican motherhood," and "true womanhood."[7] In prescriptive literature such as women's magazines, writers have used these words to glorify ideal feminine types.[8] The degree to which the majority of women have imbibed and exhibited these prescriptions in their everyday lives is often unclear and difficult to tease out of the historical evidence. What is most significant is the fact that regardless of how individual women accept or contest the concept of a gendered division of labor, it has been a popular standard, often disseminated through the media, by which they have been and continue to be evaluated through their roles as wives and mothers. The quality of a child's school lunch or spouse's work lunch makes a particularly public statement about a woman's domestic abilities and dedication to her loved ones.

Women's magazines provide an interesting glimpse into the evolving cultural expectations of women in the United States. Over the years, articles and advertising in these magazines have contributed to the construction of women as caretakers and consumers. An examination of their content during the twentieth century reveals interesting shifts in women's roles.

During the early years of the twentieth century, some magazine articles acknowledged the lunchtime difficulties faced by the "businesswoman." In November 1911, Bertha Stevenson published "The Young Business Woman's Lunch" in *Good Housekeeping*. Stevenson paid particular attention to the health requirements of the successful businesswoman. In her estimation, lunch was a vital element of the health regimen and needed to be intelligently planned, neither comprised of "anything on the bill of fare that happens to be novel, or that promises to be toothsome," nor sacrificed to "the inspection of the bargain pile" at the local shop. Stevenson encouraged women to look through the helpful articles on diet and health available in magazines, so that they would learn to "stick to plain food, and to cultivate a relish for it." After all:

> Food for working efficiency is the question before the business woman. If she cannot maintain her physical well-being, she cannot take the first step toward success. How can a girl who feeds herself on cream puffs be anything but mercurial? The whole world recognizes that in a crisis women are unequaled for endurance and nerve. But in spite of this there is a tendency among business people to look upon girls as an unreliable and uneven proposition for the long pull. The typical girl laughs easily and cries easily. For business she needs an emotional thermostat.

Ultimately, Stevenson concluded that lunch time for the working girl needed to be used to the best advantage: "Make it furnish food that really feeds, a breath of outdoors, and a restful mood. These are great friends of good looks, good temper, and good health."[9]

In a 1920 *Delineator* article, "The Dinner-Pail of the Business Girl," authors H. M. Conklin and P. D. Partridge argued that the high cost of meals in tea rooms and hotels and the poor quality of food available in delicatessens (éclairs, potato salad, raisin buns, and dill pickles, for example) meant that the dinner pail was the best alternative. At issue was the quality of food within the dinner pail. If packed by the girl herself, it was likely to be insufficient due to being prepared in the haste of the morning rush. If "some other member of the family" put the lunch together, this person, "who has never been in the habit if carrying a lunch," might make the packing part "merely a routine of getting together anything that is convenient and quick to prepare." The authors proceeded to offer menus and packing tips to help make the luncheon meal enticing and filling.[10]

While these earlier articles never broached the possibility of the working woman being a wife or mother, they at least acknowledged the likelihood that some women, or "girls," were employed outside of the sphere of home or domestic service. By the 1930s, however, such articles dedicated to the needs of working women disappeared from the pages of popular women's magazines. What came in their stead was a deluge of articles that focused on the lunch-packing duties of American mothers. These pieces emphasized the significance of a well-planned and well-packed lunch toward the nutritional health of the children of America. They did not, however, mention women packing lunches for themselves.

The Mystique of the Lunch Packer

The ideal American woman, according to the prescriptions laid out in mid- to late-twentieth-century magazines, was one dedicated to her family's health and well-being above all else. This type of woman was the one described in Betty Friedan's 1963 consciousness-raising book *The Feminine Mystique*. Friedan, having herself worked as a writer for such women's magazines as *Redbook* and *Ladies' Home Journal*, decried the way that magazines, advertising, and other popular culture media and the pseudo-scientific proponents of popular sociology and psychology had turned an image of the "happy suburban housewife" into the ideal American woman. Friedan described this phenomenon:

> The suburban housewife — she was the dream image of the young American woman and the envy, it was said, of women all over the

world. The American housewife — freed by science and labor-saving appliances from the drudgery, the dangers of childbirth and the illnesses of her grandmother. She was healthy, beautiful, educated, concerned only about her husband, her children, her home. She had found true feminine fulfillment. As a housewife and mother, she was respected as a full and equal partner to man in his world. She was free to choose automobiles, clothes, appliances, supermarkets; she had everything that women ever dreamed of.[11]

Many of the mid-twentieth-century articles aimed at female lunch packers indicate that lunch packing is an important aspect of a mother's work and, as such, it is one in which she should invest her time, energy, and love. This message often appears alongside information on one or more of the following topics: child nutritional guidelines and daily requirements, including food safety; suggestions for avoiding monotony in the boxed lunch for both luncher and packer; descriptions of the different types of boxes available commercially; an enumeration of the paraphernalia necessary for efficient packing, including ways to increase the convenience and reduce the expense of the process; ideas for special extras to include as a surprise to the lunch eater; sample menus and advance preparation plans; and recipes for foods conducive to packing and carrying.

In much the same way as earlier writers on the penny lunch movement capitalized on women's sense of fear and responsibility for their children's future, writers at midcentury used these same concerns to promote the importance of the home-packed lunch. In brief, they tried to imbue women with a sense of the gravity of the task at hand. A child who had the freedom at school to make à la carte selections from a vendor or even the school-sponsored cafeteria might not make wise nutritious choices. A 1933 *Hygeia* article commented on this problem:

> Years of careful training presumably influence the child to choose and consume a well balanced meal. He may see that his lunch always includes a hot food or beverage, a fruit or vegetable, and a meat or meat substitute, usually as the sandwich filling. However, the young citizen away from the parental roof and watchful eyes may toss his lunch into the wastebasket, buy a hamburger and run out to play. Hence it is up to mothers to pack lunch boxes which are so intriguing that they will be investigated and their contents devoured with avidity.[12]

How, then, to perform this feat of culinary artistry and stealthy nutrition was the subject of the packer advice genre. One of the first indications of a good lunch was its outward appearance. For the boxed lunch, this meant that the box itself was sturdy, "adequate and attractive." The vacuum bottle, which might or might not be sold with the box as a part of a lunch kit, should also exhibit the qualities of neatness and durability. Finally, the various odd containers, whether constructed out of heavy-duty paper or cardboard, glass, metal, or enamel, should be of high quality and be aesthetically pleasing. One author believed that "the influence of one such box and a well-planned lunch" would raise "the standard of the entire class."[13] Another writer noted that it was "very easy to equip a cheap basket after the fashion of the expensive automobile luncheon baskets now on the market." This author, having recommended "light-weight enameled ware dishes," observed: "Fortunately they are not unbeautiful. They usually come in good shapes and have just a little blue for decoration."[14] In matters of box assemblage, a 1933 article in *Hygeia* made extensive notes on the best methods for preparing and wrapping food. The author suggested using decorated sheets of waxed paper "made especially for sandwich wrapping." Some of her other ideas included purchasing special paper products with "Mother Goose decorations," and, for older children, mothers might buy paper cups complete with handles and designs "copied from Dresden china, with all the original lovely colors."[15]

With all of this lively advice, writers attempted to generate a sense of commitment to the home production of well-balanced lunches. By attributing health, safety, and well-being to the contents of a lunch box, writers gave women a feeling of accomplishment and pride in their efforts to send spouses and children out the door with adequate and attractive meals. A 1936 article in *Good Housekeeping* transformed the lunch packing process into something of an art, albeit a time-consuming task. The author encouraged readers to approach this duty "in a spirit of adventure." She observed that leafing through magazines and cookbooks, tarrying in food shops "with their enticing bottles and jars, boxes and cans," and "even careful scouting of soda-fountain menus" might lead packers to "perfectly grand luncheon ideas" that they had "never dreamed of before." She continued:

> Say to yourself, "Monday's lunch is going to be scrumptious," and
> make it so with the very best sandwich mixture you can concoct; add
> crisp celery, some moist and velvety chocolate cake, and a big juicy
> pear. Tuesday's, in contrast, might be homey with pink slices of cold
> ham baked as your family think only you can bake it, sweet and spicy

with brown sugar and clove. It's always a grand old favorite for sand-wiches, tucked with lettuce leaves between slices of whole-wheat bread. A nice big tomato would go well, too, and that perfect gingerbread from your special recipe. Wednesday's lunch can be thrifty, but with a thrift so toothsome that Dad may even suspect that you are exceeding the budget. And it's only left-over meatloaf that has taken a new lease on life with carrots and — well, you find out for yourself. It's the Left-over Meat Sandwich recipe we give you on page 164. We are so grateful to the reader in Missouri who sent it to us. And so on through the week until, before you know it, Saturday has come, and you find your-self looking forward to next week with new lunches to conquer.[16]

In 1964, Bonnie Lehman, a woman who had clearly taken her job as a lunch packer seriously, wrote "Readin', Writin', and Lunchboxes," for *Parents* magazine. Lehman described a morning routine that was not at all harried, but in contrast, found her rising on some mornings

bright and shiny eyed with energy to spare ... and when morning greets me with a smile in return, I like to tuck a little surprise in the lunch-boxes. (This happens seldom enough, I might add, that my surprises don't lose their surprise). These are whatever strikes my fancy at the moment, such as a candy bar, a brand-new pencil or (for my husband) a funny picture or joke cut from a magazine.

Lehman commented that she found it necessary to prepare a different luncheon menu for her children and her husband. Although he appears in the photographs that accompany the article, Lehman's husband is not an active participant, but merely looks on lovingly as his wife stirs a pot of his favorite chili. Lehman demonstrated the importance of the lunch box to marital bliss when she cautioned read-ers:

May I suggest these dishes make their first appearance at the dinner table rather than in the lunchbox? I can well remember the time, after we were first married, when I tried two new dishes in my husband's lunch. He disliked them both (intensely!) and I still get kidded about it sometimes. A new food stands or falls on its own merits when eaten out of a lonely lunchbox. When the new dish is shared, a dash of wifely enthusiasm can make it taste better. As my mother says, "Salt and psychology make the best seasoners."[17]

Alice D. Hanrahan, author of "Your Child's First Lunch Box" in the September 1954 issue of *Parents*, noted in her byline: "Four of the author's seven children are lunch-toters, so she advises you from con-siderable lunch-packing experience." To an uncertain young mother, such credentials might have placed this author squarely within the ranks of the lunch box experts. Hanrahan clearly had her finger on the pulse of lunch room culture. In her piece, she observed that the lunch box for a young child needed to be particularly well planned and attractive for "this one link with home should give him a feeling of security and being loved." She suggested allowing a child to go to the store to select a special lunch box. A good way to avert potential lunch room embarrassment, she continued, was to stage a mock lunch at home "to acquaint your child with his lunch box and the type of lunch he'll take to school." Hanrahan also commented that in spite of the many ideas on lunch packing to be found in magazines and cookbooks, many children preferred stability and sameness in their food, so she advised that mothers not try to "enforce variety." Finally, she urged them to take special care in their packing routines because children compare and discuss their lunches among themselves. She closed with this nugget of wisdom: "Send your child to school with a lunch box he can display proudly, a nourishing lunch he'll enjoy and an occasional surprise to keep him interested in this important midday meal."[18]

Hanrahan described a substantive responsibility for mother. She had to provide tasty nutritious treats and love in a portable format. The child's lunch, in her estimation, symbolized his status among his peers and expressed the mother's caring ability and child-focused life. Prescription and force were no ways to win a child's affections. The best solution was to empower the child with a sense of control over the box and the fare within it. A November 1956 *Parents* article took this process one step further. In "Candidates for School Lunches," the magazine provided a "ballot" for children allowing them to select what would go in to their school lunch boxes. While their parents were choosing between Democrat Adlai Stevenson and Republican Dwight D. Eisenhower in the presidential election of that year, children, too, could exercise their decision-making power by selecting among categories including sandwiches, soups and hot dishes, salads and finger foods, desserts and fruits, and beverages. The last column, "Dark Horses," was a checklist for mothers of "good will ambassadors to add warmth and fun to your child's school lunch box." Among the ideas offered were: special napkins; a typed menu for the lunch of the day where, "to promote good food habits," the mother could "explain briefly what each food offers nutritionally"; labels on sandwiches and maybe an extra "to share"; homemade fudge; a "pocket puzzle"; a set of jacks;

or, finally, a "shiny coin — to buy something special — perhaps for you."[19] Here, the ideal mother could reap the rewards of her child-centered life as she garnered a material manifestation of her child's love.

Many of the lunch packing articles from the 1960s down to the present day continue to emphasize the mother's responsibility to make her children healthy and happy. In 1987's "Packed with Love: Lunch-Box Foods Kids Will Eat," *Parents* magazine told readers: "Packing lunch for her children must surely be one of the supreme tests of a mother's love."[20] According to the prescriptions offered in advice articles, this love is best demonstrated through foods that are homemade and home packed. In 1999, on the Web site marthastewart.com, Martha Stewart, the modern good-living guru and self-appointed expert on all things domestic, proposed her ideas for packing love in the lunch box that were nothing short of food as art. Among her ideas was an apple cup that involved nearly as much work as a main course dinner. The recipe instructed the chef to cut an apple in half and then use a melon baller to scoop out the flesh. Next, the would-be artist was to use a lemon stripper to "carve the child's initial into the flesh of the apple. This takes only moments but is guaranteed to bring a smile to your child's face." The final stage of the production process involved filling the exposed cavity with chicken salad and then placing the whole works into "a plastic container until it's time to say goodbye." Stewart had other ideas as well, such as making a cereal bracelet out of Cheerios or Fruit Loops and then attaching a note to the edible jewelry such as "Have a Great Day."[21] With these ideas, Stewart assumes that mothers both cook in a kitchen equipped with such specialized tools as melon ballers and lemon strippers, and that they have the time necessary to devote to preparing special lunch box menus.

The New Lunch Packers Mystique

An analysis of lunch packer advice literature in women's magazines from the 1930s to the 1970s reveals sparse references to working women packing a lunch for themselves. Authors of articles instead focused on the fulfilling role of stay-at-home lunch packer. One article in the February 1930 issue of *Woman's Home Companion*, "Lunching Alone" took as its focus the lunch of the homemaker:

> If you eat alone at noon doubtless you have read many articles about
> the importance of the food your husband chooses at lunchroom or

restaurant, many discussions of the foods that should comprise the school lunch. But how much attention have you ever given to your own problem? The problem of the woman who eats at home is not the same as that of the business man or woman. His is simply one of spending his lunch money wisely. Your problem is one of utilizing left-overs, of choosing food which can be prepared with that minimum of time and trouble you are willing to spend on yourself.

Too often the woman who eats alone makes no attempt to convert leftovers into more palatable form, gives no thought to the proper nutritional balance of her meal — if indeed her collection of odds and ends can be graced by so substantial a name. Such a procedure is wrong, physically and psychologically. For men and women in business lunch time brings a certain relaxation, a chance to turn the mind away from the business of the morning. Lunch time should have a compara-ble meaning for the woman who lunches at home.[22]

A *Better Homes and Gardens* article from March 1963, "What the Men Are Having for Lunch!" further illuminates the type of people having lunch in public places. The "out-to-lunch" crowd was made up of men, not women. The article surveyed eleven of the "top-notch" restaurants across the country to find out which luncheon dishes were most popular with men. Author Myrna Johnston commented: "Some of their favorites are elegant enough for dinner when you invite the boss; others are downright delicious for a family supper or a casual buffet."[23]

Beginning in the 1970s, however, some recognition of the diverse roles played by women began to creep back into magazines in general and lunch packing articles in particular. The birth of two new maga-zines during this decade, *Working Woman* and *Working Mother*, under-scored the fact that many readers of women's magazines had to reconcile the demands of work and family life with the cultural prescriptions for ideal American womanhood.

Articles from the 1970s exhibit an increased sense of the need for different types of lunches for different types of people. For example, in "Lunch-To-Go," a 1976 article in *Ladies' Home Journal* by Sue Huffman, the magazine's Food and Equipment Editor, large photo-graphs sent a visual message about matching carrier, container, and con-tents. The first three images show what are clearly masculine hands grasping respectively: an attaché case, a brown bag, and a traditional workman's style domed lunch box. The final three images show more feminine hands holding two different purse-style bags and a children's

Disney school bus metal lunch box. Along with these pictures, the author provides sample menus for what she described as a "festive, teen, hearty, diet, junior," or "health" lunch. While the menus and the boxes are not explicitly linked to the words below, the sample menu for a "hearty" meal appears beneath the workman's box and the "diet" and "health" menus are to be found under the purse-style representations. The author commented that there had been a resurgence in carried lunches because they were "suddenly the most satisfying way to get better food that's better for you — at better prices." The article presents a paradox between its visual cues and its verbal ones. According to the introduction, the recipes provided would yield food that was amenable to transport to school, office, or factory; yet like the wives and mothers assumed to be doing the preparation, the aforementioned foods could "happily stay at home as well."[24]

An article with a similar message appeared in the September 1977 issue of *Good Housekeeping*: "These days, everyone is brown-bagging it! Lunch at the desk or out on the job saves time and money, helps watch calories too." Although this article also showed different carriers and their meals, unlike the previous article, it included a head shot of each luncher: a young female athlete with her baseball cap, ball, and glove at her side, a male construction worker, and male and female office workers. Under each image appeared a sample menu. For the young athlete, a "School Lunch"; for the construction worker, "Hearty Fare"; for the female office worker, "Calorie Counter's Delight"; and for her male counterpart, an "Attaché Case Lunch." The article included other recipes designated as "Portable Breakfast" and "Shopper's Special."[25]

While each of these articles acknowledged that a woman might have to pack a lunch for her own day on the job as well as for her husband and children, they made strong gender-based distinctions about the types of food and containers that a woman should use. The dieter's lunch and the purse-style bags were clearly feminine while anything hearty and professional was masculine.

Another interesting feature of these two articles is the fact that neither made any suggestion of culinary assistance from a husband. The preparation of lunch was still a woman's job. During World War II, as many women moved out into the workforce for the first time, an article in *Parents* in October 1943 pictured Alan Bunce, the popular star of the radio serial *Young Doctor Malone*, in the kitchen with his two sons as they prepared the boys' lunches for the day. Bunce, complete with an apron, smiled as he busily prepared sandwiches for the open boxes that lined the table. The article advised women that if they desired to receive any such assistance from their husbands, they had a responsibility as well: "If you want Dad and the children to help in packing their own lunch boxes remember to make it convenient — the chances are they're not as familiar with the kitchen as you are!"[26] Interestingly, my investigation did not turn up another image of a man actively participating in lunch preparations until a September 1992 issue of *Working Mother*. In that article, similar to the one from 1943, the author constructed a scenario whereby mom had done the background preparations: "Now you can please everyone without being a short-order cook! Just whip up a batch of any of these terrific, easy recipes, then let your gang choose their favorite add-ins and garnishes to pack along with lunch. Here, Dad jazzes up a Classic Chicken Salad with mango chutney and slivered almonds."[27]

How, then, could a woman, burdened with the responsibility for providing love and nutrition in a lunch box, cope with the time pressures of being a working mother? Enter convenience products and advertising.

Buying In: Convenience and Love at the Grocery Store

Women's magazines depend on a combination of advertiser dollars and subscription fees to make a profit.[28] In her study of women's magazines from the early 1980s, Ellen McCracken employs critical techniques from the field of literary analysis to "decode" the messages sent by women's magazines. Her main point is that women are active readers who can accept, reject or interpret content according to individual needs and desires, but, according to Stuart Hall's neo–Gramscian model which views ideology as a site of struggle, there is a consistent set of underlying tropes at work in the meanings these magazines and advertisers employ to sell products. In essence, the magazines are agents of cultural hegemony that help make a social system that equates women with consumption. McCracken ultimately agrees with Stuart Hall that magazines are a "leaky system," because the reality of life is often in direct contrast to what readers see in the pages of a magazine. In

McCracken's estimation, advertisers may take advantage of this situation, using the very "unreality" to sell products.[29]

In many women's magazines, advertising worked along with editorial content to construct idealized American women. For example, an advertisement beside a 1951 *Good Housekeeping* article, "From Freezer to Lunchbox," was for McCormick/Schilling Pure Vanilla Extract. The article told readers that with a home freezer, they could prepare sandwiches and desserts ahead of time and "store enough lunches for a week in one free morning." While the idea of putting up lunches in advance might save time at one end, the preparation of homemade breads, fillings, and desserts still required a significant time commitment.[30] The advertisement provided a recipe for "Date-Nut Sandwiches," using, of course, one teaspoon of vanilla, and asserted that the vanilla "puts extra goodness in school day sandwiches and desserts ... adds richer, fuller flavor that won't cook out, bake out or freeze out!" The article and ad, therefore, complemented one another.

By the 1970s, however, the tension between articles and advertisements had become more pronounced. In the September 1977 *Good Housekeeping* article "Lunch Box Specials," discussed earlier, amid the various recipes for homemade sandwiches, cakes, and other lunch box delights appeared several small advertisements for the Betty Crocker product Hamburger Helper, which had appeared on supermarket shelves in 1970.[31] As more women entered the workforce and new technologies allowed food processors to develop time-saving meal alternatives, the messages broadcast by magazine articles and advertiser seemed increasingly at odds.

This trend continued into the 1980s. As in previous decades, lunch packing articles continued to assume that the wife and mother was also the chief lunch packer. "Lunches Kids Will Love," in the September 1989 issue of *Parents* magazine, offered ideas for ways to increase the child appeal of boxed lunches. The author suggested trying special finger foods and other labor-intensive, bite-sized treats. Rather than being concerned with specific foods in the lunch box, the author told readers to concentrate on overall nutrition quality and food safety. The most interesting aspect of this article was its proximity to a full-page advertisement for ready-made Jell-O Pudding snacks. The advertisement consisted of a collage of three pudding cups, a handwritten note, an open lunch box, and a Polaroid picture of a young boy, sitting before an open book, a look of smug satisfaction on his face. This youngster is pleased with himself for he, in the guise of the "school board," wrote a note to his parents requesting three extra pudding snacks be placed in his lunch from this time forward. The reason being that he, as the star student in an accelerated reading class, had used up so many brain cells that only a Jell-O snack could replace them. The advertising agency responsible for this advertisement employed a creative approach to reach the parents. Naming neither mother nor father, the ad could be addressed to either one, though the placement of the ad in *Parents*, which was read primarily by women, suggests women as the intended audience. The ad itself is humorous. The boy has clearly attempted to manipulate his parents by invoking the authority of the school board. The subtext of the ad demonstrates who truly holds the power to influence family purchasing decisions — the child.

The interplay between this ad and article is interesting because of the juxtaposition of a mass-produced convenience product next to the time-consuming ideas such as the crafting of animal-shaped sandwiches with cookie cutters. The consistent message to women is clear: that either through culinary artistry or consumer activity, the lunch box is more than a meal; it is a symbol of love. The one is a valid symbol of the other. This advertisement plays on a key element in selling convenience products to women — guilt. This sense of maternal guilt stems from the idealized image of mother as caretaker and homemaker that continues to dominate women's magazines even as more women find themselves living lives that require them to balance these domestic duties with other tasks and responsibilities outside the home.[32] Indeed, advertisers have responded to the increasing numbers of working mothers by redefining "homemade" to include foods carried from home but that originated on the grocer's shelf.

In recent years, manufacturers have begun to offer a new alternative to the lunch box and the school cafeteria — the "lunchable." Lunchables are convenient, commercially produced, complete ready-to-go lunches in disposable boxes. Although the brainchild of product developers at the Oscar Mayer meat processing company in 1988, today many other companies distribute similar products under different labels.[33] In addition to the market explosion in other brands of lunchables, there has been a tremendous increase in the variety of meals available. The original Lunchable was comprised of a simple combination of different meats, cheeses, and crackers. Today, they range from make-your-own pizza and taco kits, to waffles with syrup and dessert packs of cookies, frosting and toppings.

According to a June 1995 article in the trade publication *Supermarket News*: "It was a breakthrough concept, an early hit with both consumers and marketing gurus. Having since settled in as a fixture, the lunch kit still reigns from a marketing standpoint as one of the few consistently dynamic impulse items in the processed meat case." A representative from Oscar Mayer stated: "From a consumer standpoint, one of the keys to success for lunch combinations is that moms are challenged with what to make for lunch every day. Kids get bored, and it is a convenient solution to those two consumer problems."[34] In addition, another Oscar Mayer executive has noted that the products were initially marketed toward children "as the eaters, and parents as the buyers." With the passage of time, however, their marketing strategy has evolved to include adult consumers. Product developers, for instance, hit on low-fat options as the way to entice adult lunch carriers.

While children might like the foods in Lunchables and parents might enjoy their convenience, nutritionists have criticized the trend toward such products because they are often high in fat, sodium, and sugar. According to a 12 October 1999 article in the *Atlanta Constitution*, Oscar Mayer, as the leader in the lunch kit category, had sold some 1.6 billion Lunchables since the line debuted, with an annual increase in sales of 15 percent. Moreover, in a survey of Atlanta-area elementary students, children preferred Lunchables over home-packed or cafeteria food. While one third-grader was "happily eating his pizza Lunchables," one of his comrades was "ignoring his homemade peanut butter and jelly sandwich because it was 'smooshed.'"[35] Some schools, in an effort to maintain student participation in the school lunch program, have begun to include a Lunchable-type meal in their menu rotations.

Although a 1999 survey of home-packed school lunches in Fairfax County, Virginia, revealed that the lunch provided by the school cafeteria was the most nutritious option for students, the dietary intern who conducted the study found that when competing against most home-packed lunches, the Lunchable was actually superior in nutrition. Most home-packed lunches contained no fruit or vegetables and too many sweets. The typical home-packed lunch was: a ham sandwich on white bread with mayonnaise, a bag of pretzels, a six pack of peanut butter crackers, and a Capri Sun brand fruit drink. According to the intern, a child with a home-packed lunch was "no better off than with a Lunchables; in fact, it could be worse."[36]

Advertisers have capitalized on the fun factor and child-pleasing qualities of the prepackaged meals. One advertising campaign that was disseminated through both women's magazines and television commercials pitted the Lunchables product directly against the home-packed lunch. It featured children peering discontentedly into paper bags while one smiling child proudly displayed his Lunchables. Another ad that appeared in the February 2002 issues of both *Better Homes and Gardens* and *Woman's Day* showed a smiling boy holding his Lunchables Cracker Stackers with the words "Groovy Mom" above his head. The advertisers are sending a clear message through those two words: "good" mothers buy Lunchables.

Gilding the Lunch Box

Lunch boxes are invested with special meaning and significance by both packers and carriers. A curious phenomenon of late has been the increasing nostalgia attached to old metal and even plastic lunch boxes. Dubbed as collector's items, authentic boxes from the 1930s to 1980s can claim price tags into the thousands of dollars. The market for such treasures has grown so large that reproductions are now widely available. The Hallmark greeting card company has begun to market a line of miniature tin lunch box ornaments sporting such popular cultural heroes as Super Man, Howdy Doody, Hot Wheels race cars, and the Lone Ranger, among others. Similarly, many gift shops are selling miniature candy-filled reproductions featuring images such as the Candy Land board game, Mickey Mouse, and GI Joe, to name just a few. For those hard-core collectors unsatisfied by reproduction boxes, there are innumerable antiques stores and Web sites that specialize in the sale of authentic lunch boxes. Why do lunch boxes conjure up such a sense of nostalgia? Certainly part of the reason has to do with the near disappearance of tin lunch boxes after a mythical "mother's crusade" in Florida petitioned the state government to eliminate metal boxes.[37] Still, the eclipse of metal boxes does not alone account for their collectability, nor does it explain why people seek out older plastic boxes as well. Perhaps the old-fashioned boxes evoke memories of an era before Lunchables and other convenience foods had made inroads into the nation's lunch rooms. The metal boxes that saw their heyday during the 1950s and 1960s might represent in part the notion of an ideal wife and mother, investing her time and energy into packing a well-balanced, appetizing lunch for her charges. Feminists such as Betty Friedan might contend that these boxes are symbolic of the feminine mystique that denied women an identity outside the domestic realm. In this sense, the lunch box is tied to modern Americans' perception that today's women are busier with work outside the home and less family-oriented than in the past. It may, in fact, be an image of a family that never existed in reality.[38]

Much as early lunch containers represented the movement of men and children away from the home, modern convenience products, lunch-related material culture and dining habits connote motion and the dispersal of the family to work and school. In the latter decades of the twentieth century and now into the twenty-first, it is the manufacture and distribution of convenience products, rather than food containers, that have seen growth. From drinkable yogurt in a tube to prepackaged individual servings of crackers, potato chips, and even carrots and dip, the explosion in single-serving food items demonstrates that a large and growing market exists for foods that require little or no preparation. Even when eating at home, Americans seem to be less interested in spending time preparing meals. At the 2001 Food Marketing Institute trade show in Chicago, food processors unveiled more new products in the "home meal replacement" category. Sagging supermarket sales in recent years have demonstrated a trend toward more fast-food dining and takeout-style meals. The Food Marketing Institute conducted a survey of consumers in which they found that three out of four consumers cooked at home at least three times a week, but of that number, fewer than half reported making a meal from scratch. In fact, less than a third of people under the age of forty listed themselves as "scratch cooks." A newspaper reporter covering the convention commented: "Convenience used to mean condensed soup, TV dinners or ready-to-eat breakfast cereals. Then came Hamburger Helper. Now it's bagged salads to go with a pre-basted pork tenderloin that requires little cooking, casseroles out of a box or the no-refrigeration-needed spaghetti dish that heats in the microwave."[39]

Maternal Love within a Box of Boxes

Over the course of the twentieth century, changing family structures, work and meal patterns have forced many women to develop new ways of fulfilling their responsibility for family food. Still, as the women's magazines continue to show, and the trend toward more convenience products attests, the persistence of social prescriptions that place the bulk of responsibility for family meals on women mean that many women must seek out alternative ways to fulfill that role. Advertisers and manufacturers have responded to the changing situation in ways that have made the balancing of one's domestic responsibilities somewhat easier. Whether for good or ill, the trend in the direction of convenience continues. While the lunchbox represents a mythical golden age; the Lunchable is a symbol of the postmodern era: no box, no packing, just pure consuming at the economic and physical level.

The obento of the Japanese school child is a miniaturized version of a five- or six-course meal. Both the containers and the food within them are highly stylized and reflect general Japanese attitudes about the proper presentation and contents of a meal. The food and its container are coded messages about "social order and the role that gender plays in sustaining and nourishing that order."[40] Like the Japanese obento box, the lunch box of an American school child is a powerful material representation of a mother's love. The lunch box is, in a sense, a metaphor or synecdoche of maternal love. During the twentieth and into the twenty-first centuries, the ideological function of the lunch box has been the contested ground of various individuals and groups ranging from scientists and educators to the government and advertisers. Despite their often different purposes and approaches, these interests have shaped the way American women view their maternal responsibilities.

The colonization process that has affected lunch in general has also had a profound effect on the modern American child's school lunch box. Through the efforts of early school lunch advocates and federal nutrition education campaigns, the lines of communication among schools, the government, and parents were established. With such lines open, a whole host of interests gained access to mothers — the gatekeepers of the family table. With regard to women's roles in packing school lunches, the food manufacturers and marketers have had the most influence. Playing on the ideology of true motherhood, commercial products are marketed in such a way as to render maternal love a purchasable commodity. Typified by the Lunchable, the lunch box of the modern American student has become a collection of small boxes, bags, or other containers that are the products of a trip to the grocery store rather than the result of hours of slavish maternal labor. In essence, it has been reduced to a "box of boxes" that when taken as a whole provides evidence of the ideological manipulation of food and gender achieved through the interaction of colonizing forces.

Conclusion:
Blame Not the Oreo

On 27 July 2002, a troubling and telling news story broke. It appeared under the headline, "Obese Diabetic Sues Fast Food Restaurant." Caesar Barber, a fifty-six-year-old man from the Bronx, had filed a suit in the Bronx Supreme Court in which he named McDonald's, Wendy's, Burger King, and Kentucky Fried Chicken as responsible for his weight and other "serious health problems." Barber was quoted: "They said '100 percent beef.' I thought that meant it was good for you." Barber, who at five-foot-ten weighed 272 pounds, had had heart attacks in 1996 and 1999 and continued to suffer from diabetes, high blood pressure, and high cholesterol. He told reporters that he had consumed fast food for "decades, thinking that it was good for him until his doctor cautioned him otherwise."[1] On the advice of his lawyers, Barber later dropped the suit.

Even so, at the McDonald's corporation over the past several years, there has been little cause for celebration. Since the first lawsuits aimed at fast-food chains, not only have the summons continued to roll in, but the corporation and the food industry at large have faced additional scrutiny and attacks. Journalist and social commentator Eric Schlosser wrote a 2001 nonfiction best-seller *Fast Food Nation: The Dark Side of the All-American Meal*. Although highly critical of the fast-food industry in general, Schlosser was particularly disparaging of McDonalds's employment practices, food quality, and supply-purchasing habits.[2] With many more American consumers ranting against big business and protesting against the insidious nature of advertising and commercial culture, filmmaker Morgan Spurlock fed the flames when in 2004 he released his documentary/feature film *Super-Size Me*. The first-time filmmaker was nominated for an Academy Award for the production about which he stated:

> *Super Size Me* is one man's journey into the world of weight gain, health problems and fast food. It's an examination of the American way of life and the influence that has had on our children, the nation and the world at large.... Leading up to my sadistic epiphany, you couldn't turn on the TV without hearing about the "obesity epidemic in America" or of the girls who were suing McDonald's. It seemed as though all of America and the world had suddenly gotten "Fat Happy."[3]

In 2005, as a part of its effort to bounce back from the attacks, McDonald's launched a new advertising campaign featuring a Ronald McDonald who has undergone an extreme makeover. No longer sporting baggy pants and hocking hamburgers and fries, Ronald now talks about the importance of good health and a sensible, balanced diet. Toward that end, the restaurant chain has even modified its menu, adding more options such as salads and fruit, and even introducing the choice of fruit or milk as a part of the Happy Meals marketed to children.

Such legal and cultural actions followed by industry reactions raise questions about where or with whom responsibility for a person's food choices and their consequences rest. During the twentieth century, as reformers, corporations, the state, schools, and the media entered American kitchens, each claiming to have the answer to nutritional health and well-being, the issue of what to eat and why was muddied rather than illuminated. Even before World War II, colonizers, or ideology shapers, in the guise of efficiency experts and progressive reformers, endeavored to influence how people thought about and consumed food. Because of industrialization and the advent of systems of mass education, lunch, as the most public and hence most visible meal of the day, became the focus of their efforts. Late-nineteenth- and early twentieth-century progressive reformers expressed early interest, bringing concerns about the relationship between nutrition and industrial or educational efficiency into the public spotlight. Their work set the stage for business and government leaders during World War II who relied on the exigencies of wartime mobilization to try to improve civilian eating habits. The war lent a new sense of urgency to the problem of poor nutrition. In the past, advocates of the colonization process had seen the eating habits of the poor and immigrants as contributing to health problems and bad working habits; under the strain of war, however, nutrition became an issue of patriotism that had implications for our national security. From then on, the language of nutritional advice and advertisement was melded as new public/private partnerships participated in the formation of an American eating ideology.

Following the war, the efforts to rationalize and routinize lunch did not abate but only shifted to accommodate new circumstances. In many workplaces, lunch became the terrain of union-management conflicts. Meanwhile, in American schools, the government, businesses, dieticians, and education experts worked both independently and cooperatively to develop new standards of child nutrition and new measures of student achievement. Their efforts helped push the school lunch to the core of equal opportunity programs. Finally, during the twentieth and into the twenty-first centuries, broad changes in women's roles at home and in the workplace rendered the packed lunch an arena of conflict over the nature of motherhood itself.

While it is simple to define modern American eating habits as the product of twentieth-century ideology shapers, providing a concise definition of what that ideology is becomes less clear-cut. In fact, American eating ideology is constantly changing and ever contested. The way Americans think about food and their eating habits is the product of the complex interplay of different social, economic, and political factors. It is clouded by mixed and sometimes antagonistic messages. For example, while one nutrition guru promotes a diet high in fat and protein, another warns that such a regime will result in heart disease. America's progression from an agricultural to industrial to informational economy is chronicled through the story of the colonization of lunch. The players have changed little over time, but they have been joined by a new teammate who grew out of their combined efforts — the market researcher.

"And Now a Word from Our Sponsor": Marketing the American Dream

The notion that we inhabit a consumer society is difficult to dispute. Indeed, the literature and historiography of American consumerism is vast. As an interpretive tool, "consumerism" is rather in vogue in both history and material culture studies. Sociologist Manuel Castells unites some of the popular themes in historical and material cultural research in his effort to understand the changing face of capitalism in the postindustrial world. In his discussion of modern life, he tells us that beginning in the mid–1970s, a new technological paradigm and a new organizational logic began to converge and came to constitute the historical basis for a new economy, which he defined as "informational." Within this model, one of the key elements is the dispersal of production along networks of firms as opposed to traditional, old-style, vertically integrated corporations.[4]

One of the significant effects of this transformation is its role in altering the relationship between producers and consumers. As much as the organization of work and the relationship between employers and employees has evolved since the publication of Frederick Winslow Taylor's *Principles of Scientific Management* in 1911, the changing relationship between producers and consumers has kept apace. In many industries, extracting a profile of the average consumer has taken precedence over the utility of time and motion studies once aimed at increasing productivity and efficiency. Now, when manufacturers reach a certain level of reliability in production, the urgent task for management shifts from one of manpower to one of market share. The customer may always be right, but the issue becomes finding out just exactly what he is right about. Knowledge about the consumer is a product in and of itself.

Armand and Michèle Mattelart, authors of *Theories of Communication*, also broach this topic. They try to show how the trend away from Fordism and Taylorism, with their emphases on rationalizing production, has been replaced in "contemporary cybernetic rationality" by an effort to manage both production and consumption. What they describe ultimately is in fact a commodification of the consumer profile wherein data on individuals and groups are collected and analyzed through "computerized production technologies." The knowledge about needs and desires gained from these studies is not treated in a linear producer-to-customer fashion, but in contrast, "informs and feeds the circular movement of programming, production and consumption, which, though always unstable, tends none the less towards functional and affective integration of the consumer into the mechanisms of the market economy."[5] In short, the consumer becomes a vital link in a new flexible network, as the integration of system and user blurs what were once rigid distinctions.[6] Ultimately, consumers are commodified and homogenized into markets based on common characteristics, needs, and desires.

So how did we arrive at this juncture — where the avatar of the consumer is as much the product as any material object or service? Thanks in large part to the fusion of science, statistics, and strategy into a new field of study — market research. In the 13 October 2004 issue of *USA Today* newspaper, an article, "This Man Is Watching You Eat," provides a useful lens into the relationship among producers and consumers. The subject of the article, one Harry Balzer, an employee of the NPD Group, described as "one of the nation's leading market research firms," has spent the past twenty-six years studying facts and statistics about the nation's eating habits. He and his colleagues utilize a range of techniques to study how Americans eat at home and in various restaurant settings. The "information" they glean from surveys, food diaries, and other statistics is then packaged into a reference work, complete with charts and tables, and sold to "almost all the leading food and beverage marketers, including manufacturers, restaurant chains and supermarket chains."[7] The data collected in their studies, in turn, helps industry leaders predict where trends are heading and they can then tailor their products and services accordingly. Such information helps mitigate the effects of unpredictable consumer behavior.

Building a New Pyramid: The Culmination of Colonization

This is not a conspiracy. Today's colonizers, mirroring those of the past include members of the government, media, industry, assorted experts from the worlds of science and medicine, and now the market researcher, each continue to exercise their specialized and particular influence over the way Americans eat. They feed on each other's efforts in a complex web of tangled messages. Sometimes their goals harmonize, while at other times they conflict. What is clear, however, is that they continue to build on the foundation constructed by earlier colonizers. Each player helps propel the process forward.

Much as malnourishment at all economic levels disturbed progressive reformers, and later World War II food planners, similar concerns today center around the so-called obesity epidemic. The potential consequences of obesity include diabetes, heart conditions, high blood pressure, and many others. A recent study by the International Obesity Task Force found that 67 percent of Americans now fall into the obese category based on scores on the Body Mass Index chart. The study also concluded that obesity is a problem in much of western Europe. In fact, topping the list above the United States were Greece, Germany, the Czech Republic, Cyprus, Slovakia, Malta, and Finland. Finishing just below the United States were Slovenia, Ireland, and Britain.[8] "So what?" you might say. Why should the government care about how much a person weighs? Is that not a matter of personal responsibility? The answer to that question is "sort of." There is no doubt that what a person introduces into his or her body is a matter of personal choice. However, due in large part to the legacy of the early colonizers and the continued efforts of later reformers, food continues to be both a personal and a political issue.

The reasons behind the public interest in individual heath are manifold, and echo the refrains sung by past activists and experts. A well-nourished, healthy worker or student is more productive and efficient and better able to face the challenges of the day. Another important benefit of good nutrition is the decreased risk of disease and sickness. For industry and government, a healthy population ultimately costs less money to maintain. How, then, to produce a healthy citizenry? Education is the key. Not surprisingly, education is the new focal point and meeting ground of all modern colonizers.

In early 2004, the Department of Agriculture announced plans to revamp, revise, and update the federal food pyramid. The pyramid, which made its debut in 1992, was in need of an overhaul to reflect the changing lifestyles of Americans and the evolution of scientific and medical research on the subjects of nutrition and health. The department invited suggestions and comments from the general public, special interest groups, scholars, industry, and lobbyists. The goal of the revised food code was the same as it had been in 1992: to reduce the amount of information about food and diet into a simple, easily digestible set of guidelines. According to an Associated Press article from 6 April 2004, the department had received hundreds of comments from interested and concerned citizens across the nation, one of whom hoped that the government would include a warning regarding the "poisonous" nature of vegetables. Aside from the pipe dreams of picky eaters everywhere, the article noted that both industry and lobbyists had "seized the opportunity to weigh in with changes, hoping to prove that people can't live well without their products." In that vein, the walnut industry took the prize for persistence, sending more than twenty letters "touting the nut's alpha-linolenic acid, an essential fatty acid that cannot be manufactured by the body." Even more interesting were the letters from representatives of industries that manufacture high-carbohydrate products. Reflective of the current national obsession with carbohydrate intake and its effect on weight loss or gain, these industry insiders were quite concerned that their products not be positioned at the top of the pyramid. The logic behind the food pyramid is that those items in the largest base section should be the biggest component of one's diet, to be supplemented by items from the higher levels of the structure. The 1992 pyramid placed bread, cereal, rice, and pasta in the lowest position, followed by a second level of fruits and vegetables, a third of milk, cheese, meat, fish, eggs, and nuts, topped off, at the summit, by fats, oils, and sweets.[9]

With every major food industry lobbyist, vegetarian activist, and vegetable-hater waiting in anxious expectation, at long last, in April 2005, the Department of Agriculture unveiled its new, colorful and user-friendly guide. So, who wound up in the dreaded top spot? No one at all. The new pyramid takes an entirely different approach to healthy eating and food selection. According to the Department's press release, the pyramid is but one element in an "overall food guidance system that emphasizes the need for a more individualized approach to improving diet and lifestyle." The "MyPyramid" system incorporates the newest dietary recommendations established jointly by the Departments of Agriculture and Health and Human Services, and "was developed to carry the messages of the dietary guidelines and to make Americans aware of the vital health benefits of simple and modest improvements in nutrition, physical activity and lifestyle behavior." One of the improvements to the pyramid came in the area of portion size. The 1992 version used suggested serving sizes that were somewhat amorphous and difficult for nonchefs to translate into tangible amounts

The new food pyramid as released by the Department of Agriculture in 2005.

of food. Now, in contrast, the guidelines utilize common household measurements, such as cups and ounces.[10]

Another strikingly modern, new feature of the pyramid allows computer-savvy Americans to navigate the Web to www.MyPyramid. gov, where they are offered online tools allowing them to estimate the quantities one should eat from the various food groups based on age, gender, and activity level. Still, even if one has limited computer knowledge or access to the Internet, the new pyramid will quickly become a familiar symbol thanks to the efforts of the media and marketers. Shortly after the new pyramid became public, the Associated Press noted: "Food companies announced Tuesday they will distribute posters and guides for teachers and parents next fall aimed at reaching 4 million students. Materials for students to take home will be in both English and Spanish, and will include math, nutrition and science activities."[11]

So the colonization process continues — the government's guidelines, provided to educators by food companies, travel to the homes of American parents where they may have their greatest impact on the family diet. Recently, the children's television program *Sesame Street* joined the crusade for better health and nutrition when producers announced that the upcoming thirty-sixth season (set to begin in summer 2005) would focus on health and overall well-being. Even Cookie Monster will get into the healthy lifestyle act through his new song, "A Cookie Is a Sometimes Food." A press release described the new approach:

> Sesame Street's newest curriculum is a part of a larger Sesame Workshop company-wide initiative, "Healthy Habits for Life," created in response to the growing crisis of childhood obesity among children. The preschool years are a crucial time in children's lives to foster healthy habits. Recent data reflect both the immediate and long-term consequences of poor dietary behaviors. Tackling the critical issues of health and well being, Sesame Workshop continues to set the benchmark in educational television with Sesame Street storylines that guide preschoolers and their caregivers through lessons related to healthy eating, the importance of active play and other key activities such as hygiene and rest.[12]

The staff and advisors of the Sesame Workshop, the nonprofit foundation which supports and produces the *Sesame Street* program along with many other children's programs, include "academic experts" from various American universities, leading medical practitioners, the assistant secretary for health from the Office of Disease Prevention and Health Promotion, the assistant surgeon general, and even an Olympic gymnast, Dominique Dawes. This team is charged with the oversight of the health initiatives that are part of the new *Sesame Street* season. Among the other organizations partnering in this effort are the U.S. Department of Health and Human Services, the Corporation for Public Broadcasting, the YMCA of the United States, the Ad Council, and the National Association for the Education of Younger Children. Together, these players will work to disseminate healthy messages through public service announcements, "outreach and advocacy events," and the funding of additional research. Their influence will be felt in other areas as well due to corporate sponsorships, branding, merchandizing, and marketing. From books and magazines, to videos and DVDs, to traveling stage productions, to advertisements on packages of cereal, juice, and applesauce, the *Sesame Street* health initiative will work its way into American homes.[13]

Do not be surprised if the box of Sesame Street brand cereal on your grocer's shelf bears the seal of the Whole Grains Council (WGC). The Hain/Celestial Group, manufacturers of the cereal, has a representative member of the WGC. This "consortium of industry, scientists, chefs and Oldways Preservation Trust" is committed to increasing Americans' consumption of grains toward the goal of better health. The group was organized in 2002 at the instigation of the Oldways Preservation Trust. Oldways is a self-described "nonprofit 'food issues think tank' praised for translating the complex details of nutrition science into 'the familiar language of food.' This synthesis converts high-level science into a consumer-friendly health-promotion tool for consumers, health professionals, chefs, farmers, journalists, and the food industry."[14] Not surprisingly, the WGC emphasizes the health benefits of consuming whole grains:

> The medical evidence is clear that whole grains reduce risks of heart disease, stroke, cancer, diabetes and obesity. Few foods can offer such diverse benefits.
>
> People who eat whole grains regularly have a lower risk of obesity, as measured by their body mass index and waist-to-hip ratios. They also have lower cholesterol levels. Because of the phytochemicals and antioxidants, people who eat three daily servings of whole grains have been shown to reduce their risk of heart disease by 25–36%, stroke by 37%, Type II diabetes by 21–27%, digestive system cancers by 21–43%, and hormone-related cancers by 10–40%.[15]

The WGC's membership agreed early on that one of its primary focuses needed to be maintaining both whole and refined grains as the base of the federal food pyramid. Their initiatives to achieve this and other goals have been and continue to be carried out through the channels of "school feeding programs, government programs, retail markets, and media."[16]

While no one food group now occupies the coveted bottom level of the new pyramid, the WGC must have been pleased by the recommendations for grain consumption found at MyPyramid.gov: "Make half of your grains whole. Eat at least 3 oz. of whole-grain cereals, breads, crackers, rice or pasta every day."[17] General Mills, the nation's largest producer of whole grain products and a member of the WGC, praised the new guidelines and embarked on a "major nutrition education initiative" in conjunction with their release. The company's vice president for marketing had this to say: "The cereal box is one of the most read items in the home, read on average 2.6 times. With cereal consumed in 93 percent of American households and with the information on more than 100 million General Mills cereal boxes, this is a powerful step forward in nutrition education."[18] The company announced in June 2005 that it was kicking off yet another new campaign: this one aimed directly at children. The "Choose Breakfast" advertising materials and Web site will be a "nonbranded" campaign in that the ads themselves will not be for any one specific product, although the theme will be rotated among several cereal brands primarily consumed by children, including Cinnamon Toast Crunch, Lucky Charms, Cocoa Puffs, and Trix. The chief marketing officer described the program:

> We are excited about the opportunity to use our expertise to communicate important health messages to kids in their terms.... Our goal is to not have kids walk away from breakfast in the morning. It is our job to communicate the benefits — the opportunity for a healthier body weight and to perform better in school — in a way that will resonate with kids and make a difference.[19]

Rediscovering the Golden Mean

Back in Washington, D.C., in February 2005, Representative Ric Keller, a Florida Republican, introduced the Personal Responsibility in Food Consumption Act. The aim of this legislation is clear from its formal title:

> An Act To prevent legislative and regulatory functions from being usurped by civil liability actions brought or continued against food manufacturers, marketers, distributors, advertisers, sellers, and trade associations for claims of injury relating to a person's weight gain, obesity, or any health condition associated with weight gain or obesity.[20]

The act, popularly dubbed the Cheeseburger Bill, was reported to the Committee on Judiciary in June 2005, and on 19 October 2005 it passed the House with a vote of 306–120. The Senate received the act the following day, read the text twice, and on 21 October placed it on the Senate Legislative Calendar.

In the text of the act, the House enumerates its findings and purpose. The version passed in that body in October 2005 stated that the food and beverage industries are a significant part of the national economy; that they affect both interstate and foreign commerce; that a person's obesity, weight gain, or ill health is the result of numerous factors, including genetics, lifestyle, and fitness, and as such cannot be attributed to the consumption of specific foods or beverages; and finally that "fostering a culture of acceptance of personal responsibility" is important to the promotion of a healthy society, and hence, lawsuits seeking to place blame on members of the food industry for a person's overweight or ill health are "not only legally frivolous and economically damaging, but also harmful to a healthy America." Accordingly, the House declared its purpose to be the securing to Congress and regulatory agencies the power to establish the laws, rules, and regulations necessary to address issues related to weight gain, obesity, and health.[21]

Even before the House had passed the act, the National Restaurant Association, an organization with an admitted self-interest in its successful passage, issued this statement:

> The nation's 900,000 restaurants have long provided and will continue to offer a wide variety of choices and options that meet any individual's dietary needs. Experts agree that all foods can be part of a healthy lifestyle, which can best be attained through balancing energy in and energy out. Emphasis needs to be placed on education, personal responsibility, moderation and healthier lifestyles — not on expensive and frivolous litigation.[22]

Cheeseburgers, Choices, and Consequences

This book has told the story of how various reformers over the course of the past century have endeavored to improve the quality of the food consumed by workers and schoolchildren. Many of these reformers hoped that the improvements integrated into schools and workplaces would carry over to homes and entire families. There have indeed been many laudable effects of this process, including national nutrition guidelines, improved dining conditions in many workplaces and schools, and the federal free and reduced price lunch programs. There have been consequences as well.

The colonization of food has introduced scientists, advertisers, manufacturers, and legislators, among others, into the decisions Americans make about food and nutrition. The resulting cacophony of opinions has certainly introduced a significant element of homogeneity to Americans' diets, but it has not rendered this decision-making process any easier. This begs the question: "Have the colonizers succeeded?" The answer to that is yes and no. Over the course of the twentieth century, reformers were clearly successful in raising the national level of nutritional awareness. In addition, they helped establish the cooperative networks by which nutritional information, including scientific/medical data and advertising, is disseminated to the American people. The colonizers' most enduring success has been the transformation of food into both a public and a political issue. However, despite their efforts to make schools, corporations, and the state more responsible for people's dietary health, they ultimately could not colonize and control the variable that is constantly present — individual choice. With recent efforts like the revised dietary guidelines and the Cheeseburger Bill, and the increasing cooperation of food manufacturers, processors and distributors in making nutritional information available, reformers have begun a shift back toward individual responsibility for food choices and their consequences. None of this releases the colonizers entirely of their responsibilities in relation to the promotion of health and the distribution of nutritional information. Responsibility is indeed the key, but it is a two-sided proposition.

Corporations have a responsibility to consumers to be honest in their disclosure of product information. Government and the media have a responsibility to act as overseers of the disclosure process, regulating and publicizing facts and fictions. Regulation of food label content and standards must continue so that consumers have a basis for evaluating the nutritional quality of food products. Clearly, this is a public health concern of staggering proportions, one toward which no one can afford to turn their back. It is not a problem that can be solved by individuals, although it requires the commitment and cooperation of everyone for success. Now, perhaps more than ever, the colonization process needs to focus on education so that people can make choices within a framework of information. The most positive action the government can take is to set standards for and ensure the education of all Americans.

Education remains our most effective personal and national defense against the ravages of poor nutritional health. In a world so full of differing opinions about what, when, why, where, and how to eat, it is all the more important that we educate children about the range of choices available so that they can make good decisions. In a November 1999 article, "The Lunch Box as Battlefield," in *Gourmet* magazine, author Perri Klass related a telling experience she had while packing lunches for her young children. Her eldest son attended a day-care center where "unhealthy" foods had been banned from lunch boxes as the result of an unfortunate situation where one child traded his winter coat for the Oreo cookie of a classmate. Klass responded:

> I have a message for you all: Stay out of my child's lunch box; stay away from his plate! You are, of course, free to take the whole-grains-and-lentils route, or to raise your children to think that anything highly spiced is strange and icky and likely to lead to immoral behavior. It may turn out to be an extremely clever strategy, for which you'll pat yourselves on the back someday when you realize you've created adolescents who can act out full-scale rebellions merely by scarfing down Mounds bars. But you can't remove temptation from your child's path by legislating what mine can eat. It's a misguided notion anyway. The food choices that children will grow up to make have to be choices — if there is a food you don't want your child to eat, she has to be able to watch someone else eating it without going into a frenzy.[23]

Clearly, we need to be concerned over what our kids are eating at school and what messages they are receiving about food from the school curriculum, their peers, the media and advertisers. Still, if American eating ideology can be said to be based on anything, it is freedom of choice and personal responsibility. Supermarkets, fast-food restaurants, and convenience products show no signs of disappearing anytime in the near future. Eating choices are a right that we, as Americans, enjoy. With that right, like any, comes responsibility. Schools can provide information about how to make good choices, but it is not the responsibility of the school to control the choices individual children make.

In January 2003, U.S. District Court Judge Robert Sweet took a stand in this spirit when he dismissed a class action lawsuit against several fast-food chains. The suit alleged that the chains should be held accountable for obesity among Americans. Although the case involved, Sweet noted, presented "unique and challenging issues," including questions of "personal responsibility, common knowledge and public health," he ruled that if "consumers know (or reasonably should know) the potential ill health effects of eating at McDonald's, they cannot blame McDonald's if they, nonetheless, choose to satiate their appetite with a surfeit of super-sized McDonald's products."[24] Some words by Thomas Jefferson may shed additional light on this sentiment: "I know no safe depository of the ultimate powers of the society, but the people themselves: and if we think them not enlightened enough to exercise their controul with a wholsome discretion, the remedy is, not to take it from them, but to inform their discretion by education. this is the true corrective of abuses of constitutional power."[25] Indeed, education is the true corrective and preventive of all manner of abuses. As a nation, we have a responsibility to ensure the education of all Americans, to have faith in their informed decisions, and to allow them to accept responsibility for their choices — only then will the battle over lunch end in a victory for everyone.

Chapter Notes

Preface

1. Septimia Anne Randolph Meikleham, manuscript: "Everyday Life at Monticello," Thomas Jefferson Library, Thomas Jefferson Foundation, Charlottesville, Virginia.

Introduction

1. L. Frank Baum, *Ozma of Oz* (Reilly and Britton, 1907; repr. New York: Dover Publications, 1985), 40.

2. Jurgen Habermas employed the colonization metaphor in his two-volume work *The Theory of Communicative Action*. 2 vols. (Boston: Beacon Press, 1984–1987).

3. On the general issues of ideology and power, see Craig Calhoun, ed., *Habermas and the Public* Sphere (Cambridge, MA: MIT Press, 1992) and Terry Eagleton, *Ideology: An Introduction* (London: Verso, 1991). Specifically on the triangle of food, ideology, and power, see Sidney Mintz, *Sweetness and Power: The Place of Sugar in Modern History* (New York: Penguin Books, 1985).

4. Mary Douglas, "Deciphering a Meal," in *Implicit Meanings: Essays in Anthropology* (London: Routledge and Kegan Paul, 1975), 249.

5. David R. Roediger and Philip S. Foner, *Our Own Time: A History of American Labor and the Working Day* (New York: Greenwood Press, 1989), chapter 1.

6. Elaine McIntosh, *American Food Habits in Historical Perspective* (Westport, CT: Praeger,

1995), 154. McIntosh notes that more current usage of these terms marks those who eat lunch and dinner as being of higher social status.

7. For broad social histories of food, see Harvey Levenstein, *Revolution at the Table: The Transformation of the American Diet* (New York: Oxford University Press, 1988); and Levenstein, *Paradox of Plenty: A Social History of Eating in Modern America* (New York: Oxford University Press, 1993). See also Evan Jones, *American Food: The Gastronomic Story* (New York: Overlook Press, 1990); McIntosh; *The American Heritage Cookbook and Illustrated History of American Eating and Drinking* (New York: Simon and Schuster, 1964). There are also numerous focused studies that illuminate the history of American foodways, for example, Kathryn Grover, ed., *Dining in America: 1850–1900* (Amherst: University of Massachusetts Press and Margaret Woodbury Strong Museum, 1987).

8. See Marjorie DeVault, *Feeding the Family: The Social Organization of Caring as Gendered Work* (Chicago: University of Chicago Press, 1991); Catherine Manton, *Fed Up: Women and Food in America* (Westport, CT: Bergin and Garvey, 1999); and for the British equivalent, see Nickie Charles and Marion Kerr, *Women, Food, and Families: Power, Status, Love, Anger* (Manchester: Manchester University Press, 1988). Each of these works deals with the association of women with the responsibility for family feeding.

9. Leila Rupp, *Mobilizing Women for War: German and American Propaganda, 1929–1945* (Princeton: Princeton University Press, 1978), 6.

10. Catherine E. Beecher and Harriet Beecher Stowe, *The American Woman's Home* (New York: J. B. Ford, 1869).

11. See, for example, Linda K. Kerber, *Women of the Republic: Intellect and Ideology in Revolutionary America* (Chapel Hill: University of North Carolina Press, 1980).

12. See Laura Shapiro, *Perfection Salad: Women and Cooking at the Turn of the Century* (New York: Farrar, Straus and Giroux, 1986).

13. See Alan Trachtenberg, *The Incorporation of America: Culture and Society in the Gilded Age* (New York: Hill and Wang, 1982) for a discussion of how American life changed in important ways during the years after the Civil War.

14. Levenstein, *Paradox of Plenty*, 91.

15. George Ritzer, *The McDonaldization of Society: An Investigation into the Changing Character of Contemporary Social Life* (Thousand Oaks, CA: Pine Forge Press, 1993), 19.

16. Jean Anthelme Brillat-Savarin, *Physiologie Du Gout* (Paris: Feydeau, 1826), 2 vols.

17. Ann Hulbert, "'I Say the Hell with It!' School Lunches Are Making Kids Fat — But Collard Greens Aren't the Solution," www.slate.msn.com, accessed 11 February 2003.

Chapter 1

1. "A Novel Hot Lunch Box," *New York Daily Tribune*, 5 July 1903.

2. See Noel Jacob Kent, *America in 1900* (Armonk, NY: M. E. Sharpe, 2000).

3. Jacob Riis, *The Children of the Poor* (New York: Charles Scribner's Sons, 1892), 1.

4. Riis, 1.

5. Crandall Shifflett, *Victorian America 1876 to 1913* (New York: Facts on File, 1996), 74.

6. Shifflett, 35.

7. Bryan, "Cross of Gold," quoted in Ronald F. Reid, *Three Centuries of American Rhetorical Discourse* (Prospect Heights, IL: Waveland Press, 1988), 601–606.

8. Bryan, "Cross of Gold," quoted in Reid.

9. Lewis L. Gould, "Introduction: The Progressive Era," in Lewis L. Gould, ed., *The Progressive Era* (Syracuse: Syracuse University Press, 1974), 1.

10. See Gould, ed., *The Progressive Era*; Richard Hofstadter, ed., *The Progressive Movement* (Englewood Cliffs, NJ: Prentice Hall, 1963); and John Whiteclay Chambers II, *The Tyranny of Change: America in the Progressive Era, 1890–1912,* 2d ed. (New Brunswick, N.J.: Rutgers University Press, 2000).

11. See Stanley P. Caine, "Origins of Progressivism," in Gould, *The Progressive Era*.

12. Glad, 93.

13. Stanley Jones, *The Presidential Election of 1896* (Madison: University of Wisconsin Press, 1964), 170–71.

14. L. Frank Baum, *Ozma of Oz* (Reilly and Britton, 1907; repr, New York: Dover Publications, 1985), 15, 19.

15. Baum, *Ozma of Oz*, 38–40.

16. Baum, *Ozma of Oz*, 67–8.

17. Baum, *Ozma of Oz*, 44, 47–48.

18. Frank Joslyn Baum and Russell P. MacFall, *To Please a Child: A Biography of L. Frank Baum, Royal Historian of Oz* (Chicago: Reilly and Lee, 1961), 65.

19. Baum and MacFall, 74. The authors speculate that Baum may have had this scenario in mind when he later penned *The Wonderful Wizard of Oz*, as prior to entering the Emerald City, Dorothy and her fellow travelers don green spectacles.

20. William Leach, *Land of Desire: Merchants, Power, and the Rise of a New American Culture* (New York: Vintage Books, 1993), examines Baum's wizard story as evidence of a different allegorical message. In Leach's estimation, the story is an "Americanized" fairy tale that was an expression of "mind cure" spiritualism popular at the turn of the century (248–60).

21. For specific works on the allegorical nature of *The Wonderful Wizard of Oz*, see Henry M. Littlefield, "The Wizard of Oz: Parable on Populism," *American Quarterly* 16 (Spring 1964): 47–58; Suzanne Rahn, *The Wizard of Oz: Shaping an Imaginary World* (New York: Twayne Publishers, 1998); Gretchen Ritter, "Silver Slippers and a Golden Cap: L. Frank Baum's *The Wonderful Wizard of Oz* and Historical Memory in American Politics," *Journal of American Studies* 31 (1997): 171–202; and Hugh Rockoff, "The Wizard of Oz as a Monetary Allegory," *Journal of Political Economy* 98 (August 1990), 739–760.

22. Lewis L. Gould, *The Presidency of William McKinley* (Lawrence, Kansas: Regents Press, 1980), 207.

23. Baum, *Ozma of Oz*, 40.

24. Sir William A. Craigie and James R. Hulbert, eds., *A Dictionary of American English on Historical Principles* (Chicago: University of Chicago Press, 1942), III, 1460.

25. See Daniel Boorstin, "Condense! Making Food Portable through Time," in *The Americans: The Democratic Experience* (New York: Vintage Books, 1974), 309–16, for an enchanting description of American contributions to the science of food processing.

26. On material culture study, see Clifford Geertz, *The Interpretation of Cultures* (New York: Basic Books, 1973); Daniel Miller, *A Theory of Shopping* (Ithaca: Cornell University Press, 1998); and Thomas Schlereth, *Material Culture Studies in America* (Nashville: Association for State and Local History, 1982).

27. See for example, Arjun Appadurai, ed., *The Social Life of Things: Commodities in Perspective* (Cambridge: Cambridge University Press, 1986); Colin Campbell, *The Romantic Ethic and the Spirit of Modern Consumerism* (London: Basil Blackwell, 1987); Daniel Horowitz, *The Morality of Spending: Attitudes toward the Consumer Society in America, 1875–1940* (Chicago: Ivan R. Dee, 1985); Grant McCracken, *Culture and Consumption: New Approaches to the Symbolic Character of Consumer Goods and Activities* (Bloomington: Indiana University Press, 1988); and Neil McKendrick, John Brewer, and J. H. Plumb, *The Birth of a Consumer Society: The Commercialization of Eighteenth-Century England* (Bloomington: Indiana University Press, 1982).

28. Several case studies of material culture and consumers proved enlightening for this project. Among them were: Scott Bruce and Bill Crawford, *The Cerealization of America: The Unsweetened Story of American Breakfast Cereal* (Boston: Faber and Faber, 1995); Alison J. Clarke, "Tupperware: Product as Social Relation," in *American Material Culture: The Shape of the Field*, ed. Ann Smart Martin and J. Ritchie Garrison (Knoxville: University of Tennessee Press, 1999), 225–50; Karal Ann Marling, *As Seen on TV: The Visual Culture of Everyday Life in the 1950s* (Cambridge, MA: Harvard University Press, 1994); and Margaret Visser, *Much Depends upon Dinner* (New York: Grove Press, 1986).

29. Craigie and Hulbert, II, 764.

30. Robert Grant, "Search-Light Letters: To a Young Man or Woman in Search of the Ideal," *Scribner's Magazine* 25 (1899), 106 and 107.

31. Trachtenberg, 139.

32. For more on the growth of advertising and consumerism, see Chambers, *The Tyranny of Change*; Kent, *American in 1900*; Leach, *Land of Desire*; Susan Strasser, *Waste and Want: A Social History of Trash* (New York: Metropolitan Books, 1999); Susan Strasser, Charles McGovern, and Matthias Judt, eds., *Getting and Spending: European and American Consumer Societies in the Twentieth Century* (Washington, DC: German Historical Institute, 1998); and Warren I. Susman, *Culture as History: The Transformation of American Society in*

the *Twentieth Century* (New York: Pantheon Books, 1984).

33. Trachtenberg, 69.

34. Baum, *Ozma of Oz*, 55, 70.

35. Trachtenberg, 87.

36. Trachtenberg, 135.

Chapter 2

1. Upton Sinclair, *The Jungle* (1905; repr., New York: Harper, 1951), 56–57.

2. Theodore Dreiser, *Sister Carrie* (1900; repr. New York: Bantam Books, 1992), 48.

3. Dreiser, 387

4. Bruce and Crawford, *Cerealizing America*, 66.

5. "Nobody Counted Calories: Travel on the Chesapeake Bay Steamboats," *Weather Gauge: The Magazine of the Chesapeake Bay Maritime Museum* 35 (Fall 1999), 6.

6. Strasser, *Waste and Want*, 72.

7. Roy Rosenzweig, *Eight Hours for What We Will: Workers and Leisure in an Industrial City, 1870–1920* (Cambridge: Cambridge University Press, 1983), chapter 2, "The Rise of the Saloon."

8. Harper Lee, *To Kill A Mockingbird* (1961; repr. New York: Harper Collins, 1995), 21–22.

9. Lizabeth Cohen, *Making A New Deal: Industrial Workers in Chicago, 1919–1939* (New York: Cambridge University Press, 1990), 161.

10. Ernest F. Hoyer, "The Canteen Versus the Cold Dinner Pail," *Industrial Management* (1 June 1921), 440.

11. "Decline and Fall of the 'Full Dinner Pail,'" *Literary Digest* (3 November 1923), 54–55.

12. See Levenstein, *Revolution at the Table*.

13. See Levenstein, *Revolution at the Table*, and George Rosen, *A History of Public Health* (Baltimore: Johns Hopkins University Press, 1993).

14. Mary Alden Hopkins, "The Disappearance of the Dinner Pail," *Independent* (1 January 1917), 18.

15. "Decline and Fall of the 'Full Dinner Pail,'" 52.

16. "Decline and Fall of the 'Full Dinner Pail,'" 52–54.

17. See Daniel Horowitz, *The Morality of Spending: Attitudes Toward the Consumer Society in America, 1875–1940* (Chicago: Ivan R. Dee, 1985). Horowitz examines the shifts in social theorists' attitudes about morality and spending. He argues that the language Americans have used to talk about consumption have long been informed by moral judgments with an emphasis on how materialism results in a

loss of self control and leads to moral decadence.

18. "Decline and Fall of the 'Full Dinner Pail,' " 52 and 54.

19. "The Factory Lunchroom and Equipment," *Industrial Management* (May 1918), 418–19; "Factory Lunchroom," *Industrial Management* (September 1918), 254–55.

20. "Lunch Rooms in Industrial Establishments," *Monthly Labor Review* (March 1927), 484.

21. "Lunch Rooms in Industrial Establishments," *Monthly Labor Review* (March 1927), 483.

22. D. R. Wilson, "When the Dinner-Bell Rings," *Factory and Industrial Management* (March 1930), 568.

23. Joel H. Spring and Edgar B. Gumbert, *The Superschool and the Superstate: American Education in the Twentieth Century* (New York: John Wiley and Sons, 1974).

24. Maris A. Vinovskis, *Education, Society, and Economic Opportunity: A Historical Perspective on Persistent Issues* (New Haven: Yale University Press, 1995), 175.

25. Sol Cohen, *Progressives and Urban School Reform: The Public Education Association of New York City, 1895–1954* (New York: Teacher's College, Columbia University, 1964).

26. Agnes Fay Morgan, "How Schools Improve the Nutrition of Pupils," *Journal of Home Economics* 34 (December 1942) 721.

27. Emeline E. Torrey, "The Penny Lunch Movement," *Good Housekeeping* 52 (1911), 242.

28. Gordon W. Gunderson, "The National School Lunch Program: Background and Development," *www.fns.usda.gov*, accessed 19 September 2000.

29. Gunderson.

30. Torrey, 242.

31. Torrey, 242–244.

32. George B. Masslich, "The Beginnings of a Penny Portion Lunch," *Journal of Home Economics* (May 1919), 212.

33. Anna L. Steckelberg, "Planning for the Hot Lunch in Rural Schools," *Journal of Home Economics*, November 1923, 642; 645.

34. "The School Lunch in Rural and Urban Districts," *American City* 27, no. 1 (July 1922), 43.

35. "The School Lunch in Rural and Urban Districts," 43, 45.

36. J. Mace Andress, "The Educational Value of a School Cafeteria," *Hygeia* 7 (October 1929), 1030.

37. Albertina Bechmann, "The First Penny Lunch," *Journal of Home Economics* (November 1933), 761.

38. Catharine M. Leamy, "The Rural School Lunch," *Journal of Home Economics* (February 1940), 87.

39. Reinette Lovewell, "Substitute for the Dinner Pail," *Technical World Magazine* (September 1914), 52.

40. Irene Hume Taylor, "The Rural School Lunch," *Hygeia* (October 1926), 573–574.

41. "Aladdin's Bottle of Milk," *Hygeia* 6 (May 1928), 278–280.

42. "Aladdin's Bottle of Milk," 280.

43. "Aladdin's Bottle of Milk," 281.

44. W. J. Hilty, "Lunch-Room Management in the County School," *Journal of Home Economics* (April 1935), 214.

45. *Good Housekeeping's Book of Meals: Tested, Tasted, and Approved* (New York: Good Housekeeping, 1930), 14; emphasis in original.

46. Lydia Roberts, *Nutrition Work with Children* (Chicago: University of Chicago Press, 1927), 3.

47. Roberts, 235.

48. Roberts, 300.

49. Ethel Austin Martin, *Roberts' Nutrition Work with Children* (Chicago: University of Chicago Press, 1954), 347.

50. Martin, 466.

51. Morgan, "How Schools Improve Nutrition of Pupils," 725.

52. Morgan, 722.

53. Blanche M. Stover, "The School Lunch and Your Child," *Parents* 33 (October 1958), 73.

54. Pauline Berry Mack, "Nine-Year Study of the School Lunch," *Journal of Home Economics* 39 (February 1947), 76.

Chapter 3

1. There are several informative general studies of society and culture in the World War II era. Among them are John Morton Blum, *V Was for Victory: Politics and Culture During World War II* (New York: Harcourt, Brace, 1976); Richard R. Lingeman, *Don't You Know There's a War On? The American Homefront, 1941–1945* (New York: G. P. Putnam's Sons, 1970); Richard Polenberg, *War and Society: The United States 1941–1945* (Philadelphia: J. B. Lippincott, 1972); Geffrey Perrett, *Days of Sadness, Years of Triumph: The American People 1939–1945* (New York: Coward, McCann and Geoghegan, 1973); and William Tuttle, *Daddy's Gone to War: The Second World War in the Lives of American Children* (New York: Oxford University Press, 1993). Portions of this and the following chapter come from my master's thesis, "'I Will Waste Nothing': American Women's Patriotism Seen Through World War

II Era Cookbooks," Kent State University, 1997.

2. See Blum, *V Was For Victory*, 90–116. Blum argues that although the war introduced new demands on family income in the form of price controls, rationing, and income taxes, "the wartime surge of buying was exciting in part because for so long most Americans had had to stint. It was also frustrating because wartime shortages denied Americans much of what they wanted" (92).

3. The Lend-Lease Act was signed by President Franklin D. Roosevelt in 1941. Under the terms of this act, the United States agreed to assist its Allies through loans of military supplies that were to be returned or paid for at the close of the war.

4. See Maureen Honey, *Creating Rosie the Riveter: Class, Gender, and Propaganda during World War II* (Amherst: University of Massachusetts Press, 1984), for a detailed study of the cooperation of the government and the media. Honey focuses on images of women in popular fiction and advertising from wartime issues of *The Saturday Evening Post* and *True Story*.

5. "No Rush at Stores to Buy Tinned Food Before Rationing," *New York Times* (29 December 1942).

6. For detailed information about food control during World War I, see William Ahlers Nielander, *Wartime Food Rationing in the United States* (Washington, DC: World Trade Relations, 1947), 4–9.

7. See Levenstein, *Paradox of Plenty*, 80–81.

8. As Nielander points out, during World War I, food shortages were less acute than those during World War II. He noted that while the World War I Food Administration was able to rely on voluntarism, compulsory rationing was necessary to distribute supplies adequately during World War II (6–9).

9. For example, see John Smith's observations from his voyages in the New World in Karen Ordahl Kupperman, ed., *Captain John Smith: A Select Edition of His Writings* (Chapel Hill: University of North Carolina Press, 1988).

10. John D. Black, *Food Enough* (Lancaster, PA: Jacques Cattell Press, 1943), 1.

11. See Levenstein, *Paradox of Plenty*, 55, 62–63, 78–79, 81–83 for information of food surpluses in the 1930s and 1940s.

12. Levenstein, *Paradox of Plenty*, 80–100.

13. Nielander, 4.

14. Nielander, 4–9.

15. Nielander, 19.

16. Nielander, 21.

17. See Harold Vatter, *The U.S. Economy in World War II* (New York: Columbia University Press, 1985), 1–2.

18. Nielander provides a good overview of the development of the various agencies associated with wartime rationing (21–37). The first chapter of Vatter is a useful outline of the events leading up to U.S. involvement in the war (1–31). In addition, general literature about the United States and the war, such as Blum, *V Was for Victory* and Polenberg, *War and Society,* provide valuable information about the impact of war on American society, politics, and culture.

19. Alonzo Hamby, *Liberalism and Its Challengers: FDR to Reagan* (New York: Oxford University Press, 1985), 32.

20. Vatter, 34.

21. In Nielander's estimation, the vacancy left by the absence of a centralized power to deal with food rationing caused inefficiency and confusion in the overall administration of the wartime food program (31–37). See also Vatter's section titled "The Administration of 'Control by No One' " (32–42).

22. See Nielander, 25.

23. Nielander, 21–37.

24. Nielander, 106.

25. Nielander, 39.

26. Barbara McLean Ward, "A Fair Share at a Fair Price: Rationing, Resource Management, and Price Controls During World War II," in *Produce and Conserve, Share and Play Square: The Grocer and the Consumer on the Home-Front Battlefield during World War II,* ed. Barbara McLean Ward (Portsmouth, NH: Strawbery Banke Museum, 1994), 82.

27. Information in this paragraph comes from Ward, 82–83. See also Nielander.

28. "Canned Food Rationing Explained in OPA Replies to New Questions," *New York Times* (5 January 1943).

29. Nielander, 48–9.

30. Maxwell Stewart, *The Smiths and Their Wartime Budgets,* Public Affairs Pamphlets, Number 88 (New York: Public Affairs Committee, 1944), 33.

31. Stewart, 1–2.

32. Stewart, 3.

33. Stewart, 5.

34. "U.S. Gearing Homes to Economy in War," *New York Times* (7 December 1942).

35. Perhaps the most useful sources on the notion of wartime obligation are Mark H. Leff, "The Politics of Sacrifice on the American Home Front in World War II," *Journal of American History* 77, no. 4 (March 1991): 1296–1318; and Robert B. Westbrook, " 'I Want a Girl, Just Like the Girl That Married Harry James': American Women and the Problem of Political Obligation

in World War II," *American Quarterly* 42, no. 4 (December 1990), 587–614. Leff argues that during the war, the relationship between the government and American industry was significant in shaping Americans' conception of wartime sacrifice. He further points out that the experience of war helped establish industry's position in postwar U.S. culture and its role in setting the parameters of the "good life." Westbrook notes that during World War II, political obligation was not well defined, so the government had to resort to arguments that drew on Americans' sense of duty toward their own private interests. He employs pin-up posters to demonstrate the notion of the ideal woman and shows how these images stirred American soldiers to protect their girlfriends, wives, and mothers — "those worth fighting for" (600).

36. Charles Egan, "Housewives 'Catch on' to Food Points Quickly," *New York Times* (7 March 1943).

37. Holt, "News of Food," *New York Times* (30 December 1942).

38. "Point Ration Plan Coming Next Month," *New York Times* (3 December 1942).

39. "Text of Wickard's Broadcast Announcing the New Food Rationing Regulations," *New York Times* (28 December 1942).

40. On civilian interpretations of and reactions to the rationing system, see Blum, 15–52; Amy Lynn Bentley, *Eating for Victory: Food Rationing and the Politics of Domesticity* (Urbana: University of Illinois Press, 1998); Levenstein, *Paradox of Plenty*, 80–89; Polenberg, 131–153; and Lautenschlager, chapter 4, "The Ant and the Grasshopper: Conservation and Thrift Versus Hoarding."

41. "Rationing of Canned Fruits, Soups and Vegetables Starts in February; Halt in Retail Sales to Come First," *New York Times* (28 December 1942).

42. "Hits Advance Notice of Food Rationing," *New York Times* (28 December 1942).

43. "Says Japanese Benefit," *New York Times* (10 January 1943).

44. "Asks House Inquiry on OPA 'Meat Mess,'" *New York Times* (27 January 1943).

45. "U.S. Food Stocks Huge," *New York Times* (30 January 1943).

46. "To Release Big Stocks of Evaporated Milk," *New York Times* (23 December 1942).

47. "Food Dealers See Federal Hoarding," *New York Times* (6 March 1943).

48. "OPA Explains Rationing of Foods," *New York Times* (28 December 1942).

49. "If You Haven't Applied for Ration Book No. 2 Today Will Be the Last Chance for a Month," *New York Times* (5 March 1943).

50. "2,004,310 in City Get Ration Books; Long Lines Form," *New York Times* (24 February 1943).

51. "Declares 1,000 Cans of Food," *New York Times* (24 February 1943).

52. "Bryn Mawr Family Hoards 4,502 Cans," *New York Times* (25 February 1943).

53. See "Five Cans a Person to Be Ration Free," *New York Times* (27 January 1943).

54. The general information on Ration Book 2 in the following two paragraphs comes from various articles which appeared in the *New York Times* during the period between December 1942 and March 1943.

55. Quoted material from, "Regional Basis Urged for Food Rationing to Allot Canned Goods Where Most Used," *New York Times* (17 February 1943). See also "Canners Warn OPA on Food Rationing," *New York Times* (4 February 1943).

56. "Canned Goods Rush Clears Shops Here," *New York Times* (21 February 1943).

57. Prentiss Brown, "How to Make Rationing Work," *New York Times* (21 February 1943).

58. "Food Hoarders Face Penalties in 2 Laws," *New York Times* (29 December 1942).

59. "Searching Homes for Hoards Barred in New York Area," *New York Times* (8 March 1943).

60. "Hitlerism Seen Here," *New York Times* (6 March 1943).

61. "The Pantry Is a Castle," *New York Times* (9 March 1943).

62. "Rationing Methods Protested," *New York Times* (8 January 1943).

63. Holt published OPA's "Golden Rules of Food Rationing" along with her 20 February 1943, column. Other city newspapers carried similar food columns. See for example, the *Akron Beacon Journal*, an Ohio newspaper featuring Glenna Snow.

64. "Holiday Meal For 6 to Cost $2.46 More," *New York Times* (21 November 1942), 9.

65. Holt, "News of Food," *New York Times* (21 November 1942).

66. Many meat packers blamed OPA for failing to enact price ceilings on livestock soon enough to avoid dramatic price increases on fresh meat. See "Asks House Inquiry On OPA 'Meat Mess,'" *New York Times* (27 January 1943), and Levenstein, *Paradox of Plenty*, 83.

67. Holt, "News of Food," *New York Times* (19 December 1942).

68. Holt, "News of Food," *New York Times* (24 December 1942).

69. Holt, "Little Things for a Big Christmas," *New York Times Magazine*, 13 December 1942, 22.

70. Holt, "News of Food," *New York Times* (15 December 1942). Chocolate chip cookies were "invented" by Ruth Wakefield of Whitman, Massachusetts, in 1933. Wakefield and her husband owned the Toll House Inn and ran a restaurant. In 1939, the Nestle company began selling chocolate morsels for use in baking and purchased the rights to use the Toll House name. See James Trager, *The Food Chronology* (New York: Henry Holt, 1995), 476.

71. Holt, "The Cook's New Leaf," *New York Times Magazine* (27 December 1942), 14.

72. Holt, "Rationed Cookery," *New York Times Magazine* (17 January 1943), 20.

73. Holt, "How to Like a Turnip," *New York Times Magazine* (10 January 1943), 20.

74. Holt, "Shape of Meals to Come," *New York Times Magazine* (24 January 1943), 22.

75. Holt, "News of Food," *New York Times* (5 January 1943).

76. Holt, "News of Food," *New York Times* (16 January 1943).

77. Holt, "News of Food," *New York Times* (10 February 1943). Department of Labor figures on the cost of living are available in E. Eastman Irvine, ed. *The World Almanac and Book of Facts for 1944* (New York: New York World Telegram, 1944), 843. The same volume includes a cost of living analysis for New York City (897). The 1945 volume contains similar information regarding cost of living increases as well as a chart listing meat production and consumption figures for the United States (542, 538).

78. Holt, "News of Food," *New York Times* (4 February 1943).

79. Holt, "News of Food," *New York Times* (6 February 1943).

80. Holt, "News of Food," *New York Times* (20 February 1943). For working women, being flexible in grocery shopping was often not an option. Some of these women expressed the hope that once point rationing began they would have a better opportunity to get the foods that they desired. One working woman commented: "At least I will know that I can get what I am entitled to ... instead of wasting time looking around for what I can't get." "Women in War Jobs Still Find Time to Have Fun and Run Households," *New York Times* (3 March 1943).

81. Holt, "The ABC of Point Rationing," *New York Times Magazine* (21 February 1943), 22.

82. Holt, "ABC," 22.

83. "When Rationing Comes," *New York Times* (4 January 1943).

84. "Expects Housewives' Cooperation," *New York Times* (8 December 1942).

Chapter 4

1. Useful sources on women in the World War II era include Karen Anderson, *Wartime Women: Sex Roles, Family Relations, and the Status of Women During World War II* (Westport, CT: Greenwood Press, 1981); D'Ann Campbell, *Women at War with America: Private Lives in a Patriotic Era* (Cambridge: Harvard University Press, 1984); William H. Chafe, *The Paradox of Change: American Women in the Twentieth Century* (New York: Oxford University Press, 1991); Susan Hartmann, *The Homefront and Beyond: Women in the 1940's* (Boston: Twayne Publishers, 1982); Leila Rupp, *Mobilizing Women for War: German and American Propaganda, 1939–1945* (Princeton: Princeton University Press, 1978); Doris Weatherford, *American Women and World War II* (New York: Facts on File, 1990); and Nancy Baker Wise and Christy Wise, *A Mouthful of Rivets: Women at Work in World War II* (San Francisco: Josey-Bass, 1994).

2. The authors of several recent historical works on women's domestic and social roles have investigated the subject of women and the food situation during World War II. See especially Amy Lynn Bentley, *Eating for Victory: Food Rationing and the Politics of Domesticity* (Urbana: University of Illinois Press, 1998); Joanne Lamb Hayes, *Grandma's Wartime Kitchen: World War II and the Way We Cooked* (New York: St. Martin's Press, 2000); Sherrie A. Inness, *Dinner Roles: American Women and Culinary Culture* (Dubuque: University of Iowa Press, 2001); Mary Drake McFeely, *Can She Bake a Cherry Pie? American Women and the Kitchen in the Twentieth Century* (Amherst: University of Massachusetts Press, 2000); and Jessamyn Neuhaus, *Manly Meals and Mom's Home Cooking: Cookbooks and Gender in Modern America* (Baltimore: Johns Hopkins University Press, 2003). I also addressed this subject in a chapter of my master's thesis, "Grandmother Knew Best: Connecting Modern Women and the Women of America's Mythic Past through Patriotism and Invented Tradition."

3. For more detailed arguments regarding women's status in the United States, see Jeanne Boydston, *Home and Work: Housework, Wages, and Ideology in the Early Republic* (New York: Oxford University Press, 1990); Ruth Schwartz Cowan, *More Work for Mother: The Ironies of Household Technology from the Open Hearth to the Microwave* (New York: Basic Books, 1983); Glenna Matthews, *"Just a Housewife": The Rise and Fall of Domesticity in America* (New York: Oxford University Press, 1987); Laura Shapiro,

Perfection Salad: Women and Cooking at the Turn of the Century (New York: Farrar, Straus, and Giroux, 1986); and Susan Strasser, *Never Done: A History of American Housework* (New York: Pantheon Books, 1982).

4. On the concept of republican motherhood, see Linda K. Kerber, *Women of the Republic: Intellect and Ideology in Revolutionary America* (Chapel Hill: University of North Carolina Press, 1980). On changing perceptions of women's roles, see Matthews, *"Just a Housewife."*

5. Levenstein, *Paradox of Plenty*, 33–34.

6. Matthews, chapters 6 and 7.

7. See Shapiro, *Perfection Salad.*

8. Margot Murphy, *Wartime Meals: How to Plan Them, How to Buy Them, How to Cook Them* (New York: Greenburg Publishers, 1942), 36–37.

9. "Menus for These Times," *New York Times Book Review* (23 August 1942).

10. Helmut Ripperger, "Cookery Books of 1942," *Publisher's Weekly* (2 January 1943), 23.

11. Murphy 1, 2.

12. Murphy, 72.

13. Murphy, 1, 35.

14. Susan J. Leonardi, "Recipes for Reading: Pasta Salad, Lobster à la Riseholme, Key Lime Pie," in *Cooking by the Book: Food in Literature and Culture,* ed. Mary Anne Schofield (Bowling Green: Bowling Green State University Popular Press, 1989): 126–137. Quoted material from 130–31.

15. Murphy, 6, 7, 11.

16. Murphy, 11, 12, 37–38.

17. Murphy, 12, 15–16, 41, 54–55.

18. Murphy, 58.

19. Murphy, 66, 68.

20. Murphy, 66, 68.

21. Murphy, 88–89, 92.

22. Murphy, 29–30, 38.

23. Murphy, 114, 115.

24. Murphy, 135.

25. For an interesting interpretation of the connections between morality and spending, see Daniel Horowitz, *The Morality of Spending: Attitudes Toward the Consumer Society in America, 1875–1940* (Chicago: Ivan R. Dee, 1985.) Although Horowitz does not carry his study through the World War II era, he comments that some reform writers of that time viewed the war as "another opportunity to commit the nation to a less materialistic way of life" (135).

26. Murphy, 115, 116–7.

27. Murphy, 71.

28. Murphy, 59.

29. For current historiography on the golden age myth, see Stephanie Coontz, *The Way We Never Were: American Families and the Nostalgia Trap* (New York: Basic Books, 1992), and John R. Gillis, *A World of Their Own Making: Myth, Ritual, and the Quest for Family Values* (New York, Basic Books, 1996). See also Hayes, *Grandma's Wartime Kitchen*; and the discussions of wartime cookbooks and the mythic past in Inness, *Dinner Roles*, 136–37; and Neuhaus, *Manly Meals*, 140–41.

30. Murphy, 164.

31. "Menus for These Times," *New York Times Book Review* (23 August 1942).

32. Inness and Neuhaus both discuss the dual focus of homefront propaganda. See especially Inness, chapter 7, "Rosie the Riveter in the Kitchen," Neuhaus, part two "'You are First and Foremost Homemakers': Cookbooks and the Second World War."

33. Alice Winn-Smith, *Thrifty Cooking for Wartime* (New York: Macmillan, 1942), vii; Betty Crocker, *Your Share: How to Prepare Appetizing, Healthful Meals with Foods Available Today* (Minneapolis, MN: General Mills, 1943), i.

34. Florence Brobeck, *Cook It in a Casserole* (New York: M. Barrows, 1943), 14.

35. Hazel Young, *The Working Girl Must Eat,* rev. ed. (Boston: Little, Brown, 1944), v.

36. Young, 10.

37. *The Good Housekeeping Cookbook* (New York: Periodical Publishers Service Bureau, 1943).

38. Brobeck, 14.

39. Harriet Hester, *300 Sugar Saving Recipes* (New York: M. Barrows, 1942), 98–103.

40. Helen Robertson, Sarah MacLeod, and Frances Preston, *What Do We Eat Now? A Guide to Wartime Housekeeping* (Philadelphia: J.B. Lippincott, 1942), 313.

41. The "Basic Seven" was the result of the work of the National Research Council's Food and Nutrition Board. Although it is frequently mentioned in other books, it is printed in chart form in Miriam Williams, *Home Canning Made Easy* (New York: Macmillan, 1943), and *The Kerr Home Canning Book* (Sand Springs, OK: Kerr Manufacturing, 1943).

42. She advised that soup be packed in a special vacuum container.

43. Hester, 159.

44. Harris, 33.

45. Robertson, 313.

46. Harris, 34–35.

47. Dorothy Marsh, "A Wonderful Lunch in a Box," *Good Housekeeping* (January 1943), 99.

48. Jane Giesler, "Nothing Fancy About These Box Lunches," *Good Housekeeping* (October 1943), 95.

Chapter 5

1. In Levenstein, *Revolution at the Table*, the author examines the economic, social, and ideological forces that helped bring about dramatic changes in American eating patterns from 1880–1930. Boorstin, *The Americans: The Democratic Experience,* 309–31 also explores the theme of changing eating habits as a result of improvements in preservation and transportation technology.

2. See Harvey Green, *Fit for America* (New York: Pantheon Books, 1986), 283–317.

3. Levenstein, *Revolution at the Table,* 148–49.

4. Levenstein, *Paradox of Plenty,* 65.

5. *Proceedings of the National Nutrition Conference for Defense* (Washington, DC: U.S. Government Printing Office, 1942), 67.

6. See Levenstein, *Paradox of Plenty,* 64–79, for a discussion of the complex history of the Recommended Daily Allowance and the various boards and committees that dealt with national nutrition.

7. Jane Holt, "News of Food," *New York Times* (6 March 1943).

8. "Housewife Urged to Buy Best Food," *New York Times* (12 November 1942).

9. Levenstein discusses the redistributive effects of rationing in *Paradox of Plenty,* 86–89. See also Black, 193–203 and 206–7; and Richard Cummings, *The American and His Food: A History of Food Habits in the United States* (Chicago: University of Chicago Press, 1940), 247–49. Nielander states that although rationing in theory equalized the distribution of scarce goods, it could not achieve "perfect equity" because the administrative means were simply "not available" (39).

10. Nielander, 137–222; and Office of Temporary Controls, Office of Price Administration, *Studies in Food Rationing* (by Judith Russell and Renee Fantin, 1948), 1–69, are detailed studies of coffee rationing that include information about consumer reactions. Russell and Fantin also include studies of processed food rationing and fats, oils, and dairy product rationing. These reports were produced for the OPA and are highly detailed, but they are useful for information about the technical process of rationing.

11. Nielander, 200.

12. *American National Biography,* s.v. "Paul V. McNutt."

13. *Proceedings of the National Nutrition Conference for Defense* (Washington, DC: U.S. Government Printing Office, 1942), 1–2.

14. *Proceedings of the National Nutrition Conference for Defense* summarized points from pp. 96–100; other material, p. 82.

15. *Proceedings of the National Nutrition Conference for Defense,* 5–6.

16. See for example, Levenstein, *Revolution at the Table* and *Paradox of Plenty*; Elizabeth Capaldi, ed., *Why We Eat What We Eat* (Washington, DC: American Psychological Association, 1996); Roy C. Wood, *The Sociology of the Meal* (Edinburgh: Edinburgh University Press, 1995); and Richard Pillsbury, *The American Diet in Time and Place* (Boulder, CO: Westview Press, 1998).

17. For more background on the focus of nutritional reform movements in the United States, see Levenstein, *Revolution at the Table,* and Green, *Fit for America.*

18. Committee on Food Habits, Food Research Council, *The Problem of Changing Food Habits.* Bulletin of the National Research Council 108, October 1943 (Washington, DC: National Research Council, 1943), 10–11.

19. Kurt Lewin, "Forces Behind Food Habits and Methods of Change," in *The Problem of Changing Food Habits,* 63.

20. Margaret Mead, "The Problem of Changing Food Habits," in *The Problem of Changing Food Habits,* 27–28.

21. Carl E. Guther, "History of the Committee on Food Habits," in *The Problem of Changing Food Habits,* 15.

22. Kurt Lewin, "Forces Behind Food Habits and Methods of Change," in *The Problem of Changing Food Habits,* 37.

23. Lewin, 35.

24. Lewin, 42.

25. Lewin, 51.

26. Lewin, 54.

27. Lewin, 43.

28. Mead, "The Problem of Changing Food Habits," 24.

29. Lewin, 43–44.

30. Mead, 26.

31. Lewin, 63.

32. Lewin, 44.

33. Study cited in Mead, 28.

34. Mead, 28.

35. Mead, 29.

36. "Better Lunch Box," *Business Week* (12 September 1942), 39.

37. Robert A. Crosby, "Improving Nutrition of War Workers," *American City* (June 1942), 103.

38. Helen Morgan Hall, "Pack a Lunch a Man Can Work On!" *Hygeia,* 20 (1942), 900.

39. Hall, 901.

40. Hall, 928.

41. Hall, 929.

42. Hall, 930.

43. "In-Plant Feeding," *Business Week* (19 August 1944), 106.

44. "Better Lunch Box," 42.

45. "Better Lunch Box," 42.

46. Gertrude York Christy, "The Lunch Box Derby," *Journal of Home Economics* (May 1943), 285.

47. Christy, 286.

Chapter 6

1. For a fascinating study of family life in the postwar United States, see Elaine Tyler May, *Homeward Bound: American Families in the Cold War Era* (New York: Basic Books, 1988).

2. More information of the National School Lunch Program appears in the next chapter.

3. E. P. Thompson, *Customs in Common* (London: Merlin Press, 1991), 359. Emphasis in original.

4. Thompson, 368.

5. Thompson, 388.

6. Frank Adams, *Then Ya Just Untwist* (Rialto, CA: Rialto Publishing, 1951). Because this book contains no page numbers, future references will not be noted.

7. Ida Bailey Allen, *Mrs. Allen's Book of Sugar Substitutes* (Boston: Small, Maynard, 1918). Allen, *Mrs. Allen's Book of Wheat Substitutes* (Boston: Small, Maynard, 1918).

8. *Contemporary Authors Online*, Gale, 2005. Reproduced in *Biography Resource Center*, *New York Times* (17 July 1973).

9. Ida Bailey Allen, "The Nation's Lunch Box," *Today's Health*, 33 (September 1955), 24–25; 44–51.

10. Nelson Lichtenstein, "Conflict over Workers' Control: The Automobile Industry in World War II," in *Working Class America: Essays on Labor, Community, and American Society*, ed. Michael H. Frisch and Daniel J. Walkowitz (Urbana: University of Illinois Press, 1983), 284–304.

11. "On-the-Job Food," *Business Week* (1 September 1944), 65.

12. "Lunchbox Is No Picnic for Telephone Workers," *Business Week* (5 December 1953), 164.

13. "Lunch with Pay," *Business Week* (30 June 1951), 34.

14. "Food at the Bargaining Table," *Monthly Labor Review* (September 1979), 58.

15. Maria Gallagher, "Tote Cuisine," Knight-Ridder/Tribune News Service (10 September 2001).

16. Kemba Johnson, "Brown Baggin' It," *American Demographics* (January 2001), n.p.

17. Anne Lear, "The Great Lunch Box Caper," *Gourmet* (March 1985), 126.

18. Susan Hodges, "A Lower-Cost Menu," *Nation's Business*, 86 (August 1998), 26.

19. Bryan Miller, "Earning It," *New York Times* (18 June 1995).

20. Bill Husted, "Three-Martini Lunch Alive at the Palm," *Denver Post* (26 October 2001).

21. Marian Burros, "High Noon: Restaurants Fight to Draw a Crowd," *New York Times* (7 July 1999).

22. "This Brown Bag Crowd Could Surprise You," *Restaurant Business*, 92, no. 15 (10 October 1993), 30.

23. "LTV, Union Row Over Lunch," *American Metal Market* (13 January 1994), 102.

Chapter 7

1. "Truman Approves School Lunch Bill," *New York Times* (5 June 1946).

2. J. D. Ratcliff, "Eating Their Way to Health and Learning," *Reader's Digest*, 38 (February 1941), 94–95.

3. Ronald Edsforth, *The New Deal: America's Response to the Great Depression* (Malden, MA: Blackwell Publishers, 2000), 47.

4. Gordon W. Gunderson, "The National School Lunch Program: Background and Development," www.fns.usda.gov, accessed 19 September 2000.

5. "School Lunches in Country and City," *Farmer's Bulletin* (Washington, DC: Department of Agricultural Economics, 1942), 3.

6. "School Lunches in Country and City," 4.

7. Ellen Woodward, "WPA School Lunch Program," *School and Society*, 46 (17 July 1937), 91.

8. Gunderson.

9. "School Lunches in Country and City," 6.

10. "School Lunch Cost Assailed in House," *New York Times* (20 February 1946).

11. "House Votes Fund for School Meals," *New York Times* (22 February 1946).

12. "House Votes Fund for School Meals."

13. "School Lunch Fund Doubled by Senate," *New York Times* (27 February 1946).

14. "Ponder Racial Issue in School Lunch Bill," *New York Times* (21 February 1946).

15. National School Lunch Act, Public Law 396.

16. Jean R. Komaiko, "The Shocking Failure of the School Lunch Act," *Parents*, 45 (March 1970), 59.

17. Gunderson, 31–33.

18. Gunderson, 34.

19. "Hershey Decries Low Nutrition," *New York Times* (28 March 1945).

20. "Need for School Luncheons Is Stressed as Part of Education-Nutrition Program," *New York Times* (2 March 1944).

21. "Truman Approves School Lunch Bill," *New York Times* (5 June 1946).

22. Gunderson.

23. Gregory Cerio, "Put an End to Bad Lunch," *Redbook* (September 1994), 194.

24. Scott Bruce, "The Power Lunch: It's in the Bag," *Disney Magazine* (Fall 1996), 106.

25. Bruce, *The Fifties and Sixties Lunch Box* (San Francisco: Chronicle Books, 1988), 7.

26. Bruce, *The Fifties and Sixties Lunch Box*, 9.

27. Bruce, *The Fifties and Sixties Lunch Box*, 8.

28. "The Sacred Cod Goes to School," *Practical Home Economics*, 33 (January 1955), 21.

29. "Public and Private Efforts for the National School Lunch Program," *Food Review* (May–August 1996), 54–55.

30. Diane Brockett, "School Cafeterias Selling Brand-Name Junk Food: WHO Deserves a Break Today?" *Education Digest* (October 1998), 58–59.

31. Miriam Stawowy, "Plan to Ban School Vending Unpopular," *Hampton-Newport News (Virginia) Daily Press* (31 January 2002).

Chapter 8

1. Anne Allison, "Japanese Mothers and Obentos: The Lunch-Box as Ideological State Apparatus," *Anthropological Quarterly*, 64 (1991), 198.

2. Allison, 195.

3. Allison, 195.

4. "Clubwomen Back School Luncheons," *New York Times* (28 April 1944).

5. See DeVault, *Feeding the Family;* Manton, *Fed Up: Women and Food in America* (Westport, CT: Bergin and Garvey); and Charles and Kerr, *Women, Food, and Families.*

6. See DeVault.

7. On women's roles in American history, see, for example, Nancy Cott, *The Bonds of Womanhood: "Woman's Sphere" in New England, 1780–1835* (New Haven: Yale University Press, 1977); Sara M. Evans, *Born for Liberty: A History of Women in America* (New York: Free Press, 1989); Linda Kerber, "Separate Spheres, Female Worlds, Woman's Place: The Rhetoric of Women's History," *Journal of American History* 75 (June 1988): 9–38; Mary P. Ryan, *Womanhood in America: From Colonial New York Times to the Present*, 3rd ed. (New York: Franklin Watts, 1983); and Barbara Welter, "The Cult of True Womanhood: 1820–1860," *American Quarterly*, 18 (Summer 1966): 151–174.

8. On the role of American women's magazines, see Nancy A. Walker, *Shaping Our Mothers' World: American Women's Magazines* (Jackson: University Press of Mississippi, 2000); and Mary Ellen Zuckerman, *A History of Popular Women's Magazines in the United States, 1792–1995* (Westport, CT: Greenwood Press, 1998).

9. Bertha Stevenson, "The Young Business Woman's Lunch," *Good Housekeeping* (November 1911), 695–697.

10. H. M. Conklin and P. D. Partridge, "The Dinner-Pail of the Business Girl," *Delineator*, 97, (September 1920), 36.

11. Betty Friedan, *The Feminine Mystique: With a New Introduction and Epilogue by the Author* (New York: Dell, 1994), 18

12. Mary C. Brown, "What Your Child Eats at Noon," *Hygeia*, 11 (September 1933), 807.

13. Lillian Alber, "Recess and a Square Lunch," *Delineator* (October 1922), 52.

14. Hunt, Caroline L. "The Children's Lunch at School," *Good Housekeeping* (September 1910).

15. Brown, "What Your Child Eats at Noon," 809.

16. Helen E. Ridley, "Box Lunches That Intrigue," *Good Housekeeping* (September 1936), 85.

17. Bonnie Lehman, "Readin,' Writin,' and Lunchboxes," *Parents*, 36 (September 1964), 73 and 102.

18. Alice D. Hanrahan, "Your Child's First Lunch Box," *Parents*, 29 (September 1954), 59.

19. "Candidates for School Lunches," *Parents*, 31 (November 1956), 66–67.

20. "Packed with Love: Lunch-Box Foods Kids Will Eat," *Parents* (September 1987), 170.

21. www.marthastewart.com, cooking and entertaining, accessed September 14, 1999. It is interesting that Stewart uses brand-name cereals for this project, but she (or some member of her staff), must have neglected to consult carefully with a box of "Fruit Loops" for had she done so, she would have seen that Kellogg's popular cereal name plays on the double "o" in "Loops" by misspelling *fruit* as "Froot."

22. Elizabeth Shaffer, "Lunching Alone: Addressed to the Woman Who Eats by Herself at Noon," *Woman's Home Companion*, 57 (February 1930), 78.

23. Myrna Johnston, "What the Men Are Having for Lunch!" *Better Homes and Gardens*, 41 (March 1963), 72.

24. Sue B. Huffman, "Lunch-to-Go," *Ladies' Home Journal* (September 1976), 108–109.

25. "Lunch-Box Specials," *Good Housekeeping* (September 1977), 160–167, and 227–228.

26. Eva Seldens Bank and Cecily Brownstone, "If They Take Their Lunch," *Parents*, 18 (October 1943), 52–62.

27. Diane Worthington, "Lunch to Go!" *Working Mother* (September 1992), 115.

28. Ellen Garvey, *The Adman in the Parlor: Magazines and the Gendering of Consumer Culture, 1880s–1910s,* (New York: Oxford University Press, 1996), demonstrates how at the turn of the century, magazines became increasingly driven by advertising revenue rather than editorial content. As a part of this process, advertising moved from the back matter of the journals to more prominent locations in the front and center regions. Sometimes, advertising even masqueraded as fiction, making the separation between content and commercials shady. According to Garvey, this transition in magazine style allowed for advertising to infiltrate the middle-class American home without disturbing traditional gender prescriptions. In this way, advertising moved in to what was once a private space.

29. Ellen McCracken, *Decoding Women's Magazines From Mlle to Ms* (New York: St. Martin's Press, 1993).

30. Mary Jean Leedy, "From Freezer to Lunch Box," *Good Housekeeping*, 133 (September 1951), 185.

31. Douglas E. Bowers, "Cooking Trends Echo Changing Roles of Women," *USDA Food Review* 23 (January–April 2000), 23–31.

32. For an interesting discussion of how toy manufacturers and advertisers sell to parents and children, see Ellen Seiter, *Sold Separately: Children and Parents in Consumer Culture* (New Brunswick: Rutgers University Press, 1993). Seiter examines toys in the context of the relationships among children, parents, and manufacturers. She argues that it is a middle-class delusion that children should be shielded from consumerism. She notes that people need to come to terms with the fact that parenthood and consumption are inextricably linked.

33. For the purpose of clarity, the term *lunchable* will be used to refer to the entire product category, and *Lunchable* will denote the Oscar Mayer brand product specifically.

34. Stephen Dowdell, "Oscar Mayer Sees Lunch Kits Maturing," *Supermarket News*, 45 (19 June, 1995), 28.

35. Diane Lore and Reagan Walker, "Leaning on Lunch Sets; Parents Hop on Prepackaged Meals, but Are They Nutritious?" *Atlanta Constitution* (12 October 1999).

36. Carole Sugarman, "You Call This Lunch? Lunchables are Everywhere," *Washington Post* (29 September 1999).

37. Since the early 1980s, plastic lunch boxes have eclipsed their earlier metal counterparts. The root cause of this mysterious disappearance of the meal box has long been a source of debate among lunch box collectors. Some attribute it to the activities of a group of Florida mothers who called the metal box a "killer, a classroom Corvair. After they paraded alleged victims of box 'brain-bashing' past the Florida legislature, a ban was slapped on the sale of steel boxes. Other legislatures soon fell to the inquisition." This tale of mothers on the march has achieved the status of myth in lunch box collecting circles. The actual existence of any Florida statute remains unconfirmed, and some companies have begun to manufacture the metal boxes once again. Whether the maternal protests are truth or fiction, it was most likely the health of the financial balance sheet that instigated manufacturers' shift away from metal. As plastic production techniques became less expensive, these boxes replaced metal ones. Bryan Los, "Florida Lunch Box Legislation: Law or Lore?" Lunch Box Pad, www.echoroom.com/lunchbox, accessed 29 February 2000.

38. For a thorough and interesting look at American families and the idealized past, see Stephanie Coontz, *The Way We Never Were: American Families and the Nostalgia Trap* (New York: Basic Books, 1992).

39. Philip Brasher, "What's for Dinner? Industry Hopes It'll Be Pre-Cooked, No-Fuss Entrees," *Hampton (Virginia) Daily Press* (9 May 2001).

40. Allison, 198.

Conclusion

1. "Obese Diabetic Sues Fast Food Restaurants," *Hampton-Newport News (Virginia) Daily Press* (27 July 2002).

2. Eric Schlosser, *Fast Food Nation: The Dark Side of the All-American Meal* (Boston: Houghton Mifflin, 2001).

3. Super Size Me Film Website, "Statement by Morgan Spurlock on Super Size Me," www.supersizeme.com/home.aspx?page= aboutmovie, accessed July 3, 2004.

4. Manuel Castells, *The Rise of the Network Society*, 2nd ed. (London: Blackwell Publishing, 2000), 163–83.

5. Armand and Michèle Mattelart, *Theories of Communication: A Short Introduction* (London: Sage, 1998), 125–26.

6. An important characteristic of the successful network enterprise is flexibility in production and the ability to tailor products and or services to meet the needs and desires of certain specific consumers or markets. The system of interchangeable parts, so vital to the development of American manufacturing capability during the nineteenth century, while shifting the focus from individualized production, did not necessarily limit specialization, but in fact it made some degree of specialization, albeit within a certain specified range, more efficient and cost-effective. Even Henry Ford, who was noted for his mass-production methods, is said to have told consumers that they could have their Model T's in any color — so long as it was black. Today, in contrast, the flexibility of networked production allows for greater availability of custom products, limited only by the reach of the network. For an interesting and lively discussion of the impact made by the intersection of interchangeable parts and statistical quality control, see Boorstin, *The Americans: The Democratic Experience*. Boorstin concludes that a "just make it so it works" mentality was the result of this occurrence (see 193–94).

7. Nanci Hellmich, "This Man Is Watching You Eat," *USA Today* (13 October 2004).

8. "Europeans Outweigh U.S. in Ratio of Obesity Cases," *Charlottesville (Virginia) Daily Progress* (16 March 2005).

9. "Revising the Food Pyramid," *Charlottesville (Virginia) Daily Progress* (6 April 2004).

10. U.S. Department of Agriculture, "News and Media," www.mypyramid.gov/global_nav/media_press_release.html, accessed July 3, 2005.

11. "New Food Pyramid Emphasizes Exercise," *Charlottesville (Virginia) Daily Progress* (20 April 2005).

12. Sesame Workshop, "Press Releases," www.sesameworkshop.org/press, accessed 21 June 2005.

13. Sesame Workshop, "Healthy Habits for Life Initiative," www.sesameworkshop.org/press, accessed 21 June 2005.

14. Oldways, "What Os Oldways?" www.oldwayspt.org/about/about.html, accessed 5 July 2005.

15. Whole Grains Council, "Reaping the Benefits of Whole Grains," www.wholegrainscouncil.org/Consumer%20Guide.html, accessed 6 July 2005.

16. Whole Grains Council, "Closing the Whole Grains Gap," www.wholegrainscouncil.org/index.htm, accessed 6 July 2005.

17. U.S. Department of Agriculture, "MyPyramid.gov," www.mypyramid.gov/pyramid/index.html, accessed 6 July 2005.

18. General Mills, Corporate, Health and Wellness, In the News, "General Mills Announces Major New Nutrition Education Initiative in Conjunction with New Food Guide Pyramid, 19 April 2005," www.generalmills.com/corporate/health_wellness/in_the_news_detail.aspx%3FitemID%3D10561%26catID%3D7586%26section%3Dnews+general+mills+whole+grain+initiative&hl=en, accessed 6 July 2005.

19. General Mills, Corporate Media Center, "General Mills Launches New Children's Advertising Initiative," 22 June 2005, www.generalmills.com/corporate/media_center/news_release_detail.aspx?itemID=11144&catID=227, accessed 6 July 2005. See also www.choosebreakfast.com.

20. Congress, House, Personal Responsibility in Consumption Act of 2005, 109th Congress, 1st sess., H.R. 554, thomas.loc.gov, accessed 28 October 2005.

21. Ibid.

22. National Restaurant Association, "Public Policy Issue Briefs," www.restaurant.org/government/issues/issue.cfm?Issue=lawsuits, accessed 6 July 2005.

23. Perri Klass, "The Lunchbox as Battlefield." *Gourmet* (November 1999), 244.

24. Dan Ackman, "Judge to Fat Plaintiffs: Where's the Beef?" www.forbes.com, accessed 24 January 2003.

25. Thomas Jefferson to William Charles Jarvis, 28 September 1820. Library of Congress: Jefferson Papers. This transcription retains Jefferson's idiosyncratic spelling and capitalization.

Selected Bibliography

Periodicals and Journals Cited

The American City
American Demographics
American Journal of Public Health and the
    Nation's Health
American Metal Market
Better Homes and Gardens
Business
Business Week
Christian Science Monitor
Consumer Reports
Cooking Light
The Delineator
The Disney Magazine
The Education Digest
Education for Victory
The Elementary School Journal
Factory and Industrial Management
Good Housekeeping
Gourmet
Hygeia
The Independent
Industrial Management
Journal of Educational Psychology
Journal of Home Economics
Ladies' Home Journal
The Literary Digest
Monthly Labor Review
The Nation
Nation's Business
Newsweek
Parents
Practical Home Economics
Reader's Digest
Redbook
Restaurant Business
Saturday Evening Post
Science Digest
School Life
School and Society
Scribner's Monthly
Supermarket News
Technical World Magazine
Today's Health
USDA Food Review
The Weather Gauge: The Magazine of the
    Chesapeake Bay Maritime Museum
Woman's Home Companion
Working Mother

Newspapers

The Atlanta Constitution
Charlottesville (Virginia) Daily Progress
The Chicago Sun-Times
The Denver Post
Hampton-Newport News (Virginia) Daily
    Press
Milwaukee Journal Sentinel
The New York Daily Tribune
New York Times
USA Today
The Washington Post

Selected Bibliography

Web Sites

www.echoroom.com/lunchbox
www.forbes.com
www.fsn.usda.gov (Gordon Gunderson,
    "The National School Lunch Program:
    Background and Development")
www.generalmills.com
www.marthastewart.com
www.mypyramid.gov
www.oldwayspt.org
www.restaurant.org
www.sesameworkshop.org
www.slate.msn.com
www.thomas.loc.gov
www.wholegrainscouncil.org

Popular Literature

Baum, L. Frank. *Ozma of Oz*, 1907.
Bellamy, Edward. *Looking Backward*,
    1888.
Crane, Stephen. *Maggie: A Girl of the
    Streets*, 1893.
Dreiser, Theodore. *Sister Carrie*, 1900.
Lee, Harper. *To Kill a Mockingbird*, 1960.
Sinclair, Upton. *The Jungle*, 1905.
Steinbeck, John. *The Grapes of Wrath*,
    1939.
Wolfe, Thomas. *Look Homeward, Angel*,
    1929.

Monographs and Articles

Adam, Barbara. *Time and Social Theory*. Philadelphia: Temple University Press, 1990.
Adams, Frank. *Then Ya Just Untwist*. Rialto, CA: Rialto Publishing, 1951.
Allison, Anne. "Japanese Mothers and Obentos: The Lunch-Box as Ideological State Apparatus." *Anthropological Quarterly* 64 (1991): 195–208.
The American Heritage Cookbook and Illustrated History of American Eating and Drinking. New York: Simon and Schuster, 1964.
American Social History Project. Herbert G. Gutman, founding director. *Who Built America: Working People and the Nation's Economy, Politics, Culture, and Society. Volume Two: From the Gilded Age to the Present*. New York: Pantheon Books, 1992.
Anderson, Karen. *Wartime Women: Sex Roles, Family Relations, and the Status of Women During World War II*. Westport, CT: Greenwood Press, 1981.
Appadurai, Arjun, ed. *The Social Life of Things: Commodities in Cultural Perspective*. Cambridge: Cambridge University Press, 1986. Part 1: "Toward An Anthropology of Things."
Batjer, Margaret Q., and Mimi Atwater. *Meals for the Modern Family*. New York: John Wiley and Sons, 1961.
Baum, Frank Joslyn, and Russell P. MacFall. *To Please a Child: A Biography of L. Frank Baum: Royal Historian of Oz*. Chicago: Reilly and Lee, 1961.
Beaudry, Mary C., and Stephen A. Mrozowski. *Interdisciplinary Investigations of the Boott Mills Lowell, Massachusetts. Volume III, The Boarding House System as a Way of Life*. National Park Service, 1989.
Beecher, Catherine E., and Harriet Beecher Stowe. *The American Woman's Home*. New York: J. B. Ford and Co., 1869.
Belasco, Warren. *Appetite for Change: How the Counterculture Took on the Food Industry, 1966–1988*. New York: Pantheon Books, 1988.
Bell, David, and Gill Valentine, eds. *Consuming Geographies: We Are Where We Eat*. London: Routledge, 1997.
Bentley, Amy Lynn. *Eating for Victory: Food Rationing and the Politics of Domesticity*. Urbana: University of Illinois Press, 1998.
Black, John D. *Food Enough*. Lancaster, PA: Jacques Cattell Press, 1943.
Blum, John Morton. *V Was for Victory: Politics and Culture During World War II*. New York: Harcourt, Brace, 1976.
Boortstin, Daniel. *The Americans: The Democratic Experience*. New York: Vintage Books, 1974.
Boris, Eileen. *Home to Work: Motherhood and the Politics of Industrial Homework in the United States*. Cambridge: Cambridge University Press, 1994.

Bourdieu, Pierre. *Distinction: A Social Critique of the Judgement of Taste*. Translated by Richard Nice. Cambridge, MA: Harvard University Press, 1984.

_____, and James S. Coleman, ed. *Social Theory for a Changing Society*. Boulder: Westview Press, 1991.

Boydston, Jeanne. *Home and Work: Housework, Wages, and the Ideology of Labor in the Early Republic*. New York: Oxford University Press, 1990.

Brillat-Savarin, Jean Anthelme. *Physiologie Du Gout*. Paris: Feydeau, 1826. 2 vols.

Brobeck, Florence. *Cook It in a Casserole*. New York: M. Barrows, 1943.

Brody, David. *In Labor's Cause: Main Themes on the History of the American Worker*. New York: Oxford University Press, 1993.

_____. "Workers and Work in America: The New Labor History." In *Ordinary People and Everyday Life: Perspectives on the New Social History*, ed. James B. Gardner and George Rollie Adams, 139–159. Nashville: American Association for State and Local History, 1983.

Brown, Linda Keller, and Kay Mussell, eds. *Ethnic and Regional Foodways in the United States: The Performance of Group Identity*. Knoxville: University of Tennessee Press, 1984.

Bruce, Scott. *The Fifties and Sixties Lunch Box*. San Francisco: Chronicle Books, 1988.

_____, and Bill Crawford. *Cerealizing America: The Unsweetened Story of American Breakfast Cereal*. Boston: Faber and Faber, 1995.

Brunnell, Miriam Formanek. *Made to Play House: Dolls and the Commercialization of American Girlhood, 1830–1930*. New Haven: Yale University Press, 1993.

Bryan, Mary DeGarmo. *The School Cafeteria*. New York: F. S. Crofts, 1936.

Calhoun, Craig, ed. *Habermas and the Public Sphere*. Cambridge, MA: MIT Press, 1992.

Camp, Charles. *American Foodways: What, When, Why and How We Eat in America*. Little Rock, AK: August House, 1989.

Campbell, Colin. *The Romantic Ethic and the Spirit of Modern Consumerism*. Oxford: Blackwell, 1987.

Campbell, D'Ann. *Women at War with America: Private Lives in a Patriotic Era*. Cambridge, MA: Harvard University Press, 1984.

Capaldi, Elizabeth, ed. *Why We Eat What We Eat*. Washington, DC: American Psychological Association, 1996.

Carson, Barbara G. *Ambitious Appetites: Dining, Behavior, and Patterns of Consumption in Federal Washington*. Washington, DC: American Institute of Architects Press, 1990.

Chafe, William H. *The Paradox of Change: American Women in the Twentieth Century*. New York: Oxford University Press, 1991.

Chambers, John Whiteclay III. *The Tyranny of Change: America in the Progressive Era*. New Brunswick: Rutgers University Press, 2d ed., 2000.

Charles, Nickie, and Marion Kerr. *Women, Food and Families: Power, Status, Love, Anger*. New York: St. Martins, 1988.

Cohen, Lizabeth. *Making a New Deal: Industrial Workers in Chicago, 1919–1939*. New York: Cambridge University Press, 1990.

Cohen, Sol. *Progressives and Urban School Reform: The Public Education Association of New York City, 1895–1954*. New York: Teacher's College, Columbia University, 1964.

Coontz, Stephanie. *The Way We Never Were: American Families and the Nostalgia Trap*. New York: Basic Books, 1992.

Cott, Nancy. *The Bonds of Womanhood: "Woman's Sphere" in New England, 1780–1835*. New Haven: Yale University Press, 1977.

_____. *The Groundings of Modern Feminism*. New Haven: Yale University Press, 1987.

Counihan, Carole, and Penny Van Esterik, eds. *Food and Culture: A Reader*. New York: Routledge, 1997.

Cowan, Ruth Schwartz. *More Work for Mother: The Ironies of Household Technology from the Open Hearth to the Microwave*. New York: Basic Books, 1983.

Craigie, Sir William A., and James R. Hulbert. *A Dictionary of American English on Historical Principles*. Chicago: University of Chicago Press, 1942.

Crichton, Judy. *America 1900: The Turning Point*. New York: Henry Holt, 1998.

Cross, Gary. *Kid's Stuff: Toys and the Changing World of American Childhood*. Cambridge, MA: Harvard University Press, 1997.

Cross, Gary. *Time and Money: The Making of Consumer Culture*. New York: Routledge, 1993.

Csikszentmihalyi, Mihalyi. *The Meaning of Things: Domestic Symbols and the Self*. Cambridge: Cambridge University Press, 1981.

Cummings, Richard. *The American and His Food: A History of Food Habits in the United States*. Chicago: University of Chicago Press, 1940.

Damon-Moore, Helen. *Magazines for the Millions: Gender and Commerce in the Ladies Home Journal and the Saturday Evening Post, 1880–1910*. Albany: State University Press of New York, 1994.

DeVault, Marjorie L. *Feeding the Family: The Social Organization of Caring as Gendered Work*. Chicago: University of Chicago Press, 1991.

Dittmar, Helga. *The Social Psychology of Material Possessions: To Have Is To Be*. New York: St. Martins, 1992.

Douglas, Mary. "Deciphering a Meal." In *Implicit Meanings: Essays in Anthropology*. London: Routledge and Kegan Paul, 1975.

_____, and Baron Isherwood. *The World of Goods: Towards and Anthropology of Consumption*. New York: W. W. Norton, 1977.

Dregni, Michael. "The Politics of Oz." *Utne Reader* July/August 1988, 32–33.

Eagleton, Terry. *Ideology: An Introduction*. London: Verso, 1991.

Edsforth, Ronald. *The New Deal: America's Response to the Great Depression*. Malden, MA: Blackwell, 2000.

Eichar, Douglas M. *Occupation and Class Consciousness in America*. New York: Greenwood, 1989.

Endres, Kathleen L., and Therese L. Lueck. *Women's Periodicals in the United States: Consumer Magazines*. Westport, CT: Greenwood, 1995.

Evans, Sara M. *Born for Liberty: A History of Women in America*. New York: Free Press, 1989.

Faubion, James D., ed. *Michel Foucault: Power*. New York: New World Press, 1994.

Finkelstein, Joanne. *Dining Out: A Sociology of Modern Manners*. New York: New York University Press, 1989.

Ford, Willard Stanley. *Some Administrative Problems of the High School Cafeteria*. New York: Bureau of Publications, Teacher's College, Columbia University, 1926; reprint, New York: AMS Press, 1972.

Forster, Robert, and Orest Ranum, eds. *Food and Drink in History: Selections from the Annales Economies, Societes, Civilisations*. Volume 5. Translated by Elborg Forster and Patricia M. Ranum. Baltimore, MD: Johns Hopkins University Press, 1979.

Fowles, Jib. *Advertising and Popular Culture*. Thousand Oaks, CA: Sage, 1996.

Fleming, E. McClung. "Artifact Study: A Proposed Model," in *Material Culture Studies in America*, ed. Thomas J. Schlereth. Nashville: American Association for State and Local History, 1982.

Friedan, Betty. *The Feminine Mystique*. New York: Dell, 1994.

Frisch, Michael H., and Daniel J. Walkowitz, eds. *Working-Class America: Essays on Labor, Community, and American Society*. Urbana: University of Illinois Press, 1983.

Gardiner, Martin, and Russel B. Nye. *The Wizard of Oz and Who He Was*. East Lansing: Michigan State University Press, 1957.

Gardner, Iwon, Cynthia Winder, and Alan Sharpe. *The Relationship Between Nutrition and Learning: A School Employee's Guide to Information and Action*. Washington, DC: National Education Association, 1989.

Garvey, Ellen Gruber. *The Adman in the Parlor: Magazines and the Gendering of Consumer Culture, 1880s to 1910s*. New York: Oxford University Press, 1996.

"Gee Whiz — Was the Wiz Really William McKinley," *Charlotte Observer*, 30 March 1978, 5H.

Geertz, Clifford. *The Interpretation of Cultures*. New York: Basic Books, 1973.

Gillis, John R. *A World of Their Own Making: Myth, Ritual, and the Quest for Family Values*. New York: Basic Books, 1996.

Glad, Paul W. *McKinley, Bryan, and the People*. Philadelphia: J. B. Lippincott, 1964.

Goffman, Irving. *The Presentation of the Self in Everyday Life*. New York: Doubleday Anchor, 1959.

The Good Housekeeping Cookbook. New York: Periodical Publishers Services Bureau, 1943.

Gould, Lewis L. *The Presidency of William McKinley.* Lawrence: Regents Press of Kansas, 1980.

Grier, Katherine C. *Culture and Comfort: Parlor Making and Middle-Class Identity, 1850–1930.* Washington, DC: Smithsonian Institution Press, 1988.

Grover, Kathryn, ed. *Dining In America, 1850–1900.* Amherst: University of Massachusetts Press and Margaret Woodbury Strong Museum, 1987.

Guethe, Carl E., and Margaret Mead. *The Problem of Changing Food Habits: Report of the Committee on Food Habits, 1941–1943.* Bulletin of the National Research Council, Number 108, October 1943.

Gumbert, Edgar B., and Joel H. Spring. *The Superschool and the Superstate: American Education in the Twentieth Century, 1918–1970.* New York: John Wiley and Sons, 1974.

Gutman, Herbert G. *Power and Culture: Essays on the American Working Class.* Edited by Ira Berlin. New York: Pantheon Books, 1987.

Habermas, Jurgen. *The Theory of Communicative Action.* 2 vols. Boston: Beacon Press, 1984–7.

Hall, Edward. *Beyond Culture.* New York: Doubleday Anchor, 1976.

_____. *The Dance of Life: The Other Dimension of Time.* Garden City: Anchor Press/Doubleday, 1983.

Hall, Sharon K., ed. *Twentieth-Century Literary Criticism.* Detroit: Gale Research Company, 1982. s.v. "L(yman) Frank Baum."

Hamby, Alonzo. *Liberalism and Its Challengers: FDR to Reagan.* New York: Oxford University Press, 1985.

Hareven, Tamara K. *Family Time and Industrial Time: The Relationship Between the Family and Work in a New England Industrial Community.* Cambridge: Cambridge University Press, 1982.

Harris, Florence Laganke. *Victory Vitamin Cookbook for Wartime Meals.* New York: William Penn, 1943.

Harris, Jessie W., and Elisabeth Lacey Speer. *Everyday Foods.* Boston: Houghton Mifflin, 1939.

Hartmann, Susan. *The Homefront and Beyond: Women in the 1940s.* Boston: Twayne Publishers, 1982.

Hayes, Joanne Lamb. *Grandma's Wartime Kitchen: World War II and the Way We Cooked.* New York: St. Martin's Press, 2000.

Heald, Edward Thornton. *Condensed Biography of William McKinley.* Canton, OH: Stark County Historical Society, 1964.

Hester, Harriet. *300 Sugar Saving Recipes.* New York: M. Barrows, 1942.

Hess, John L., and Karen Hess. *The Taste of America.* 3d ed. University of South Carolina Press, 1989.

Hewitt, Patricia. *About Time: The Revolution in Work and Family Life.* London: Rivers Oram Press, 1993.

Hofstadter, Richard, ed. *The Progressive Movement: 1900–1915.* Englewood Cliffs, NJ: Prentice Hall, 1963.

Honey, Maureen. *Creating Rosie the Riveter: Class, Gender, and Propaganda during World War II.* Amherst: University of Massachusetts Press, 1984.

Horowitz, Daniel. *The Morality of Spending: Attitudes Toward the Consumer Society In America, 1875–1940.* Chicago: Ivan R. Dee, 1985.

Horsfield, Margaret. *Biting the Dust: The Joys of Housework.* New York: St. Martin's, 1998.

Humphrey, Theodore C., Sue Samuelson, and Lin T. Humphrey. *We Gather Together: Food and Festivity in American Life.* Ann Arbor: UMI Research Press, 1988.

Hunnicutt, Benjamin Kline. *Kellogg's Six-Hour Day.* Philadelphia: Temple University Press, 1996.

Inness, Sherrie. *Dinner Roles: American Women and Culinary Culture.* Iowa City: University of Iowa Press, 2001.

Jones, Evan. *American Food: The Gastronomic Story.* New York: Overlook Press, 1990.

Jones, Stanley L. *The Presidential Election of 1896.* Madison: University of Wisconsin Press, 1964.

Kahn, Barbara E., and Leigh McAlister. *Grocery Revolution: The New Focus on the Consumer.* Reading, MA: Addison-Wesley, 1997.

Katz, Michael B. *Improving Poor People: The Welfare State, the "Underclass," and Urban Schools as History.* Princeton: Princeton University Press, 1995.

Kent, Noel Jacob. *America in 1900.* Armonk, NY: M. E. Sharpe, 2000.

Kerber, Linda K. "The Republican Mother: Women and the Enlightenment — An American Perspective." *American Quarterly* 28 (Summer 1976): 187–205.

_____. "Separate Spheres, Female Worlds, Woman's Place: The Rhetoric of Women's History." *Journal of American History* 75, no. 1 (June 1988): 9–39.

_____. *Women of the Republic: Intellect and Ideology in Revolutionary America.* Chapel Hill: University of North Carolina Press, 1980.

Kubler, George. *The Shape of Time.* New Haven: Yale University Press, 1962.

Kupperman, Karen Ordahl, ed. *Captain John Smith: A Select Edition of His Writings.* Chapel Hill: University of North Carolina Press, 1988.

Lautenschlager, Julie L. " 'I Will Waste Nothing!': American Women's Patriotism Seen Through World War II–Era Cookbooks." Master's thesis, Kent State University, 1997.

Leach, William. *Land of Desire: Merchants, Power, and the Rise of a New American Culture.* New York: Pantheon Books, 1993.

Leff, Mark H. "The Politics of Sacrifice on the American Home Front in World War II." *Journal of American History* 77, no. 4 (March 1991): 1296–1318.

Leonardi, Susan. "Recipes for Reading: Pasta Salad, Lobster à la Riseholme, Key Lime Pie." In *Cooking by the Book: Food in Literature and Culture,* ed. Mary Anne Schofield, 126–37. Bowling Green, OH: Bowling Green University Popular Press, 1989.

Levenstein, Harvey. *Paradox of Plenty: A Social History of Eating in Modern America.* New York: Oxford University Press, 1993.

_____. *Revolution at the Table: The Transformation of the American Diet.* New York: Oxford, 1988.

Levitan, Sar A., ed. *Blue-Collar Workers: A Symposium on Middle America.* New York: McGraw-Hill, 1971.

Lingeman, Richard R. *Don't You Know There's a War On? The American Homefront, 1941–1945.* New York: G. P. Putnam's Sons, 1970.

Littlefield, Henry M. "The Wizard of Oz: Parable on Populism." *American Quarterly* 16 (Spring 1964): 47–58.

Lyman, Bernard. *A Psychology of Food: More Than a Matter of Taste.* New York: Van Nostrand Reinhold, 1989.

MacClancy, Jeremy. *Consuming Culture: Why You Eat What You Eat.* New York: Henry Holt, 1992.

Macklin, M. Carole, and Les Carlson. *Advertising to Children: Concepts and Controversies.* Thousand Oaks, CA: Sage, 1999.

Manton, Catherine. *Fed Up: Women and Food in America.* Westport: Bergin and Garvey, 1999.

Marchand, Roland. *Advertising the American Dream: Making Way for Modernity, 1920–1940.* Berkeley: University of California Press, 1985.

Margolis, Sidney. *The Great American Food Hoax.* New York: Walker, 1971.

Mariani, John. *America Eats Out.* New York: Morrow, 1991.

Marling, Karal Ann. *As Seen on TV: The Visual Culture of Everyday Life in the 1950s.* Cambridge, MA: Harvard University Press, 1994.

Martin, Ann Smart. "Makers, Buyers, Users: Consumerism as a Material Culture Framework." *Winterthur Portfolio* Summer/Autumn 1993, 141–158.

_____, and J. Ritchie Garrison, eds. *American Material Culture: The Shape of the Field.* Knoxville: University of Tennessee Press, 1999.

Martin, Ethel Austin. *Roberts' Nutrition Work with Children.* Chicago: University of Chicago Press, 1954.

Matthews, Glenna. *"Just a Housewife": The Rise and Fall of Domesticity in America.* New York: Oxford University Press, 1987.

Maurer, Donna and Jeffery Sobal, eds. *Eating Agendas: Food and Nutrition as Social Problems.* Hawthorne, NY: Aldine de Gruyter, 1995.

May, Elaine Tyler. *Homeward Bound: American Families in the Cold War Era*. New York: Basic Books, 1988.

McAllister, Matthew P. *The Commercialization of American Culture: New Advertising, Control, and Democracy*. Thousand Oaks, CA: Sage, 1996.

McCracken, Ellen. *Decoding Women's Magazines: From Mademoiselle to Ms*. New York: St. Martin's, 1993.

McCracken, Grant. *Culture and Consumption: New Approaches to the Symbolic Character of Consumer Goods and Activities*. Bloomington: Indiana University Press, 1988.

McFeely, Mary Drake. *Can She Bake a Cherry Pie? American Women and the Kitchen in the Twentieth Century*. Amherst: University of Massachusetts Press, 2000.

McIntosh, Elaine. *American Food Habits in Historical Perspective*. Westport, CT: Praeger, 1995.

McKendrick, Neil, John Brewer, and J. H. Plumb. *The Birth of a Consumer Society*. Bloomington: University of Indiana Press, 1982.

Melder, Keith. *Presidential Campaigns from Banners to Broadcasts*. Washington, DC: Smithsonian Institution Press, 1992.

Miller, Daniel, ed. *Material Cultures: Why Some Things Matter*. Chicago: University of Chicago Press, 1998.

_____. *A Theory of Shopping*. Ithaca, NY: Cornell University Press, 1998.

_____, Peter Jackson, Nigel Thrift, Beverly Holbrook, and Michael Rowlands. *Shopping, Place, and Identity*. New York: Routledge, 1998.

Mintz, Sidney. *Sweetness and Power: The Place of Sugar in Modern History*. New York: Penguin Books, 1985.

Mintz, Sidney. *Tasting Food, Tasting Freedom: Excursions into Eating, Culture, and the Past*. Boston: Beacon Press, 1987.

Mintz, Steven. and Susan Kellogg. *Domestic Revolutions: A Social History of American Family Life*. New York: Free Press, 1988.

Mosier, Richard D. *Making the American Mind: Social and Moral Ideas in the McGuffey Readers*. New York: Russell and Russell, 1965.

Murphy, Margot. *Wartime Meals: How to Plan Them, How to Buy Them, How to Cook Them*. New York: Greenburg, 1942.

Neuhaus, Jessamyn. *Manly Meals and Mom's Home Cooking: Cookbooks and Gender in Modern America*. Baltimore: Johns Hopkins University Press, 2003.

Nielander, William Ahlers. *Wartime Food Rationing in the United States*. Washington, DC: World Trade Relations, 1947.

Office of Temporary Controls, Office of Price Administration. *Studies in Food Rationing*. By Judith Russell and Renee Fantin. Washington, DC: Office of Temporary Controls, Office of Price Administration, 1947.

Orleck, Annelise. *Common Sense and a Little Fire: Women and Working-Class Politics in the United States, 1900–1965*. Chapel Hill: University of North Carolina Press, 1995.

Palmer, Phyllis. *Housewives and Domestic Servants in the United States, 1920–1945*. Philadelphia: Temple University Press, 1989.

Perkinson, Henry J. *The Imperfect Panacea: American Faith in Education, 1865–1990*. 3d ed. New York: McGraw-Hill, 1991.

Perrett, Geoffrey. *Days of Sadness, Years of Triumph: The American People 1939–1945*. New York: Coward, McCann and Geoghegan, 1973.

Petroski, Henry. *The Evolution of Useful Things*. New York: Borzoi, 1992.

_____. *The Pencil: A History of Design and Circumstance*. New York: Knopf, 1989.

Pillsbury, Richard. *No Foreign Food: The American Diet in Time and Place*. Boulder, CO: Westview Press, 1998.

Polenberg, Richard. *War and Society: The United States, 1941–1945*. Philadelphia: J. B. Lipincott, 1972.

Price, Sally. *Primitive Art in Civilized Places*. Chicago: University of Chicago Press, 1989.

Proceedings of the National Nutrition Conference for Defense. Washington, DC: U.S. Government Printing Office, 1942.

Proudfoot, Merrill. *Diary of a Sit-In*. Chapel Hill: University of North Carolina Press, 1962.

Pulliam, John D., and James J. Van Patten. *History of Education in America*. 7th ed. Upper Saddle River, NJ: Prentice Hall, 1999.

Rahn, Suzanne. *The Wizard of Oz: Shaping an Imaginary World*. New York: Twayne Publishers, 1998.

Riis, Jacob. *The Children of the Poor*. New York: Charles Scribner's Sons, 1892.

Ritter, Gretchen. "Silver Slippers and a Golden Cap: L. Frank Baum's *The Wonderful Wizard of Oz* and Historical Memory in American Politics." *Journal of American Studies* 31 (1997): 171–202.

Ritzer, George. *The McDonaldization of Society*. Thousand Oaks, CA: Pine Forge Press, 1993.

Roberts, Lydia J. *Nutrition Work with Children*. Chicago: University of Chicago Press, 1927.

Robertson, Helen, Sarah MacLeod, and Frances Preston. *What Do We Eat Now? A Guide to Wartime Housekeeping*. Philadelphia: J. B. Lippincott, 1942.

Rockoff, Hugh. "The Wizard of Oz as a Monetary Allegory." *Journal of Political Economy* 98 (August 1990): 739–760.

Roediger, David R., and Philip S. Foner. *Our Own Time: A History of American Labor and the Working Day*. New York: Greenwood Press, 1989.

Rosen, George. *A History of Public Health*. Baltimore: Johns Hopkins University Press, 1993.

Rosenzweig, Roy. *Eight Hours for What We Will: Workers and Leisure in an Industrial City, 1870–1920*. Westport, CT: Bergin and Garvey, 1994.

Rothstein, Stanley William. *Schooling the Poor: A Social Inquiry Into the American Educational Experience*. Westport, CT: Bergin and Garvey, 1994.

Rudy, Willis. *Schools in an Age of Mass Culture: An Exploration of Selected Themes in the History of Twentieth-Century American Education*. Englewood Cliffs, NJ: Prentice Hall, 1965.

Rupp, Leila. *Mobilizing Women for War: German and American Propaganda, 1939–1945*. Princeton: Princeton University Press, 1978.

Ryan, Mary. *Womanhood in America: From Colonial Times to the Present*. 3d. ed. New York: Franklin Watts, 1983.

Santino, Jack. *New Old-Fashioned Ways: Holidays and Popular Culture*. Knoxville: University of Tennessee Press, 1996.

Scanlon, Jennifer. *Inarticulate Longings:* The Ladies' Home Journal, *Gender, and the Promise of Consumer Culture*. Routledge, 1995.

Schlereth, Thomas, ed. *Material Culture Studies in America, 1876–1976*. Nashville: American Association for State and Local History, 1982.

Schmidt, Leigh Eric. *Consumer Rites: The Buying and Selling of American Holidays*. Princeton: Princeton University Press, 1995.

Scofield, Mary Ann, ed. *Cooking by the Book: Food in Literature and Culture*. Bowling Green, OH: Bowling Green University Press, 1989.

Seiter, Ellen. *Sold Separately: Children and Parents in Consumer Culture*. New Brunswick: Rutgers University Press, 1993.

Shapiro, Laura. *Perfection Salad: Women and Cooking at the Turn of the Century*. New York: Farrar, Straus and Giroux, 1986.

Shifflett, Crandall. *Victorian America, 1876 to 1913*. New York: Facts on File, 1996.

Shortridge, Barbara G., and James R. Shortridge, ed. *The Taste of American Place: A Reader on Regional and Ethnic Foodways*. Lanham, MD: Rowman and Littlefield, 1998.

Sims, Laura S. *The Politics of Fat: Food and Nutrition Policy in America*. Armonk, NY: M. E. Sharpe, 1998.

Spring, Joel. *American Education: An Introduction to Social and Political Aspects*. 5th ed. New York: Longman, 1991.

_____. *The American School, 1642–1990*. 2d ed. New York: Longman, 1990.

_____. *Images of American Life: A History of Ideological Management in Schools, Movies, Radio and Television*. Albany: State University of New York, 1992.

_____. *The Sorting Machine Revisited: National Educational Policy Since 1945*. New York: Longman, 1989.

Stewart, Maxwell. *The Smiths and their Wartime Budgets*. Public Affairs Pamphlets, Number 88. New York: Public Affairs Committee, 1944.

Strasser, Susan. *Never Done: A History of American Housework.* New York: Pantheon, 1982.
_____. *Satisfaction Guaranteed: The Making of the American Mass Market.* New York: Pantheon, 1989.
_____. *Waste and Want: A Social History of Trash.* New York: Metropolitan Books, 1999.
_____, Charles McGovern, and Matthias Judt, eds. *Getting and Spending: European and American Consumer Societies in the Twentieth Century.* Washington, DC: German Historical Institute, 1998.
Susman, Warren I. *Culture as History: The Transformation of American Society in the Twentieth Century.* New York: Pantheon Books, 1984.
Thompson, E. P. *Customs in Common.* London: Merlin Press, 1991.
Trachtenberg, Alan. *The Incorporation of America: Culture and Society in the Gilded Age.* New York: Hill and Wang, 1982.
Trager, James. *The Food Chronology.* New York: Henry Holt, 1995.
Tuttle, William. *Daddy's Gone to War: The Second World War in the Lives of American Children.* New York: Oxford University Press, 1993.
Ulrich, Laurel Thatcher. "Hannah Barnard's Cupboard." In *Through a Glass Darkly: Reflections on Personal Identity in Early America,* ed. Ronald Hoffman, Mechal Sobel, and Fredrika J. Teute. Chapel Hill: University of North Carolina Press, 1997.
U.S. Department of Agriculture. *Farmers' Bulletin: The School Lunch.* Washington, DC: Government Printing Office, 1916; revised edition, 1922.
United States Statutes at Large. Volume 60, Part 1, 1946. Washington, DC: U.S. Government Printing Office, 1947: 230–234.
Vatter, Harold. *The U.S. Economy in World War II.* New York: Columbia University Press, 1985.
Vinovskis, Maris A. *Education, Society, and Economic Opportunity: A Historical Perspective on Persistent Issues.* New Haven: Yale University Press, 1995.
Visser, Margaret. *Much Depends upon Dinner.* New York: Grove Press, 1986.
_____. *The Rituals of Dinner: The Origins, Evolution, Eccentricities, and Meaning of Table Manners.* New York: Grove Weidenfeld, 1991.
Walker, Nancy A. *Shaping Our Mothers' World: American Women's Magazines.* Jackson: University of Mississippi Press, 2000.
Ward, Barbara McLean, ed. *Produce and Conserve, Share and Play Square: The Grocer and the Consumer on the Home-Front Battlefield during World War II.* Portsmouth, NH: Strawbery Banke Museum, 1994.
Weatherford, Doris. *American Women and World War II.* New York: Facts on File, 1990.
Welter, Barbara. "The Cult of True Womanhood." *American Quarterly* 18 (Summer 1966): 151–174.
West, Elliott. *Growing Up in Twentieth-Century America.* Westport: Greenwood, 1996.
Westbrook, Robert B. "'I Want a Girl, Just Like the Girl That Married Harry James': American Women and the Problem of Political Obligation in World War II." *American Quarterly,* 42, no. 4 (December 1990): 587–614.
Williams, Susan. *Savory Suppers and Fashionable Feasts: Dining in Victorian America.* New York: Pantheon, 1985.
Willis, Susan. *A Primer for Daily Life.* London: Routledge, 1991.
Wise, Nancy Baker, and Christy Wise. *A Mouthful of Rivets: Women at Work in World War II.* San Francisco: Josey-Bass, 1994.
Wolff, Miles. *Lunch at the Five and Ten: The Greensboro Sit-Ins.* New York: Stein and Day, 1970.
Wood, Roy C. *The Sociology of the Meal.* Edinburgh: Edinburgh University Press, 1995.
World Almanac and Book of Facts for 1944, ed. E. Eastman Irvine. New York: New York World Telegram, 1944.
Young, Hazel. *The Working Girl Must Eat.* Revised edition. Boston: Little, Brown, 1944.
Zuckerman, Mary Ellen. *A History of Popular Women's Magazines in the United States, 1792–1995.* Westport, CT: Greenwood Press, 1998.

Index

Numbers in **bold italics** refer to pages with illustrations

Aberdeen, SD 32
Aberdeen Saturday Pioneer 32
Ad Council 209
Adams, Frank 147–150
advertising 39, 104, 125, 176–179, 194–197, 213
Advisory Commission 82
Akron, OH 70
Aladdin Industries 175, 176
Allen, Ida Bailey 150–152
Allison, Anne 181–182
Alton, IL **55**
American Association of Home Economics 171
American Institute of Food Distribution 90
American Red Cross 142
The American Woman's Home 13
Armour, Philip 122
Army and Navy Munitions Board 82
Atlanta Constitution 196

Baisden, Mabel 66–68
Baltimore, MD 93
Balzer, Henry 205
Bambi 75
Barber, Caesar 201
Barbie lunch box 176
Barker Brothers 140, 142
"Basic Seven" 119–120, 124
Baum, Lyman Frank 5, 31–33, 40, 41
Baum, Maud (Gage) 32
The Beatles lunch box 176
Bechmann, Albertina 65

Beecher, Catherine E. 13, 104, 115
Better Homes and Gardens 191, 197
Birdseye, Clarence 122
black market 89, 100, 101
Bon-Vee-Von lunch box 19–20
Borden, Gail 122
Boston, MA 61, 62
The Brady Bunch lunch box 176
Bridgeport, CT 135–139, 140, 143
Bridgeport Gas Light Company 135–139
Brillat-Savarin, Jean Anthelme 16
Brobeck, Florence 117
Brookeville, MD **11**
Brown, Prentiss 92
Bruce, Scott 175, 176
Bryan, William Jennings 22, **23**, **24**, **28**, 33, 34
Bunce, Alan 192
Bureau of Agricultural Economics 164, 166
Bureau of Home Economics 96, 98, 106, 108, 126, 166
Burger King 201
Business Week 140, 153

cafeterias, workplace 49–50, 52, **53**, 55–57, 139, 153, 155
California Dietetic Association 142
California State Board of Health 142
Canton, OH 27
Capri Sun fruit drink 196
Castells, Manuel 204
Center for Science in the Public Interest 178

Cheerios (cereal) 190
"Cheeseburger Bill" (Personal Responsibility in Consumption Act) 211–212, 213
Cheyney Brothers Silk Manufactory *53*
Chicago, IL 22, 33, 44, *45*, 51, 63, 169, 170, 198
The Children of the Poor 21
Chittenango, NY 32
Christy, Gertrude York 142
Cincinnati, OH *46*, 61, 65
Cinnamon Toast Crunch cereal 211
cities 21–22, 42, 61, 63, 64, 99
Civil War 36, 79, 113
Civil Works Administration 165
Class: and food patterns 38, 45, 48–50, 108, 124–125, 130–132; and lunchboxes 38, 156–157; and school lunches 72, 169–171
class attitudes, postwar 147–155
Cleveland, OH 61
Cocoa Puffs cereal 211
colonization, metaphor of defined 2, 4, 6–8, 17
Columbia University 98
Committee on Food Habits 128–135
commodities: agricultural 22, 79, 165, 166; and distribution to schools 171–173
Commodity Credit Corporation 90
Communication Workers of America (CWA) 154
Community Service Society 126
Conklin, H.M. 185
Consumer Reports 178
consumer society: arrival of 37, 39, 43; and World War II 87, 103, 115, 125; post World War II 149–150, 204–205
convenience food products 193–198
Cook It in a Casserole 117
cookbooks *see* prescriptive literature
Cornell University 124
Corporation for Public Broadcasting 209
Council for National Defense 82
Cowan, Ruth Schwartz 183
Crocker, Betty 104, 117, 194
Crosby, Robert A. 136
Cup and Container Institute 140
currency issue 22, 23, 26
Cyprus 206
Czech Republic 206

Datamonitor 155
Dawes, Dominique 209
Delineator 185
Democratic Party 22, 26, 33–4, 167–168
Department of Agriculture: and food pyramid 206–*208*, 210; and school lunch 171, 172, 173, 177; and World War II 89, 98, 108, 126, 164, 165
Department of Health and Human Services 207, 209

Department of Labor 98
Department of Transportation 157
Detroit, MI 105
Detroit News 105
Dickinson, Mrs. LaFell 183
The Dictionary of American English on Historical Principles 38
dinner: definition 38, 42
dinner pail 29, 30, 37–38, 42, 43, 50, 52, 65, 153; "full dinner pail" slogan *27, 28*, 35, 42–43
Disney Company *see* Walt Disney Company
Douglas, Mary 8
Douglas Aircraft Company *116*
Dreiser, Theodore 45, 49

eating habits 128–135, 203, 212–214; *see also* meals, pattern of
economy, U.S. 21–22
Edsforth, Ronald 163
Egan, Charles 88
Eisenhower, Dwight D. 189
Election of 1896 21–29, 34
Election of 1900 33, 34, 35, 42
Election of 1912 42
Emergency Price Control Act 83
"empty market basket" slogan 42–43
England (Great Britain) 61, 81, 147, 206

Fairfax County, VA 196
Family Circle 150
Farmer, Fannie 13
farmers *11*, 23, 25, 26, 32–33, 34, 42, 79, 163, 210
Fast Food Nation: The Dark Side of the All-American Meal 201
Federal Emergency Relief Administration 165
Federal Security Agency 125
Federal Surplus Commodities Commission 165
Federal Works Agency 183
The Feminine Mystique 185
Finland 206
Flanagan, John W. 171
The Flying Nun lunch box 176
food: convenience products 193–198; Department of Agriculture food pyramid 206–*208*, 210; processors of 2, 51–2, 122, 127, 128, 211, 213
Food Administration 79, 115
Food Distribution Association 90
Food Distribution Committee 83
Food-for-Defense program 83
Food Marketing Trade Show 198
Food Review 177
Ford Company 154
France 82
Frederick, Christine 104

Friedan, Betty 185, 198
Froot Loops (cereal) 190
"full dinner pail" slogan *27*, *28*, 35, 42–43

Gage, Matilda 32
Gannon, Frances 94
Garland, Judy 32
Geauque, Edwin P. 113
Gelhorn, Walter 93
General Electric 140, 144
General Federation of Women's Clubs 183
General Mills 104, 117, 210–211
General Motors 153
Germany 61, 81, 206
Geuder, Paeschke, and Frey 175
Gillet, Lucy H. 126
golden age, myth of 114
Good Housekeeping 59, 121, 150, 184, 187, 192, 194
The Good Housekeeping Cookbook 118
Good Housekeeping's Book of Meals 69
Gorton's Fish Company 177
Gould, Lewis 25
Gourmet 156, 213
grandmothers, as role models 96, 99, 114, 118, 186
Grant, Robert 38
Grant, Ulysses S. 26
Great Britain *see* England
Great Depression 48, 68, 78, 79, 80, 107, 164
Great Society 179
Greece 206
Griffiths, Martha W. 170

Habermas, Jurgen 7
Hain/Celestial Group 210
Haley, Jack 32
Hall, Helen Morgan 136, 138
Hall, Stuart 193
Hallmark (greeting card company) 197
Hamburger Helper 194, 198
Hanrahan, Alice D. 188–189
hardtack 36
Harris, Florence Laganke 120
Heinz, Henry John 52
Henderson, Leon 89
Hershey, Lewis B. 123
Hester, Harriet 120
Hitler, Adolf 81, 82, 93
hoarding 89–94, 90, 100, 101, 103, 112–113
Holt, Jane (Margot Murphy McConnell) 77, 88, 94–100, 105–121, 124
Home Economics Women in Business 142
home economists: and school lunch 68–73; and women's roles 103–105; and World War II 98, 99, 129, 135, 140, 142
Hoover, Herbert 78
Hopalong Cassidy lunchbox 175

Hopkins, Mary Alden 52
Howard, Jonas 53–55
Howard, Dr. Joseph H. 137, 138
Hoyer, Ernest F. 50
Huffman, Sue 191
Hulbert, Ann 17
Husted, Marjorie 104
Hygeia 66, 136, 186, 187

Illinois Glass Company *55*
Industrial Management 55–56
industrialization: effects of 6, 10, 14–15, 20, 40–42, 57; and incorporation 41–42
Ireland 206
Island Creek Coal Company 67

Japanese-Americans: and World War II relocation camps 89
Japanese school lunches 181–182, 199
Jefferson, Thomas 1, 214–215
Jello pudding 194–195
Johnston, Myrna 191
Joseph Teshon Textile Plant *158*
Journal of Home Economics 58, 65, 71, 142
Judge *24*, *28*
The Jungle 44, 51, 52

Keller, Ric 211
Kellogg Company 122
Kentucky Fried Chicken 201
Kerr, Florence 183
Kewanee, IL 35
Klass, Perri 214
Kraft Foods 158
Kyrk, Hazel 126

labor unions 50, 139, 143, 153–155, 160
Ladies' Home Journal 150, 185, 191
Lahr, Bert 32
Lear, Anne 156
Lee, Harper 48
Lehman, Bonnie 188
Lend-Lease program 75, 83, 90
Leonardi, Susan J. 108
Lespinasse (NYC restaurant) 159
Levenstein, Harvey 14, 79
Lewin, Kurt 130–134, 135, 143
Lichtenstein, Nelson 153
The Lion King 177
Literary Digest 50, 52, 54
Logan County, WV 66–68
Long Beach, CA *116*
Look Homeward, Angel 47
Los Angeles, CA 61
Lost in Space lunch box 176
Louis, Joe 75
Low Countries 82
LTV Steel Corporation 160
Lucky Charms (cereal) 211

lunch: definition 8, 35–36, 38, 42, 146; three-martini 157, 159
lunch boxes *9*, *16*, 19–20, 29–30, 36, 43, *45*, *141*; and class 12, 49, 151–153, 156–157; as collectibles 197–198; and commercialism in schools 175–176; and gender 191–193; and ideology 181–182; packer advice 115–121, 135–139, 140–143, 152, 185–193; postwar workers' 147–*148*, *149*–155; shoe boxes used as 36, 47–48; tobacco tins used as 36, 48
Lunchables 14, 195–7, 199

magazines, women's *see* prescriptive literature
Malta 206
market research 203
Martin, Ethel Austin 70–71
Massachusetts Agricultural College Extension Service 65
material culture theory 36–37
Mattelart, Armand and Michèle 204
McCay, Clive 124
McConnell, James V. 105
McConnell, Margot Murphy *see* Holt, Jane
McCormack, John W. 168
McCormick/Schilling Pure Vanilla Extract 194
McCracken, Ellen 193
McDonalds Corporation 177, 178, 201–202, 214
McKinley, William *26*, *27*–29, 34, 42–43
McNutt, Paul V. 125–126
Mead, Margaret 128–129, 132, 134, 135, 143
meals, pattern of 1, 5, 10, 35–36, 122, 129–134; *see also* eating habits
Meeber, Carrie 45, 47, 49
Meikleham, Septimia Anne Randolph 1
Metro-Goldwyn-Mayer 31
Mickey Mouse lunch box 175, 197
middle class 21, 39, 42–43, 103, 108
Milwaukee, WI 61
Montgomery, Donald E. 89
Monthly Labor Review 57
Morrison's (NYC eatery) 160
motherhood *see* women
Mrs. Allen's Book of Sugar Substitutes 150
Mrs. Allen's Book of Wheat Substitutes 150
Murphy, Margot *see* Holt, Jane

National Association for the Education of Younger Children 209
National Conference on Nutrition 125–128
National Congress of Parents and Teachers 171
National Dairy Council 70
National Education Association 171
National Grocers Institute 113
National Nutrition Advisory Council 171

National Nutrition Conference 125–128
National Research Council 89, 123–124
National Restaurant Association 157, 212
National School Lunch Act 162–163, 167–169, 172, 177
National School Lunch Program (NSLP) 145, 169–171, 174, 178
National Union Catalog 106
National Youth Administration 164
Neill, John R. 37
New Deal 164, 165, 171
New York City 21, *58*, 61, 85, 92, 93, 94, 159, 160
New York Metropolitan Hospital 150
New York State College of Home Economics 99
New York Times 77, 87, 93, 101, 105, 106, 115, 124, 150, 160, 167
New York Times Magazine 105
Newport News, VA 178
Nielander, William Ahlers 80, 81, 84
Ninety-nine Ways to Share the Meat 98
Northwestern Bell Telephone Company 154
NPD Group 205
nutrition 111–112, 119, 122–124; Bridgeport Plan 135–139; and children 59–73, 164–166; and Committee on Food Habits 128–135; and economic status 124–125, 127; food pyramid 206–208, 210; government, industry and community effect on 139–143; and health 201, 206, 210–212
Nutrition Work with Children 70

obento boxes 181–182, 199
Office of Disease Prevention 209
Office of Education 172
Office of Emergency Management 82
Office of Price Administration (OPA) 77, 78, 80, 83, 84, 86, 88, 89, 90, 91, 92, 93, 100
Office of Price Administration and Civilian Supply (OPACS) 83
Oldways Preservation Trust 210
Omaha, NB 22
Oreo cookies 214
Oscar Mayer 196
O'Toole, Donald 90
Oxford English Dictionary 38
Ozma of Oz *3*, 5, 29–*30*, 31, 34, *40*

paper bags 47, 151
Parade 150
Parents 169, 188, 189, 190, 192, 194
Partridge, P. D. 185
Pasteur, Louis 51
patriotism 77, 112, 117, 121, 129, 134, 136, 203
Patterson, NJ *158*, *159*
Pearl Harbor, HI 75, 78, 80, 81, 85

penny lunch movement 59, 62–63, 127, 162, 186
Personal Responsibility in Consumption Act 211–212, 213
Philadelphia 61
Philippines 35
Pinocchio lunch box 175
Pizza Hut 177, 178
Plant-Restaurant Management 53–54
Poage, William Robert 168
point rationing 87–88, 91–92, 96, 98–101, 106; *see also* rationing
Poland 81, 82
political obligation 87
Pontiac, MI 57
Poor People's Institute 61
Populist Party 22, 26, 33, 42
Post Company 122
Powell, Adam Clayton 168
prescriptive literature 13–14, 103–104, 183–185; cookbooks as 108, 116–121; women's magazines as 121, 184–197
The Principles of Scientific Management 52, 204
The Problem of Changing Food Habits 129
Progressive Reform 2, 6, 16, 25, 49–51, 57, 59–63
Public Affairs Committee 85
Publishers Weekly 106
Pure Food and Drug Act 51–52

Randolph, Mary 36
rationing 15, 73–74, 76–85; *see also* point rationing
Reader's Digest 163
Reconstruction Finance Corporation 164
Redbook 174, 185
Republican Party 25–26, 167–168
responsibility: corporate 50, 57, 213; governmental 62, 164, 167, 213; parental 65, 69; personal 212–215; of social science experts 73, 126–127, 134–135, 139, 213
Reuther, Walter 153
Richards, Ellen 104
Riis, Jacob 21
Ripperger, Helmut 106
Ritzer, George 15
Roberts, Lydia 69–71
Roberts' Nutrition Work with Children 70–71
Roosevelt, Eleanor 137, 138
Roosevelt, Franklin D. 82–83, 86, 125–126, 128, 164
Roosevelt, Theodore 42, 51
Rosie the Riveter 74, 102, 108, 115
Rumford, Count *see* Thompson, Benjamin
Rupp, Leila 13

St. Louis, MO 61, 183
San Francisco, CA 142

Schlosser, Eric 201
Scholastic Company 177
school lunch 2, 6–7, **58**–59, **60**–74, 127; and commercialism 176–179; and commodity distribution 171–174; and early federal assistance 163–167; home economists and 68–73; and "junk food" 178–179, 203; reformers and 59–68
School Meals Initiative for Healthy Children 177
Scribner's Magazine 38
Second War Powers Act 92
selective service 64, 111, 123, 137, 165
Sesame Street 209
Share the Meat Program 95, 98
shoebees 47–48
Simmons, Amelia 104
Sinclair, Upton 44, 49, 51
Sister Carrie 45, 47
Slovakia 206
Slovenia 206
Smith, A. 93–94
*The Smiths and Their Wartime Budget*s 86
Snow White lunch box 175
social divide 21–29
South Manchester, CT **53**
Spanish-American War 34
Spurlock, Morgan 202
Standard Oil 50
Star Wars lunchbox 176
Stevenson, Adlai 189
Stevenson, Bertha 184
Stewart, Martha 190
Stewart, Maxwell 86
Stowe, Harriet Beecher 13, 104
Summers, Hattan W. 167
Super-Size Me 202
Supermarket News 196
Sweet, Judge Robert 214
Swift, Gustauvus 122

Taco Bell 177
Taft, Robert A. 168
Taft, William Howard 42
Tarver, Malcom C. 168
taxes: corporate 157, 159; income 86, 101
Taylor, Frederick W. 52, 73, 204
Taylor, Irene Hume 66
Team Nutrition 177
Technical World Magazine 65
television and children 175–176
Then Ya Just Untwist 147–150
Theories of Communication 204
Thompson, Benjamin (Count Rumford) 61
Thompson, Edward P. 146
300 Sugar Saving Recipes 120
Thrifty Cooking for Wartime 117
time 39, 57, 146–147, 155–156, 157, 160
To Kill a Mockingbird 48–49

Today's Health 150
Torrey, Emeline E. 59
Trachtenberg, Alan 39, 41
Trix (cereal) 211
Truman, Harry S. 162

Union Lunch Box Company 19
United Auto Workers (UAW) 153
United Steel Workers Union 160
University of Chicago 69, 70
University of Iowa 130, 132–133
USA Today 205

Vatter, Harold G. 82
The Virginia Housewife 36

Wadsworth, James 167
Wallace, Henry A. 127–128
Walt Disney Company 75, 175, 176, 177
War Food Administration 139, 172
War Manpower Commission 125
War Ration Book One 84
War Ration Book Two 90, 91, 92
War Resources Board 82
Wartime Meals: How to Plan Them, How to Buy Them, How to Cook Them 105–121
Washington, DC 94, 95, 125, 156, 211
Waston Machine Company *159*
Wendy's restaurants 201
Westinghouse 140, *141*, 144
What Do We Eat Now? A Guide for Wartime Housekeeping 119–120

White, Justice Byron 154–155
Whole Grains Council (WCG) 210
Wickard, Claude 88–89, 101, 113
Wilson, D.R. 57
Wilson, Woodrow 42
Wilson Foundry and Machine Company 57
Winn-Smith, Alice 117
Wolfe, Thomas 47
Woman's Day 197
Woman's Home Companion 105, 190
women: and motherhood 2, 6, 71–73, 123; and republican motherhood 69, 103, 183; and responsibility for family food 12–13, 15, 68–73, 102–105, 114–115, 117–119, 123–124, 129–144; working *116*, 117–119, 184–185, 191
The Wonderful Wizard of Oz 5, 31–34
Woodward, Ellen S. 165
working class 41–43, *46*, 52–*55*, 56–57
The Working Girl Must Eat 117–118
Working Mother 191, 193
Working Woman 191
Works Progress Administration *60*, 164, 165
World War I 50, 52, 64, 78–82, 114, 123, 150; Food Administration during 79, 115

YMCA 209
Young, Hazel 117–118
Young Dr. Malone 192
Your Share: How to Prepare Appetizing, Healthful Meals with Foods Available Today 117